Modern Social Theory

Modern Social Theory

Key debates and new directions

Derek Layder
University of Leicester

UCL
PRESS

H
6 l
,L345
1997

First published in 1997 by UCL Press
UCL Press Limited
1 Gunpowder Square
London EC4A 3DE
UK

and

1900 Frost Road, Suite 101
Bristol
Pennsylvania 19007-1598
USA

The name of University College London (UCL) is a registered
trade mark used by UCL Press with the consent of the owner.

British Library Cataloguing-in-Publication Data
A catalogue record for this book is available from the British Library.

Library of Congress Cataloging-in-Publication-Data
are available

ISBNs: 1-85728-385-6 HB
         1-85728-386-4 PB

Typeset in Baskerville.
Printed in Great Britain by T. J. International Ltd.,
Padstow, Cornwall.

Contents

CONTENTS

Preface

The theory of social domains represents an attempt to establish an approach to social theory and analysis which not only builds on the strengths of existing theories but also provides a systematic alternative that overcomes what I take to be the main weaknesses of these approaches. Domain theory is a culmination of ideas that I have been developing in various forms in previous publications and in this respect the present volume has close affinities with *New strategies in social research* and *Understanding social theory*. Some strands of thought and argumentative themes offered in these books – originally designed for very different purposes – are here worked through in a detailed fashion and presented as a developed and integrated framework of theoretical ideas. In a nutshell I present an account of the relations between society, social encounters and subjective experience that subscribes to the need for a dialogue between classical and contemporary social theory. In support of my thesis I argue that those approaches that have tried to "go beyond" or bridge the agency–structure and macro–micro dualisms in social analysis have done so only by wrongly characterizing social reality as a simplified "unification" of forces or elements. Domain theory seeks to counter this tendency by drawing attention to the richly textured and multidimensional nature of the social world as it is reflected in the principal social domains.

A number of people have helped me in carrying through this project by reading and commenting on parts or the whole of the book in draft and thus have contributed to its finished form. In this respect I would like to thank Jane Clarke for her careful and thorough reading of the whole draft and her perceptive and valuable comments. I am also indebted to the following: Justin Vaughan, Rosemary Crompton, Martyn Denscombe, Ian Craib, William Outhwaite and Steven Gerrard. Less directly involved but nonetheless essential have been Norbert Wiley, Dominic Strinati and John Scott. Of course the above mentioned bear no responsibility for any deficiencies or weaknesses that this book may possess.

Although not directly connected with the preparation of this book the following people have contributed greatly to my ability to finish the project: David Ashton, Annie Phizacklea, Julia O'Connel Davidson, Mick Gardiner, Silvana di Gregorio, John Williams, Alison Drewett, Jenny Strang, Sharon Higson and Philip Marlow. Finally, I should like to register the importance of the support and friendship of Barry Troyna who, sadly, died during the writing of this book.

Derek Layder, April 1996

1

Outline of the theory of
social domains

Introduction

My central concern in this book is to give an account of face-to-face encounters by showing how they are formed out of the combined effects of social and psychological factors. Face-to-face encounters are also known by other names such as "focused gatherings", "co-present encounters" and "everyday interaction". I shall use these terms interchangeably throughout the book. These are all examples of what I otherwise speak of as "situated activity" and I use this as an alternative. These terms refer to the situations that arise when two or more people share each other's company in the pursuit of a variety of purposes, for example, love, business, sport, law enforcement, selling and buying drugs, passing the time, eating food, doing work. Furthermore, these pursuits are undertaken in an equally dazzling array of settings and circumstances such as bedrooms, courtrooms, breakfast tables, bars and coffee shops, restaurants, theatres, prisons, hospitals, factories and so on. Much of everyday social life is conducted at this face-to-face level in which participants formulate their conduct in the light of the behaviour and intentions of the others present.

Although the central focus of the book is to provide an explanatory account of face-to-face encounters, my argument suggests that this is possible only by understanding how this domain of social life intersects and is interdependent with other social domains. Thus, to understand the domain of situated activity we have to place it in the broader context of social organization as a whole as well as the psychological (subjective) propensities of individuals. To this end I argue that we must view society and social life as comprising a number of important dimensions that have varying and distinctive characteristics and that these differing "social domains" are interlocking and mutually dependent on each other. Although this might seem uncontroversial to those unfamiliar with social theory and the procedures of sociological analysis, this view of society is far from settled or agreed upon by the sociological community. The detailed ramifications that follow from this apparently simple starting point will be the subject matter of the book as a whole. In order to inject variation into the stylistics of the exposition I refer to "dimensions", "domains" or "orders" almost interchangeably although I shall have occasion to distinguish between them. Similarly, I often speak of different "layerings" of society that give some sense of vertical depth to social life. This image emphasizes the faceted nature of society while at the same time drawing attention to its ontological depth.

First, let me indicate in a provisional and necessarily simplified manner what I am referring to when I speak of the "domains" of social life in the context of a "theory of social domains". There are four principal domains and I refer to them in the following terms: psychobiography, situated activity, social settings and contextual resources. The elements that bind these domains together are social relations and positions, power, discourses and practices. At this point I shall not attempt to describe any of these in detail since this can be properly done only in terms of a lengthy ongoing discussion. However, it is important to point out that the domains are related to each other not only as "layers" of social life within the same time unit, but also as stretched-out over time and space. Before the discussion becomes too abstract and complicated I shall sketch in a fairly down-to-earth way the kinds of events, situations and circumstances that are indicative of these social domains. In this respect consider the following scenarios and descriptions of various facets of social life.

(a) A woman is sitting at home in her flat reflecting on her life so far. She contemplates her recent divorce, its emotional aftermath and her future promotion prospects at work (she is a teacher). She remembers the kind of social life and friendships she had before her marital split and then envisages how she would like these things to be in the immediate future. This scenario accentuates the domain of psychobiography that focuses on the personal feelings, attitudes and predispositions of individuals. In this respect we can grasp a person's unique individuality only by understanding their identity and behaviour as it has unfolded over the course of their lives, and is currently embedded in their daily routines and experiences. These in turn have to be considered in relation to the broader context of other social domains – see below.

(b) Consider the following scenarios: two friends in a coffee bar spending their work lunch-hour chatting about work friends and family; a typical scene in a suburban household as family members prepare for their daily round of activity; an argument between two homeless itinerants; a crowded restaurant; the audience at a concert, a theatre or sporting event; the massed demonstrations that accompanied the demise of communism in many east European countries. These examples accentuate the domain of situated activity that is characterized by face-to-face transactions between people. The communicative interchanges that take place between the participants are crucial in determining the flow and outcome of the encounter as a whole. As with psychobiography, situated activity is interdependent with the other domains and while it has its own distinctive characteristics it is not entirely separate from them.

(c) With the above examples of situated activity it is clear that they all occur in particular settings that have a specific location and social organization. Such settings vary considerably in terms of their organizational features. Consider, for example, the working conditions and social status associated with certain jobs and occupational careers such as clerical work, truck driving, nursing or management. Many work settings such as hospitals, universities, trade unions and managerial hierarchies are highly organized and operate through the rules and regulations that govern working practices and authority relations within them. They often have promotional procedures, reward systems and pay scales that shape the lives of those who perform the work tasks in these settings.

Other social settings are much less formally organized, particularly family or domestic circumstances, or the private sphere of personal relations in general. Yet other settings that represent "in transit" areas of social existence such as street life, public spaces such as lifts, shops and modes of transportation like trains, planes, ships and ferries, seem even more nebulous in terms of their organizational form. None the less, the behaviour and practices that occur within them are underpinned by an elaborate social fabric of rules, understandings, obligations and expectations. These examples highlight the domain of social settings that is characterized by a concern with (reproduced) social positions, practices and discourses as well as forms of power and control. Social settings cannot be understood entirely independently of the situated activities that take place within them (or the self-identities of those involved), nor can they be separated from the wider context of resource allocation, social inequalities and the forms of signification and legitimation that underpin them.

(d) Consider the society-wide distribution and ownership of resources (goods, money, status, credit facilities, mortgages, occupations, health care and insurance, standards of accommodation, quality of life and lifestyle) along gender, racialized and class lines. Consider also the wide variety of cultural (and subcultural) resources, products and commodities that are available in society at large, including newspapers, magazines, television, video as well as the specialist or esoteric forms of knowledge and expertise that are also distributed unevenly throughout modern societies. The range of discourses and practices that surround these cultural practices is wide and encompasses phenomena such as imagery and signification as forms of communication and status (as in advertising or fashion, reading habits or other lifestyle indicators), to the signalling and transmission of social conventions and mores as well as the ideological legitimation of wealth and status.

These examples highlight the domain of contextual resources that is characterized by its focus on power and domination and the discourses and practices that undergird various forms of hierarchy and inequality on a society-wide basis. In this sense we are dealing primarily with a group or collective level of analysis in terms of the possession, distribution or ownership of cultural, material and authoritative resources throughout the whole social system. Such systemic factors directly enter into the constitution of social settings and the social encounters that take place within them. They also play a significant role in the structuring of self-identities through individual psychobiographies. However such systemic factors do not *determine* the psychologies or subjectivities of individuals nor do they "determine" the nature of interpersonal encounters or the settings in which they occur. Likewise, psychobiography and interpersonal encounters do not cause or determine the nature and functioning of social settings or the contextual resources that provide their environment. Each domain, although deeply interwoven and interdependent with the others, also has its own distinct characteristics and a certain measure of independence from the others.

Apart from the characteristics I have just mentioned we can analytically distinguish between these scenarios and descriptions in other ways. For example, they refer to quite distinct kinds of activity involving rather different things ranging from solo activity (including reflecting on one's own life and career) through intimate or routine conversations to large gatherings of people and right up to the group or collective level of resource distribution. In this sense the scenarios vary considerably in terms of "personalization". That is, some events and circumstances involve a high degree of intimacy between specific people (the coffee-bar encounter) while others are much more impersonal or at a greater remove from specific individuals (such as the description of labour market inequalities).

As I have said the domains are interconnected and in the scenarios we can see how this involves interrelated aspects of social life. This is reflected in the biographies and the trajectories traced by the routine daily lives of particular people. For instance the woman in the flat is connected with the labour market through her teaching job. She may spend many of her lunch-breaks socializing with a work colleague. In her spare time she may play basketball and enjoy going to the opera. However, these things are also related in other socially defined ways. In terms of power, culture and institutions, different forms of activities and the different settings in which they occur are connected and thus they intermesh with each other. For example, routine daily encounters between people are profoundly affected by the organizational setting in which they take place and the political and economic circumstances that provide the wider institutional backdrop.

A final point worth considering at this juncture is the manner in which the perspective on the event or scenario in question varies as we shift the point of view of the analysis or description. This is related to the question of the degree of personalization but is in fact a slightly different point concerning the standpoint of the observer and the very real differences in the way in which society and social life are constituted. In relation to the scenarios we can see the shift from the point of view of the individual woman in her flat reflecting on her biography or life-career, through to a concern with the point of view of the two conversants in the coffee-bar. The focus on the collective activities of crowds, audiences and demonstrators again moves the central focus of the analysis further from individuals as such. When we reach the description of the distribution of cultural, material or authoritative resources in society as a whole or of the labour market for various kinds of occupational skills, we are at the furthest remove from the point of view of participants in particular encounters. In this sense we are adopting the standpoint of an "independent observer" (Habermas 1987) in that as sociologists we are viewing social arrangements from a position "external" to that aspect of society or that slice of social life which is the focus of analysis. It follows from this that the adoption of the independent observer's point of view does not imply that this reflects the "objective" truth of the matter as opposed to the "subjectively biased" views of actual participants. It simply means that the analytic focus or standpoint varies significantly from different vantage points.

In very general terms the theory of social domains has much in common with other approaches to social analysis. On the one hand, it rejects the view that individuals are isolated self-sufficient "units" who remain untouched by social processes, and on the other, it eschews the view that society as a whole should be the relevant unit of social analysis. In this sense the theory of social domains insists that people are not simply automata, unthinkingly moved and moulded by social forces. In this respect it shares a lot with many other sociological approaches. However, it is on the question of the exact nature of this "middle-ground" that domain theory parts company from established approaches and in particular those that reject the notion of society as a series of distinct but interdependent layers or domains. In that domain theory attempts to account for situated activity by understanding it as one of four interdependent but partly autonomous social domains, this immediately distinguishes it from many other approaches that tend to concentrate on one or two domains or dimensions of social analysis.

Traditionally, approaches to social analysis have tended to split into two broad camps: those concerned with what Giddens calls "interpretative analysis", and those concerned with "institutional analysis" (Giddens 1984). Interpretative analysis is associated with schools of thought such as symbolic interactionism, ethnomethodology and phenomenology and has defended a view of social activity as an intersubjective phenomenon that is largely dependent on the creative and productive capacities of human agents. Those in the institutional camp (functionalism and structuralism) have tended towards the opposite extreme, viewing social interaction mainly as an effect of the workings of structural or systemic features of society. Both groups therefore tend to reduce the analysis of social phenomena either to the realm of human agency and interaction or to the macro-realm of social structures and systems. There have been broadly two kinds of responses to this situation. One has been to suggest that while action and systems approaches should be brought together, this must be undertaken in the context of a recognition that they represent different orders or domains of social reality. A number of authors have adopted this latter view, among them Habermas and Goffman who figure prominently in this book. Although I have great sympathy with this approach (Layder 1990, 1993, 1994) the theory of social domains goes further by suggesting that we deconstruct the two domains of action and systems into four and view social activity itself as an outcome of the complex interplay of them all. So although I believe this attempt to connect action and systems theories is viable up to a point, I do not think it goes far enough towards recognizing the complexity of social life.

Domain theory is most sharply distinguished from those approaches that have responded to the action (or agency)–structure (or system) divide by conceiving of society and social life as an "essential process" or "unit of analysis" that is taken to be the basic and unifying feature of social existence. Such unifying principles go under a number of different descriptive labels depending on the author and the theory in question. In this respect the term "social practices" often conveys a common theme of bringing various strands of social life together to form a synthetic unity by identifying the core features or topics of social analysis. For instance ethnomethodologists speak of "local practices" (through which people create a sense of social order), as the essential subject matter of social analysis (Hilbert 1990). Foucault (1977, 1980) speaks of the influence of "discursive practices" and their close links with power. Giddens speaks of "social practices ordered across time and space" (1984: 2), although he also uses terms like the "duality of structure" that in like manner represent the focal analytic concerns of sociology. Similarly, Bourdieu (1977) points to the central role of the "habitus" (the socially generated attitudes that dispose people to act in particular ways) in the context of his "theory of practice". Other writers do not use the term practice – Elias (1978) for instance refers to "figuration" (which indicates the ever-changing networks of relations between people), and which he and his followers believe are the basic elements of social life. On the other hand, Blumer (1969) uses the notion of "joint activity" to express the interweaving nature of various aspects of social existence.

Such terms, then, indicate the manner in which different authors and schools of social theory have sought to express the synthetic nature of society and social activity. What is at stake here is of fundamental importance to sociology. These and other authors have offered up new concepts and terms that depict what they take to be the seamlessly interrelated nature of social processes. That is, they oppose the idea of the social world as a

7

layered series of distinct but interdependent domains. I do not want to say that I reject outright these alternatives to a layered or stratified view of the social world because I believe that each of them has something to offer in terms of a fully rounded understanding of the social world. I have to add that I do think that some have more to offer in this respect than others, although this, for the moment, is a separate issue. However, I do not believe that any of these alternative frameworks, in and of themselves, supply us with anything like a full account of the nature of social existence.

The claims that have been forwarded on behalf of the notion of social practices is a good example of the dangers of this kind of strategy and is reflected in Giddens's insistence that the "basic domain of study for the social sciences . . . is social practices ordered across time and space" (1984: 2). Now while I consider social practices to be one importance focus for social study, I think it unwise to allow it to monopolize our view of social analysis in the manner that Giddens suggests. Such a myopic channelling of analytic attention drags the focus away from equally important aspects of the social world. One effect is to concentrate our attention on practices themselves so fixedly that we fail to ask questions about the varying conditions and principles under which practices are ordered. That is, by centralizing our analytic target we lose the opportunity of examining and understanding the influence of different social conditions, settings and contexts in our attempts to explain features of the social world. Although Giddens's employment of the term is very different from Foucault's (and to a lesser extent from Bourdieu's) the overall effect is the same – to occupy the centre of analytic attention to the neglect or even exclusion of other equally essential features of social life.

The same is true for the other "synthetic alternatives", although I shall stick with the example of social practices for the moment. The advantage that the theory of social domains has in this respect is that it allows us to understand other crucially important aspects of social reality. Let us be absolutely clear about the implications of this. The primary effect of holding a synthetic view that centralizes the notion of practice (or some essential process or unit of analysis) is that it imposes a flattened-out view of the social terrain. By emphasizing this vision of society it becomes very difficult to understand the different processes that work to produce the wide spectrum of practices (and their variant natures) across society as a whole. Furthermore it raises difficulties for grasping why it is that some practices become stabilized and more widespread than others. In this sense the theory of social domains possesses the further advantage of greater

flexibility, for while there are many things of value in the synthetic alternatives, I think it remains true to claim that they can be incorporated into the
wider terms of reference allowed for in the theory of social domains.

Having sketched out in rather elementary terms the manner in which
domain theory differs from a number of current sociological approaches,
let me now indicate some of the sources it draws upon and complements.
First and foremost, domain theory is related to the classical projects of
Marx and Durkheim, who sought to open up the study of social phenomena to the rigours of scientific analysis. Now while the models of science
upon which their projects were based are not subtle enough to support the
insights of contemporary social theory, there are other associated features
of their work that bear a close relation to the theory of social domains. The
first of these is a conviction that many social phenomena have "objective"
characteristics (as well as subjective ones). This particularly applies to collective phenomena like culture, institutions and organizations, but can in
principle be extended to cover various aspects of face-to-face behaviour.

To say that social phenomena possess objective characteristics implies
that they have properties that cannot be explained simply in terms of the
conduct of particular individuals or specific encounters between people.
The discovery of the objectivity of the social realm was major, if not the
major contribution of these classical theorists. However, Durkheim and
Marx did not simply underwrite the objective nature of social phenomena, they also endeavoured to grasp the relationship between objective
and subjective aspects of social existence as it is reflected in the relation
between social institutions and the practical activities of those who are
subject to their influence. In this sense Marx and Durkheim were dualists
in that they tried to reconcile the existence of an outer (objective) social
reality with that of the inner subjective consciousness of people living
within the orbit of its influence. In both Durkheim and Marx this dualism
was connected to the historical movement of societies in the sense that
the outer objective reality was regarded as the product of conditions
inherited from the past. In this fundamental sense the classical project was
intimately concerned with the conjunction of different timeframes; that of
the accumulated products of social history and that of the contemporary
activities of members of society as they are formed and influenced by these
historically emergent conditions. This dualism (and the conjunction of
time frames that it enshrines) is something that the theory of social
domains includes within its terms of reference and thus it can be understood to be continuous with the classical projects of these authors.

In domain theory the notion of an outer objective realm of social phenomena provides a counter to those approaches (including structuration theory, phenomenology and interactionism) that propose that all forms of "objectivism" must be removed from social theory. The theory of social domains insists that such sweeping rejections of objectivism are premature and as a consequence, many important properties of society and social existence have been all but lost from view in social analysis. The objective realm of social phenomena must be recognized and properly analyzed and thus domain theory is continuous with this central aspect of classical sociology. Perhaps the main author bridging modern and classical sociology in this respect has been Talcott Parsons. Parsons's work with its emphasis on the different layerings of social organization (particularly the different system levels, including the crucially important social system) has a number of significant overlaps with domain theory. There are many aspects of Parsons's theory that I regard as insufficient, particularly its lack of a conception of power as domination and its inadequate account of the textured quality of social interaction (see Layder 1994). None the less, Parsons's insistence that each system level is interdependent with the others while still having its own characteristics, manages to convey something of the interweaving nature of macro and micro aspects of society without losing sight of the independent properties of either.

With its focal concern with the problem of social integration, Parsons's approach has more in common with Durkheim's work than it does with either Weber's or Marx's. However, it is to Marx we must turn in order to capture some appreciation of the forms of power and domination based on sectional interests that shape the institutional structures of modern capitalist societies. Marx's emphasis on the historically emergent inequalities (particularly of a class nature) is an absolutely essential requirement of any social theory that hopes to reflect something of the way in which the history of a society reveals the collective forces that have shaped its principal institutional features. Moreover, Marx more than any other was aware of the utmost importance of historical struggle and conflict between social groupings in forming the contemporary context of social activity. This refers precisely to the intersection of timeframes alluded to before, in which people's attempts to transform their present circumstances meet head-on with the resources bequeathed to them by previous generations. Marx pinpointed this important facet of social existence in a famous quotation to the effect that people "make their own history, but they do not make it just as they please; they do not make it under circumstances chosen by themselves, but under circumstances directly encountered, given and transmitted from the past" (Marx & Engels 1968: 96). While this is very much in accord with some of the central axioms of domain theory it has to be recognized that Marx's quotation has been the acknowledged starting point for other, quite different approaches (particularly structuration theory – see Giddens 1984: 6). Thus it has to be conceded that Marx's words can be subject to markedly different interpretations!

The major contemporary theorist who draws on Marx and whose work shares a good deal in common with domain theory is Jurgen Habermas. Habermas's distinction between "lifeworld" and "system" is highly suggestive and in many ways cuts across the distinctions I make about the principal social domains. I would want to distance myself from several of Habermas's formulations in his general framework, but much of the spirit and intention of his theory of "communicative action" fits comfortably with what I have to say about the theory of social domains. A central feature of Habermas's approach is his reliance on, and interpretation of the work of Marx, Durkheim and Weber and in this sense he too is at pains to fashion a continuity between some of the assumptions of classical sociological analysis and contemporary theory. In particular Habermas tries to forge a link between "systems theories" (like Parsons's), which centralize the role of the "objective" institutional features of society, with "action theories", which concentrate on understanding the nature of interpersonal encounters. In this respect Habermas's attempt at synthesis includes the work not only of Parsons but also of Mead, Wittgenstein and Austin.

The theory of social domains attempts a similar sort of marriage between action and systems (or "structural") approaches to social analysis and thus it bears some close affinities with Habermas's work. However, a significant point of difference is that domain theory borrows much more from the work of Erving Goffman. In my view Goffman's ideas have often been misrepresented simply as a form of interactionism. But it is clear from scattered comments and in particular from his presidential address to the American Sociological Association in 1982, that Goffman held a view of society in which the "interaction" order and the "institutional" orders are accorded equal importance. In this respect I would argue that Goffman's work has to be understood as a unique amalgam of influences that cannot be easily assimilated into the fold of action theories (see Meltzer et al. 1975). Goffman's work must be viewed as an attempt to trace the ligatures that bind institutional constraints and resources with those that are specific to the interaction order itself, and in this regard his work carries a direct link with that of Durkheim. However, whereas Durkheim was preoccupied with the realm of institutional constraint, Goffman concentrates on the dynamics of interpersonal encounters while locating them in a wider institutional context. This continuity with the dual preoccupations of classical theory – the nature of social activity and the nature of the social conditions that provide its environment – means that Goffman's ideas occupy a central place in the theory of social domains. I build on some of Goffman's formulations in order to develop a model of the relations between interpersonal encounters and the more encompassing settings and contexts in which they are played out.

Goffman's approach is important for domain theory in another sense. His fascination with the details of face-to-face encounters brings our attention firmly back to the realm of everyday life. It is this domain that is often neglected by approaches (like Parsons's and Marx's) that emphasize the more impersonal, collective and large-scale "macro" features of society. Domain theory underscores the importance of the arena of everyday life and the active human beings who are at its core and in this sense is quite at odds with those structuralist and post-structuralist theories that have attempted to "decentre" the human subject. The overall effect of these theories is virtually to abandon any concern with the "inner" social psychological resources and dispositions of individuals. While it is absolutely crucial not to make our social theories reducible to statements about the behaviour of individuals – the initial concern of the movement away from the subject in socal theory – it is equally important not to follow this train of logic to its opposite extreme. That is, it is essential not to dissolve an interest in individuals into a generalized concern with the social conditions and constructions that play an important role in modern social life. In this sense the domain of psychobiography as the site of the partly independent characteristics of individuals must be a key plank in any theory that endeavours to unravel the interweaving of society and face-to-face conduct.

There are two separable issues here. The first concerns the pivotal role of face-to-face conduct in everyday life, and as I have said, the work of Goffman and that of interactionist and phenomenological writers is essential for teasing out the texture, dynamics and details of interpersonal encounters. Thus these aspects of action theories must, and do play a part in the synthetic thrust of domain theory. The second issue concerns the fact that sociologists of quite different persuasions (including Goffman, Foucault, Althusser, Elias and Blumer) have overlooked the psychological dimension of human existence in their zeal to highlight the undeniable importance of social forces. It is this latter aspect that is often underplayed by sociologists, especially those who have taken the decentring of the human subject to an extreme. In this connection the work of Giddens is much closer to my own in so far as he pushes to the forefront the notion of human agents as actively engaged in grappling with, and transforming to varying degrees their immediate social circumstances. In more general terms, however, domain theory is quite unlike structuration theory in so far as it regards Giddens's uncompromising rejection of all forms of objectivism and dualism as premature and a hinderance to an in-depth account of the relations between social domains.

Power and emotion

Power, as Foucault has observed, is ubiquitous; its influence is everywhere in society from the level of the state to the finest capillaries of the routines of everyday life. In this sense power is not just a commodity possessed by an individual or a group and which confers control over others. The effects of power are diffuse and do not simply prohibit or limit the actions of others. Through its link with knowledge and social practices, power enables and disciplines minds and bodies, it gives substance to the capacities of some groups (such as professionals) and provokes resistance in those subjected to it. In short, power is productive and not simply a negative force. In very general terms I agree with Foucault's construal of power and its nature – particularly its everpresent and diffuse effects. In this respect Foucault has been responsible for enhancing our understanding of the nature of modern forms of power and certainly his vision must be part of any comprehensive theory of power. In so far as Foucault understands power to operate through discourses and the practices they are associated with, he views power as essentially a social construct that exists and operates beyond the sway of individual motivation and reason. In this particular sense I believe that there is a great deal of substance to Foucault's view because it precisely indicates a level of objectivity in social life. In this circumscribed sense the notion of a "subjectless" social analysis commands a well-founded sympathy.

However, it is all too easy to accept this poststructuralist position as the only viable analytic stance to take. Thus those influenced by Foucault often imagine that the analysis of discourses and practices that unify

13

various fields of power exhausts the possibilities of the investigation of power. However, by identifying power so closely with the level at which various forms of knowledge and discourse operate, Foucault limits his conception of power in two distinct senses. First all routes to the individual or "the person" are closed off and thus power as an aspect of agency is precluded from analysis. This is very unfortunate since there is no logical or substantive reason to suppose that the modern forms of power – notably disciplinary power and bio-power – do not exist alongside, and are related to other forms, including power as an aspect of human agency. By defining power exclusively as a social force that exists only at a level beyond the reach of individuals, Foucault arbitrarily excludes one of the most pervasively felt aspects of the experience of power in the modern world – the way in which people deploy the resources they have at their disposal to achieve certain ends. This is a common feature of everyday life in which people constantly jostle for status and attention by drawing on both personal and social resources to achieve those ends. Giddens has rightly drawn attention to this phenomenon in his notion of a "dialectic of control" (see Ch. 4 for an extended discussion). In order to tap into this interpersonal power it is necessary to include power as an aspect of human agency and not preclude it as Foucault does.

Let me hastily point out that there is often a reverse form of denial in which those who identify power exclusively with agency tend to reject the idea that it may operate at a level beyond the controlling orbit of particular individuals or groups. Giddens's view of power (along with those of Weber and various interactionist writers such as Luckenbill 1979) tends to do just this. By tying power to the asymmetrical relations between two or more people (or groups) and the alterations in the balance of power that result from the "give and take" effects of their quest for control, this action-centred view of power effectively denies the existence of other modes and sources of power. Not only does it rule out the Foucauldian notion of power as the objective effects of discourse, but also it suppresses the idea of power as a property of structural relations of domination. On this view, since power can be linked only with action then it cannot, by definition, be associated with purely structural, systemic or institutional (that is, non-acting) phenomena.

Strangely enough Foucault's image of power also tends to suppress the importance of a purely structural dimension since in his view this is overly identified with a more general structuralist account of society that relies on the notion of power as emanating from one principal source (such as the state or the bourgeoisie) and which in a further sense determines the form and content of all other power relations. However, in this respect Foucault overlooks the possibility of understanding power as a feature of relatively stable forms of structural domination that do not determine other power relations in any strong sense. (This, of course, implies a distinction between strong or complete determinism, as against a weaker sense that only implies some influence.) Thus, structural forms of power may be dispersed, fragmented and localized in the same manner as discursive forms. There is no need to suggest, as Foucault does, that modern forms of power operate in a continuous (rather than discontinuous) manner in advance of empirical investigation. In other words, the questions of how power operates and the form it takes are likely to be answered only as a result of accumulated evidence, rather than as a consequence of some general characteristic that all power is said to possess.

I believe that if power is understood as existing in the different senses covered in the above discussion, then we have a conception flexible enough to meet the requirements of a comprehensive theory of power. That is, one that attends to the need to capture power as a process at the same time as it reflects the multi-layered nature of society – its ontological depth. This embracing conception means that power can be understood as taking on multiple guises and operating simultaneously within different domains. That is, we can understand it as an integral part of the structural (or systemic) parameters of society at the same time as it can be considered as a discursive practice, an aspect of human agency and an element in the psychological make-up of individuals (see Crespi 1992). Such a multi-faceted conception of power is needed in order adequately to represent its ever-present and ubiquitous nature.

In this sense domain theory takes seriously Foucault's idea that power reaches into the finest capillaries of society and that it is not solely a privilege of those who are conventionally thought of as the "power-holders" in society. Foucault is quite right to jettison the idea that power is something that is possessed only by particular people, positions or groups in society. Unfortunately, however, Foucault's own rather restrictive view of power (and social analysis) makes it impossible for him to appreciate and absorb its multi-form character in his general approach. This, I would argue, is the proper destination of Foucault's vision of power that his own prior assumptions prevented him from reaching. It is an extremely important place to fix the conceptual net of power – to hold the line, so to speak, against further postmodern debilitations. I refer here to the purported

15

"disappearance" of power heralded by writer such as Baudrillard. I believe Foucault's radical conception of the diffuseness of power is as far as we can go conceptually without losing grip on the very phenomenon that we wish to understand. However, if all that is meant by "disappearance" is that the overt manifestations of power have been driven underground to be overlain and disguised by the signs and symbols of modern consumer society, or that signs themselves have come to take over some of the functions that other forms of power serve, then this is a more appropriate scenario. But if it is meant to imply the literal disappearance of forms of power then it is an immediately redundant proposition both theoretically and in terms of empirical evidence.

If power threads everywhere in society then it is a key element in the interweaving of social domains. The self and its psychobiography connect intimately with the domain of interpersonal behaviour (the "interaction order" in Goffman's terms) that fashions the contours of everyday life, and clearly, issues of power and control are central to this coupling. Similarly, those tracts of social life that stretch away from the immediacy of face-to-face encounters which constitute the routinized and sedimented aspects of social relations that have emerged in the historical context of particular societies (often referred to as "system" elements) reach back into, and are informed by the more personalized features of social life. Power in its different guises is the lubricant that allows the multitude of interdependencies and couplings of domains to take place.

However, power is not the only "essential ingredient" that precipitates and choreographs the movements of the social elements. I want to suggest that emotion too is a similar, behind-the-scenes co-ordinator. Although Goffman himself has done some pioneering work on the emotions, Scheff (1990) has pointed out that this area has been considerably neglected by sociologists and that even Goffman tended to limit his analysis to that of face-to-face relations between people (the interaction order). As such he neglects the psychological level of analysis and omits consideration of motives (Scheff 1990: 29–30). Scheff's own work on this topic goes some distance in rectifying this situation and I draw on it in good measure in this book. Like power, emotion infiltrates far into the social fabric colonizing every crevice and cranny that it encounters. As Scheff has observed though, the massively emotional tenor of social life is generally obscured by repression, bypassing and the typical invisibility of much emotion work. The vast underground network of emotions is subtly and silently implicated in social life and is thus rarely acknowledged.

In the theory of social domains emotion is understood as something closely akin to power in so far as the two are frequently allied. The distribution of occupations requiring emotional labour in society (teaching, the "caring" professions like social work, nursing and so on), closely mirrors the gender distribution and thus is implicated in patriarchal power. The structural asymmetry of gender divisions is a feature of all modern societies (if not all societies) and this insinuates itself into the social fabric as a whole through a number of access points and at several domain "levels". Thus emotion can also be seen as a discursive order in which "feeling rules" shape the social responses of people in daily conduct. The deployment of such rules and the manipulation of deference and demeanour in social interaction is, as Goffman has shown, intimately related to status and power. In like manner the emotions of shame and pride at a psychological level are associated with feelings of inferiority or superiority that, in turn, are closely linked to relations of power in the class structure (Leonard 1984).

Most forms and instances of power bear a complementary relation to emotion in social life. Sometimes emotion is the object of power plays and strategies, as in the attempt to manipulate one person's feelings by another, or a national government's endeavour to influence the populace's emotional attachment to particular leaders, or their commitment to a political regime. At other times emotion is simply an accompaniment to the effects of power as in the example of the abandonment of children by their parents or the neglect or abuse of prisoners by their captors or gaolers. In yet other instances emotion itself may be a constitutive feature of power as in the example of charismatic personalities who command large followings of devotees be they religious leaders or popular entertainers. As Scheff has observed, pride and shame are the principal social emotions and are to be found everywhere in social life. This, I would suggest, is precisely because power itself is ubiquitous and everpresent and that emotion is its natural partner.

By understanding power and emotion as intrinsically linked in this manner across the different domains from systemic (or structural) to individual levels of analysis, we are more easily able to connect them with issues of gender, racialization and subjectivity. This is because gender relations hinge around questions of power and control in so far as women are generally subordinated to men in modern societies. Feminists have pointed out (for example Lengermann & Niebrugge-Brantley 1992) that it is important that the individual's interpretations should be taken into account especially in the case of women because as subordinates they often experience the world in very different ways from those who dominate (men) and the established cultural representations that reflect this domination. Thus, it is argued, subjectivity should form a distinct level of analysis in its own right. This would provide a means of documenting the forms of exclusion from particular areas of interaction and social life that women (or other subordinate groups including racialized groups and oppressed minority groups such as mentally ill or disabled people), experience in sociallife. Very often sociological analysis glosses over questions of subjectivity in its endeavour to concentrate on the operation of "purely" social forces.

Also it is frequently assumed that subjective factors are somehow "biased" and undermine the objectivity of sociological accounts. In particular subjective responses such as emotional reactions are thought to be unscientific because they undo the rational and logical form of many sociological approaches and the methods of research on which they are based (Stanley & Wise 1983, Harding 1987, Smith 1988). Much the same point has been made by postmodernists (Denzin 1990, Rosenau 1992), who suggest that the dominant logic of the sciences must be challenged since it itself is an element of the system of power that contributes to the oppression of various groups. Thus they call for attention to be paid to the local narratives, subjectivities and emotional viewpoints of various subordinated groups in modern society.

Such attention is important and domain theory underscores this emphasis. However, a crucial rider to this is that it must not be forgotten that subjectivities and emotional responses while important in their own right, directly reflect, and are implicated in, the objective distributions of power and resources in society – its institutional structure. So in this sense there are macro counterparts to the micro events including the subjective experience of social encounters and these must not be omitted in the clamour to include such subjective elements. This is where domain theory diverges from some feminist and postmodernist writing. Postmodernists reject any possibility of "scientific" knowledge based on rational or objective assumptions, thus they wish to replace it with the voices of excluded groups who articulate their subjective experiences of oppression. Domain theory does not reject the notion of systematic and objective knowledge, but neither does it preclude the analysis of subjectivity.

Similarly, domain theory does not go along with those feminists who dismiss macro-sociological knowledge as flawed because it is based on

18

male notions of objectivity and rational theorizing. Such views simply restrict themselves in their explanatory scope by arbitrarily excluding whole areas of knowledge and this is surely ironic since their original purpose was to question the validity of such forms of exclusion. Also since by its very nature the theory of social domains endorses the enterprise of theorizing, it is at odds with those postmodernists and feminists who believe that such theorizing is impossible, fruitless or misguided. Again these views simply restrict the parameters of knowledge and limit the boundaries of validity and legitimate debate when much of their original impetus derived from a questioning of such arbitrary restrictions.

Some basic propositions

Having talked in a rather general manner about the nature of the theory of social domains and how it fits in with some of the existing approaches and diverges from others, let me conclude this chapter by spelling out some of its more specific implications in the form of a series of propositions and conceptual strategies. These will act as initial formulations of ideas and issues that will receive systematic attention in the chapters that follow.

1. Domain theory is primarily concerned with understanding the nature of social activity in general and interpersonal encounters in particular. It is not a theory of society as such, although it "draws in" elements of such a theory. It is concerned with society in a larger sense only in so far as it is crucial to the understanding of face-to-face conduct.

2. The viewpoint of the human actor is taken to be of critical importance. Examining social life from the standpoint of how it is experienced is essential to understanding encounters in a more general sense. However, it is crucial to note that this does not imply that the viewpoint of the actor is the only or the primary vantage point. The ability to adopt the point of view of an "external observer" is vital (Habermas 1984,1987). Also the importance of the actor's viewpoint should not lead us to suppose that social life is a purely intersubjective phenomenon.

3. There are collective properties of social life that historically emerge to form objective features that provide the wider background context and the immediate settings of activities. These features constitute part of the social organization of society and typically pre-exist and

outlast particular individuals' lifetimes. That is, they are part of the ongoing ensemble of social insitutions, cultural traditions and patterns of social relationships that people are compelled to take into account in their daily lives. So although domain theory is interested in encounters from the actor's point of view, it understands the actor to be located within an enveloping social fabric with its own special characteristics. Thus its approach is rather unusual since most theories that concern themselves with social interaction from the actor's point of view (symbolic interactionism, ethnomethodology, phenomenology, structuration theory), all strongly deny or reject the existence of objective elements of social life in this sense.

4. The previous point leads to consideration of the kind of objectivism that domain theory endorses. It is best characterized as a "moderate" rather than an extreme form of objectivism. This is important because those who reject objectivism invariably concentrate on the extreme form and thus they overlook the possibilities inherent in the more moderate version. There are five main criticisms of the extreme version of objectivism. I shall take each in turn and show how none of them applies to the moderate version.

(a) A common criticism of objectivism is that it reifies social phenomena. This suggests several related things. First, that society is produced by non-human forces – possibly mystical or religious entities. Of course domain theory, like most sociological theories views social phenomena as the product of human activity. Secondly, reification implies that society has an objective form that is completely autonomous or beyond the reach of individuals. In domain theory as I have just said, society is understood as the outcome of human activity and therefore it follows that even though objective aspects may emerge over time, they are still susceptible to people's attempts to change or rearrange them. Therefore the criticism of reification is not applicable to this moderate form of objectivism.

(b) Another criticism of the extreme version is that it is implicated in an "imperialism of the object" (Giddens 1984: 2). In other words it is said that objectivism proposes that human practices are explained in terms of society-wide (macro) features that are thought to be primary or the most important aspects of social life. Domain theory rejects this because it is based on the assumption that objective and subjective aspects of social life are interdependent and mutually influential in shaping social practices. So in this sense objectivism simply points to an objective realm as an important constitutive feature of social life. It does not suggest that it is the most important or that everything else can be explained in terms of this realm alone.

(c) An associated criticism is that objectivism implies and is necessarily coupled with determinism – the view that human activities are the outcome of the constraining nature of external structures and systems. However, as in the above point the moderate version simply says that human activity is the outcome of the dual influence of external (macro) and situational (micro) factors. There is a mutual influence not a one-way determinism.

(d) It is often assumed that objectivism is automatically tied to the view that sociology is a science that is in principle the same as the natural sciences like chemistry, physics, biology and so on. These sciences deal with an inert and independent subject matter about which generalizations and universal laws can be made. It is true that some schools of theory and approaches in sociology have emphasized the similarities between the social and the natural sciences and that they have also been those that have stressed the importance of macro-analysis or society as a totality.

However, there is no logical entailment here. The moderate objectivism that I speak of recognizes that a large part of the subject matter of the social world comprises people and their activities. Thus it recognizes the importance of interpretive methods and strategies in social research. This form of objectivism takes the view that social research must be sensitive to both the objective and subjective realms of social life. Each must be understood at and approached from its own level in order to preserve its distinctive features. Otherwise there is the real danger of either collapsing the objective level into the subjective level or absorbing the subjective component into an objective frame of reference. Both of these forms of "reductionism" seriously misrepresent social analysis.

(e) The final critique of objectivism holds that it is inevitably yoked to functionalist and structuralist schools of social theory – and therefore suffers from the same shortcomings (many of which are covered in points (a), (b), (c), and (d) above). Again there is no logical reason why it should be that all forms of objectivism should be linked to functionalism and structuralism. The moderate version is simply committed to recognizing the importance of an objective level of analysis; it has no commitments whatsoever to functionalist or structuralist theories and therefore cannot be said to possess the same weaknesses.

5. Social constraints must be understood in a dual sense as both constituent features of people's reasons and motives as well as part of an "external" set of cultural resources and obstacles to the fulfilment or achievement of objectives and which "compel" people to take them into account. This is directly counter to Giddens's view that social constraint cannot be understood independently of people's reasons and motivations. Such a position confuses and conflates psychological and social phenomena that although intimately related have essentially different characteristics.

   External constraints do not operate independently of people, but they have properties that are not reducible to people or the reasons and motives that they give for their behaviour. Of course, we are not compelled by social forces until we are psychologically engaged with them and this may occur voluntarily or through some measure of coercion. However, even voluntary compliance does not override the compelling character of social constraints. Individuals are free to decide whether to pursue certain goals or ambitions – such as achieving high career status or escaping from poverty – or to give up on them, but they cannot ignore the need for specific credentials or refuse to take account of the social obstacles that must be overcome if they decide to go ahead. Once an objective has been decided upon, then conformity with socially defined means of achieving it is a precondition of success. In this sense the external compulsion facilitates an individual's motives and reasons. Thus, both psychological and social constraints are intrinsically linked but they impact quite differently on the activity in question.

6. In domain theory power is regarded as a variegated phenomenon. It threads through the different social domains and takes on different guises in the process. I have said quite a bit about power already in this chapter so I shall not elaborate any further at this point. It simply needs to be borne in mind that domain theory challenges the assumption that power is a unitary phenomenon – an impression fostered by certain schools of thought that define power in very specific terms and that exclude other possibilities.

7. It is important to distinguish between the reproduced and emergent aspects of social relations and practices. The reproduced aspects represent the "circumstances transmitted from the past" (in Marx's phrase) and which people are forced to take into account in social life

even when they are actively trying to change or transform social arrangements. By contrast, the emergent aspects of social relations and practices draws our attention to the innovative character of face-to-face encounters. There is an intersection of timeframes involved here. The "pastness" of the inherited circumstances transmitted through reproduced relations and practices is brought into the "presentness" of unfolding encounters between people. Social activity has to be understood in the context of the intermingling of these very different timeframes and social process and it is important not to lose sight of their distinctive features, even though activity itself is an untidy amalgam of their influences.

8. The theory of social domains is against what Giddens (1984) calls the "phoney war" between action and structure (or systems) theorists who insist on separation and opposition between these social domains. Clearly these domains are implicated in, and deeply inter-fused with each other. However, Giddens's proposed resolution of this problem by analytically merging the domains into a synthetic "duality of structure" is quite unsuitable. This is because it entails the abandonment of any form of objectivism and this means an inevitable overweighting of the action (subjective, micro) side of the equation. Equally important it loses sight of, and analytic purchase on, the distinctive characteristics of different social domains and the extent of their mutual influences (Archer 1995).

Instead, domain theory understands the co-mingling of different timeframes and ontological features in the context of what Goffman (1983) calls a "loose-coupling" between the interaction order and the institutional order. Although Goffman's general views are in need of elaboration and amendment, his specific argument about the nature of the interaction order as a domain in its own right is important for an adequate understanding of the processes of social production and reproduction. By compacting or dissolving the distinct characteristics of the domains, many sociologists and schools of theory overlook or omit a special consideration of the workings of the interaction order in this respect. As a result they do not adequately deal with questions bound up with this issue concerning the extent to which human beings are creative agents involved in the construction of social reality (see Berger & Luckmann 1967). The existence of distinct domains (and in this case, principally situated activity) requires us to think in terms of different kinds of creativity in relation to the construction of social reality. At the same time it demands that we think of social reproduction as the outcome of different kinds of processes having varying effects on the everchanging character of social life.

9. It may be easier to apprehend the notion of social processes evolving "horizontally" over time since the experience of social life itself closely mirrors the emergence and development of behaviour and the passing of temporal markers in the movement from place to place in everyday life. However, this ease of "empathetic understanding" should not blot out the significance of a vertical dimension to social analysis and which is reflected in the layering of domains. This is perhaps made even more difficult since the best way of "visualizing" the depth dimension is by "freezing the frame" so to speak – by artificially examing action from the point of view of a fixed moment in time. This is acceptable as long as we acknowledge that it is simply an analytic device that allows access to the depth dimension and does not imply that we can "halt" social processes or that social reality is in some way static rather than continuously emergent. The real point is that the two dimensions operate simultaneously from the point of view of ongoing social activity and we should therefore be aware of the significance of them both.

This is important because it distinguishes domain theory from approaches that overstress the importance of social processes. By putting on process "blinkers" as it were, these approaches overlook or ignore the differentiation of social reality in a "vertical" sense and propose images or models of the social world based on a flattened ontology. In their different ways Elias, Giddens, Foucault (as well as interactionists and phenomenologists) all tend to offer images of societies as undifferentiated process. This strategy has the apparent advantage of overcoming any false distinctions and separations that may be lurking as a residual effect of the influence of objectivism in sociology. However, at the same time it fails to register the parameters of the distinct domains themselves, the roles they perform and the effects they produce within and between their principal areas of influence.

10. The social actor is a complex and contradictory being who has an emotional and cognitive depth. One important implication of this statement is that while there is much of value to be learned from interactionist and phenomenological schools of thought, we should

24

not be tempted to cling to their overly rational or cognitive view of the person. There is no need to exclude a notion of the unconscious that draws on deep wells of emotion of which we have little, if any, conscious awareness and rational control. However, in so doing the unconscious must not understood as a deterministic entity that completely replaces our conscious intentions and plans. Thus we do not have to follow Sartre's (1966) critique of Freud to its radical conclusion and adopt a purely phenomenological account of social being. I think it is both possible and necessary to retain many, if not all, the insights of those schools of thought (including existentialism) that highlight the rationality and "freedom" inherent in human activity without abandoning the notion of the unconscious altogether.

This offers us an image of individuals as beings who are always at least partly aware of what they are doing and why. To say that we are always partly aware implies that there are motivational elements that circle in and out of our conscious awareness and that impinge on our behavioural responses to others. These "unconscious" (perhaps "pre-conscious" may be a better word) elements are a historical residue of memories, emotions, wishes, imaginative phantasies and so forth, that have accumulated over the lifetime of the individual. As both the psychoanalytic and psychotherapeutic traditions have emphasized, childhood experiences are of key moment here since they contain primary experiential material acquired during our earliest and perhaps most formative years of life. However, I would go along with those (neo-Freudian) schools of thought that have sought to play down the overwhelming importance that Freud attached to childhood experiences in general (and infantile sexuality in particular). This involves balancing up our account of the individual by stressing the equally formative influences of later years and the continuing importance of current bonds and relationships as inputs into our emotional experiences.

In short this storehouse of emotionally charged memories, basic feelings and primary attachments plays a critical role in shaping our dispositions and orientations to the social world. I think that the term "psychobiography" aptly conveys the sense in which the unfolding of an individual's life provides a recurrent source of feedback that adds to and modifies the ballast of emotional energies that fuels our social responses and attitudes. The term also has the advantage that it conveys both the social and private senses of individual existence. This fundamental duality is of significance in so far as it indicates the basic point of intersection and articulation between the social and psychological worlds. To understand and register this nodal point is an important counterweight to those approaches that centre their attention on either one or the other of these worlds.

Clearly there are many psychologically orientated approaches that tend to view the individual as a separate atom split off from the social environment and this is also reflected in some political philosophies that emphasize the significance of individualism and self-reliance. Such views are erroneous in so far as they accord far too much in the way of freedom of action to individuals and their ability to manipulate social circumstances. However, some sociologists are also prone to this mistake by assuming too great an ability of the individual to create and transform their social circumstances. These schools of thought (notably interactionism and phenomenology) have been critical of the image, reflected in the work of many macro-sociologists, of an individual whose thoughts and actions are almost wholly determined by the social system. Unfortunately this image has been substituted by them for one in which social system influences are either non-existent or severely muted. As such, interactionism and phenomenology tend to stress that social life is conducted entirely at the face-to-face level and hence overplay the degree to which people can change or rearrange social circumstances at will.

Other thinkers such as Foucault and Elias, for very different reasons and with contrary theoretical implications, have focused on the socially constructed nature of individuals as a direct response to the "individualist" theories that they see as responsible for a "wrong turn" in social analysis. However, these writers and the interactionists mentioned above have over-reacted to the threat of psychological reductionism by proposing views that tend to obliterate the notion of individuals as effective single agents in the social world, or as "private", emotionally unique persons who are in a significant sense "separated" from the social world at the same time as being part of it. It is essential not to lose sight of this aspect of human existence in our zeal to avoid a preoccupation with individuals as fundamentally cut-off from social involvements. This tendency is very much at the heart of postmodern attempts to insist on the socially constructed nature of "subjectivities" without a parallel concern to rescue some notion of individual agency as standing apart from and resistant to social forces.

Although of course the person is material entity – a body in a biological and physiological sense – and this is the bedrock upon which the distinctively human and social characteristics of people are erected, the duality between the psychological and social worlds is of pivotal importance. Habermas has drawn attention to the distinction between what he calls the social and subjective worlds and I would want to endorse his ideas on them as distinctive domains. However, it must be borne in mind that Habermas has a tendency to overdraw certain distinctions and I would not want to follow him along this particular path. Thus while there are distinct properties associated with the different worlds it would be inaccurate to understand them as clean-cut and neat separations. The seam between them is fairly untidy and rather indefinite with regard to their overlapping influences, but I think that the intrinsic connection between them can be expressed in terms of what I shall call the "dialectic of separateness and relatedness".

I believe that this duality expresses the contradictory tensions involved in the intersecting ties of the social and psychological worlds. Thus the mental interior of a person is intrinsically both psychological and social in nature. That is, an individual's subjectivity (expressed through their psychobiographical career) is an amalgam of both psychological dispositions developed out of their unique biographical circumstances and the habits, customs and orientations that reflect their involvements in particular social groupings. Bourdieu (1977) refers to the latter as the social "habitus" and for him it expresses the medium through which social agency is linked to objective social structures. This is a very useful concept that does indeed reflect something of the duality of social existence although it does not readily express the idea of the individual as a unique psychological reality and thus suggests an undue weighting of social influences. It is absolutely crucial to stress the egocentric nature of human beings as well as their socio-centric tendencies. The individual is simultaneously situated within and beyond society – there is a private and separate aspect of the individual that co-exists with the "public" involvements entailed in social life. Conversely, society exists both within individuals (as a mutuality of influences) and outside and beyond the reach of particular individuals and groups (as reproduced relations). Thus it is essential for a sociological approach to incorporate some notion of a separate ego as part of the duality between psychological (subjective) and social realms.

Since the tensions and dynamics between the forces of separateness and relatedness are such that individuals can never bring them into perfect alignment, then they are constantly embroiled in struggles to control the effects of one or the other. Social involvement brings with it the possibility of being controlled or in some way being overly influenced by others and yet a quest for aloneness or separateness underlines the issue of our routine dependence on others. Ronald Laing (1969) has discussed some of these problems in relation to people suffering from schizophrenia and this directly links up with the issue of self-identity. Those who are mentally ill often suffer from violent oscillations between the poles of separateness and relatedness in a vain attempt to maintain a sense of identity. Closely associated with this is what Laing calls "ontological security" – an individual's basic trust in the reality and worth of themselves as these are reflected in the responses of others. Giddens (1984, 1990, 1991) has also effectively employed the term to make a general point about its importance in all social behaviour. Giddens's main concern, however, is with the issue of ontological security and its relation to risk factors in modern society. My own emphasis will be on the centrality of this basic form of security from the point of view of the maintenance of self and self-composure during face-to-face conduct.

Coda

In some respects the theory of social domains borrows heavily from other approaches and attempts to build on them. In other respects the theory takes its shape from a concerted attempt to provide an alternative to approaches that argue for an abandonment of all forms of objectivism and the use of macro-structural (or system) concepts as a means of understanding social activity and face-to-face encounters. While there is some point to retaining a critical outlook on some aspects of objectivism it is premature and unwise to engage in the kind of wholesale rejection sanctioned by some sociologists. The point of attempting to construct a coherent alternative based around a moderate notion of objectivism is to highlight that so much of explanatory value would be lost to social theory (and thus to social research) if we simply ruled it out of court.

2

The contours of everyday life

Let me begin the discussion by focusing on some of the issues raised at the end of Chapter 1. Since the point of view of the actor is of critical importance in the theory of social domains, this chapter charts some of the more detailed ramifications of this in relation to a broader context of institutional and structural issues. That is, while the actor's perspective and the inner texture of face-to-face conduct in everyday life are the main topics here, my discussion will spread outwards, so to speak, to connect with issues of a broader systemic nature. This is because my basic assumption is that all domains are simultaneously implicated in each other, but that for purposes of exposition it is best to concentrate on one while temporarily bracketing the others. In Chapter 3 I shall reverse this procedure by focusing on a foreground of what are conventionally thought of as macro (structural or systemic) issues while constantly referring back to the world of interpersonal encounters.

Language, communication and self-identity

That human beings have selves is something of a commonplace observation, a taken-for-granted assumption about the nature of social existence although questions concerning the nature of the self and how it is constituted are perhaps less obvious. The notion of a self is a key idea in understanding the nature not only of individual human beings but also of the social ambience in which most human activity is played out. Much of the "work" that goes on in face-to-face interaction has to do with the presentation, protection and maintenance of selves in social life. Thus, it is important to view the self as a unit of social organization in its own right. Here, I shall not attempt anything like a comprehensive discussion of the nature and development of the self since this would take us away from the primary concerns of the book. Instead I shall simply indicate the basic outlines of the self as they feed into the later topics of awareness, trust, security, emotion and the dialectic of separateness and relatedness.

Mead's (1967) discussion of the self is a useful starting point since he views it as a truly social construct. I shall go on to dispute the idea that the self is entirely social in this sense, but there is no question that the self is firmly anchored in the social domain. For Mead the self also represents the distinctively human nature of social behaviour because of its intrinsic link with linguistic communication. Only human beings (as opposed to insect or invertebrate societies) have minds and selves, the possession of which allows them to respond in a much more subtle fashion to their environment than other animals. In this sense human beings cannot be understood in terms of a behaviourist psychology (proposed by the likes of Watson & Skinner) as if they were mere organisms reacting mechanically to stimuli in the environment and indicating the presence of rewards and punishments (or penalties) for engaging in certain kinds of behaviour.

Human beings characteristically respond to their social environment in a much more complex way involving the kinds of inner mental processes that behaviourists reject. For Mead this fact reflected the workings of the human mind and self that allow individuals to think quickly through the consequences of lines of activity in terms of the meanings that various situations have for them. Humans are able to rehearse imaginatively and test out the probable consequences of various behavioural options and to anticipate others' responses to their own behaviour. The self is a crucial element in this process since an ability to self-reflect is a precondition for this kind of imaginative rehearsal of behaviour. This is made possible through linguistic communication. Instead of being restricted to "gestural" or physical signalling as are animals (such as the baring of teeth in dogs or the emission of various sounds in fighting cats), the use of language in humans allows for truly symbolic communication. This abstract feature of language enables a degree of detachment from the demands and exigencies of the immediate circumstances and this creates a cognitive space in which a considered response (rather than an immediate reaction) may occur.

Language is also a reservoir of ready-made meanings as well as a stock of raw materials (words, grammatical and syntactical rules) out of which an infinite supply of newly minted meanings and interpretations may emerge. The existence of such resources means that a high degree of flexibility and negotiation can take place in human interaction. The give and take of face-to-face conduct – the way in which individuals tolerate, or try to override others' demands and feelings – is very much dependent upon the ability to oscillate between the "outer" immediacy of an encounter and the "inner" mental checking and readjusting that takes place in the minds of the participants. The self is implicated in this very process since, as Mead says, the ability to take the role of another and to see oneself from another's point of view is an essential requirement of successful social interaction. Of course the whole process takes place very rapidly and is reliant on the competence and skills of the participants. In turn these are linked to a generalized knowledge of how to "go on in a form of life" that involves tacit understanding of the rules and appropriate forms of behaviour associated with different settings as Wittgenstein (1972) pointed out.

The close association between context, meaning and language has also been noted by writers influenced by Mead. Blumer (1969) in particular stresses that human action is closely shaped by the meanings that people impute to the situations and things that they confront in their everyday lives. He argues that these meanings arise from, and are reshaped and readjusted during, the process of interaction. For example, the meaning of a "peck on the cheek" between a man and a woman in an office corridor will mean different things if it is performed by two people doing it for the first time than if it is a regular goodbye kiss between longstanding partners. The meaning of such behaviour depends crucially on contextual particulars such as the respective statuses of those involved and how they respond to each other, the nature of their relationship and the kind of situation in which it occurs (routine, out of the ordinary, formal, casual, an emergency and so on).

Garfinkel (1967) has also noted the contextual dependence of meaning in the sense that people are always in the process of interpreting or reinventing the rules that are appropriate for, or applicable to, various situations. Also ethnomethodologists have pointed out that the manner in which things are communicated (the tone of voice, facial expression, gestures and so on) is important in conveying meaning. This idea is probably an even more radical one than that proposed by Blumer, although without doubt there is some overlapping of approach here. However, a critique of this kind of position would point to the fact that meaning cannot be extracted directly from the context of particular instances of linguistic communication (the idea that meaning is context-tied) any more than it can be "deduced" from a formal statement of the words used (the view that meaning is context-free). The upshot is that meaning arises both from within the immediate circumstances of encounters as well as from "outside" – from general linguistic resources such as discourses as well as established definitions and usages of terms and words. Neverthless, face-to-face conduct certainly plays a crucial role in the construction of meaning even if this meaning is largely tied to particular circumstances.

In Mead's view then there is a close relationship between language, meaning and self-identity. However, such a view implies that the self emerges out of and is constituted exclusively by social forces. While there is some value in viewing the self as situationally and socially anchored, it also precludes the influence of the "unconscious" in social life. In this respect we have to understand that Mead believed the self to be flexible and hence could not be the result of fixed personality traits, hereditary characteristics or instinctual drives. The self has a plasticity that is moulded, shaped and developed in the context of ongoing interaction, and does not stand immutably against the currents of social life. Mead distinguished two phases of the process of self-constitution, the "I" represents the impulsive, inquisitive and creative side of the individual – in a sense the pre-social phase of the self that initiates action in the social arena. The "me" phase represents that socialized aspect of the self that brings the impulsiveness of the "I" under the controlling influence of social constraint. It represents the internalized norms and mores and moral standards that are current in the groupings to which the individual belongs.

A person's behaviour can be understood as a composite of these two phases of the self, with the interplay between the unfettered, inquisitive spirit of the "I" continually tempered by the restraints embodied in the generalized social attitudes of the "me". However, Mead's view sets up something of a paradox around the area of social behaviour in that the individual seems to be both social and asocial. In particular his notion of the "I" tends to imply some elemental aspect of the self that, even if only momentarily, escapes the homogenizing influence of society – a phase of the self that sets it apart from the crowd so to speak. I think we can understand this tension and opposition in relation to Mead's more general view of the connection between individuals and society. The "I" after all is only the initiating phase of activity; it is never effective outside the context of the later controlling phase of the "me". Thus any "standing apart" of the self from societal influence has to be understood as taking place entirely within the parameters of existing social relations and thus cannot be said to be literally independent of them.

None the less, although he does not explicitly talk about it in this manner, Mead's distinction between the "I" and the "me" does indicate in a preliminary way a basic duality that I take to be an important generic feature of social existence. I call this the "dialectic of separateness and relatedness" and is meant to convey the paradox that the individual is an inescapably social creature yet at the same time set apart from others in existential aloneness. As I define it, an important aspect of existential aloneness – this physical and psychological apartness from others – is the notion of an unconscious. Now this immediately distinguishes what I have to say from Mead's notion of the self since in his terms it has nothing to do with any sphere beyond that of conscious awareness. The self in Mead's sense is an entirely social construct determined within the play of interaction and has no causal connection with anything innate, or biologically prior to the social arena. Furthermore, I define the idea of an unconscious realm so as to include some notion of the affectual nature of the self, and this again cuts across Mead's understanding of the self and social activity as entirely cognitive in character. Thus, my notion of the self understands it to be a conduit of both conscious and unconscious emotional freight that is deployed in activity in various ways.

Awareness, self-deception and emotion

For the purposes of the approach outlined here, I propose that the self should be construed as possessing an unconscious element and that Mead's stress on its cognitive, reasoning and rational side should be counterbalanced with an emphasis on the importance of emotion. In this sense "individuality" is not simply a social construct but has to do with an inner mental life – a psychological, affectual energy that constantly interacts with the social entanglements of the individual. To complete this amended picture these elements of the self need to be connected to some notion of biographical time as it depicts the history of a person's involvements with significant others in their lives. All these elements comprise what I shall call the "psychobiography" of the individual. This traces the career of self-identities as they emerge, develop, reconstitute and regenerate themselves as a result of a person's unique configurations of experience and social contacts over the course of their lives.

As such, I am proposing an amalgam of interactionist, phenomenolo-gical and psychotherapeutic ideas that are rarely brought together in this way. However, I believe that many of the barriers that have been thought to stand in the way of any kind of integration of these approaches have more to do with the staking out of intellectual territories and their defence. For instance it has been often asserted that the Freudian notion of the unconscious is incompatible with a view of behaviour as planful, inten-tional and purposive. This is the kind of critique that Sartre (1966) directs against Freud's ideas. In essence, Sartre argues strongly against Freud's view of human beings driven by irrational forces of which they have no conscious awareness or control.

Sartre considers this is a highly deterministic view of human behaviour that must be counterposed by a model of the person as essentially rational and free (from the determinations of unconscious forces). In this model people are always aware, at least in part, of why they are doing the things they do – they are never irresistibly driven by forces they know nothing about. Thus, instead of consulting people's unconscious in order to find out why they do the things they do, Sartre proposes that we must inquire into people's plans, intentions, hopes, fears and anxieties as they are aware of them. We must examine people's being-in-the-world – the manner in which they consciously take on projects in order to achieve certain ends. For Sartre, invoking the notion of unconscious memories, wishes and fears and so on, which have been repressed from awareness by some censoring mechanism, involves something of a logical contradiction. How can such a censoring mechanism be at work in the human mind repressing certain thoughts, ideas and feelings without the person being in some way aware of it?

Sartre discusses an example involving sexual unresponsiveness in order to develop an alternate approach. He suggests that we do not have to understand the development of sexual indifference in terms of mysterious unconscious drives. Rather, such behaviour develops for straightforward reasons such as individual's real or imagined fear that their partner is sexually interested in others. Sartre points out that what often happens in these cases is that those who have lost interest deny that this is something that they have deliberately chosen to do, and instead believe it has "hap-pened to them" like getting a cold or becoming ill. That is, people deceive themselves in order to deny responsibility for their own intentions and behaviour. To convince themselves that they are not responsible they have to engage in a kind of self-deception that Sartre describes as "living in bad faith". For Sartre this then replaces the notion of unconscious forces that may be affecting an individual's behaviour unbeknownst to them. Even though people may be strictly "unaware" of the nature of their self-deception the behaviour itself is meaningful and experienced only in a world with which they are familiar.

Instead of viewing human behaviour as a response to the dictates of irrational and unknown forces Sartre focuses on the ways in which people choose to respond to the social circumstances in which they find themselves. For instance although slaves are "unfree" in an obvious and formal sense, in another way they are free to choose to be whatever sort of slave they want to be – compliant, resistant and so on. In this sense human beings are free to choose to be whatever sort of person they wish – for instance they may choose mental illness or to pursue power ruthlessly. Whatever it is that a person becomes is in some part due to the conscious deliberations and lived experience of the individual who has taken on that persona. The reasons that individuals offer for their behaviour may be unconvincing, confused or false – but they are, none the less, reasons. Their "reasonableness" has to be judged against what we know, or observe about their mode of existence, the problems they face in their personal and social relationships, and the way they deal with them.

Sartre is right to reject the highly deterministic interpretation of the unconscious because it denies agency to the individual – the ability to take action in the light of a conscious assessment of the circumstances. However, this should not necessarily lead us to reject completely the notion of the unconscious in order to explain aspects of behaviour that reach beyond conscious awareness. This becomes more obvious when we carefully scrutinize Sartre's notion of bad faith or self-deception. To say that people are deceiving themselves implies two possibilities. First, that they are genuinely not aware of the real or underlying reasons for their behaviour and that they are therefore not "conscious" of them. This kind of self-deception involves something very much like a "lack of awareness" of the underlying reasons. Secondly, people may deceive themselves in the sense that they actually "know" what the underlying reasons are, but choose to disregard them and believe something more palatable. Here we are on uncertain ground because we have to say that in this example people are aware that they are unaware, or that some part of their mind was aware while another part was unaware. In any case is it possible to say that people really do know something at the same time as saying that they are unaware of it?

I raise these conundrums not in order to solve them or to say that they are impossible to unravel, but rather to point to the need for a notion of the unconscious that is not hedged in by the sorts of difficulties associated with the deterministic version of Freud's ideas. That is, there is a need for some notion of the unconscious that would allow us to speak of motivating factors that are not acknowledged or fully part of conscious deliberations. This would enable us to speak of underlying reasons that are prone to "drift" in and out of conscious awareness at different points in time and in relation to a person's willingness or reluctance to entertain them. Thus we need the notion of the unconscious precisely in order to deal with the issue of self-deception since we cannot be acting both intentionally and unintentionally at the same time.

The notion of the unconscious also helps us to understand conscious awareness more fully by indicating that there are some things that we may overlook and that only another person may be able to point out to us when we attempt to be self-reflexive. Emotional factors are typically of this nature. Some memories and experiences are so painful that we resist full acknowledgement. Some feelings about who we are (our identities) and our emotional responses to others (such as our parents), although felt in some way, are often carefully segregated from our awareness in routine face-to-face encounters. It is exactly these memories and feelings that are the subject of psychotherapeutic investigations, and the notion of "resistance" is pertinent here. Typically, those undergoing therapy resist acknowledgement of particular memories or feelings because of their painful nature. The whole point of therapy is to bring such factors into the conscious awareness of clients in order that they can begin the emotional work required to be able to integrate important aspects of themselves into their personality and behaviour.

Not only emotionally charged memories are of significance here (although the unconscious is primarily concerned with affect accumulated over time). Emotional freight that derives from current face-to-face encounters is also importantly implicated. One's reaction to a particular person or situation may be coloured to varying degrees by anger, shame, love, and so on. As with the influence of emotionally charged memories, such situationally generated emotion operates with different levels of acknowledgement and awareness by the person concerned (as well as those who witness it and experience its effects in the situation). As Scheff (1990) has observed, while emotions such as shame and embarrassment are pervasive in social life, their operation often remains invisible and unacknowledged by those involved. In some respects there is an active disavowal of the existence of the emotional undercurrents of interpersonal encounters.

In this sense emotion in general is subject to the "drift" I spoke of above in which it "tacks" or "shuttles" between conscious and unconscious areas of human awareness. Thus, there is no clear dividing line between unconscious and conscious levels of awareness. The ease with which mental elements pass between different levels of awareness will depend upon the intensity of their effects on particular people and the corresponding levels of repression, resistance and self-deception that are "activated" and which inhibit their effects to varying degrees. Scheff's work and evidence from psychotherapy suggests that most emotion work is managed at a level below that of full acknowledgement. That is, if challenged, a person would not be able to put into words what was actually going on in terms of emotional consequences and intensities and why particular affects had been mobilized by various parties.

This indicates that people engage in emotion work below the level of what Giddens calls "discursive consciousness" and in fact goes on at a level that has more in common with what he calls "practical consciousness". This involves what people know or believe about the social circumstances and conditions under which they act, but which they cannot express discursively. That is, they know and do what is appropriate in particular situations without necessarily being able to put this knowledge into verbal or linguistic form. People just tend to get on with doing what is required of them in encounters – such as the necessity of displaying deference to particular people – rather than discussing underlying rules, expectations and requirements associated with proper deferential behaviour. This involves the ability to "go on" in given situations by displaying tacit knowledge of the appropriate "rules of the game" and includes much of what we might call "commonsense".

It would seem that emotion work is conducted at this level of awareness since people carry it out in a semi-automatic way. However, there are subtle differences from "practical consciousness" in the case of emotions. Tacit knowledge about how to "go on" in particular situations is of a classically "practical" nature in that it seems to involve an appropriate choice of behaviour or the "right thing" to say in the circumstances. If the person is making the right choices and actually contributing to the ongoing character of the interaction, then the situation itself will have a relatively routine and predictable character (even if this involves overt conflict). However, emotion work does not necessarily produce a smoothness in the interchanges between people in encounters. Emotional incursions into the flow of face-to-face contacts introduce precipitative and unpredictable elements that may have either positive or negative effects for the situation and those present.

The introduction of "positive" emotional energies into a face-to-face situation, such as humour, lightheartedness, kidding, joking or "having a laugh", may have the effect of speeding-up the momentum and dynamics of the encounter. The whole effect may also have a ritualized quality to it if it follows a fairly established or routinized pattern that functions to structure the passage of time within the situation. This was the case with a group of factory workers observed by Roy (1973), whose day was punctuated by various ritually enacted "times" and "themes" that involved kidding, fooling around and play-acting. In this case the emotional energies were not exactly spontaneous in that they generally followed an established form and sequence. True spontaneity was limited to the inclusion of minor elaborations on tried and tested themes. Incursions of positively charged emotions into non-routinized or ritualized situations that arise genuinely on the spur of the moment, such as a sudden witty comment or effusive affection or loss of control displayed by one of the participants, are likely to facilitate the smoothness of the encounter and leave those involved with a sense of euphoria.

By contrast the release of negative emotional energies into face-to-face situations will have destabilizing effects and may disrupt what otherwise might have been a smooth and orderly encounter. The sudden development of a disagreement or an argument, or offence being taken at a comment may turn a seemingly innocuous meeting into an embarrassing incident from which all parties want to escape as quickly as possible. Such emotional outbursts are likely to produce tension, disharmony and dissonance in the situation even if they do not hasten its abandonment. Also the flow of emotions in an encounter is related to whether there are inequalities between the interactants because this will affect the continuity, atmosphere and tone of the encounter. As Collins (1983) has pointed out, when interactants of unequal power come together, a person who dominates picks up a surplus of self-confidence and energy whereas those who are dominated lose emotional energy.

Similarly J. Turner (1988) observes that people with low self-esteem work harder to sustain their sense of self in situations where others are undermining it. Unless the situation is structured by rituals or standardized by procedures for opening and closing encounters such people will experience anxiety about their lack of self-worth and thus they will seek to change or leave the situation. These examples show that certain kinds of emotional undercurrents destabilize situations and encounters and as such they pull against the idea of the continuity implied in knowing how to go on in encounters. In this sense it is not really relevant knowledge that is being applied in appropriate circumstances, rather it is an affectual accompaniment that intrudes into the encounter. That is, while obviously related to practical knowledge of how to go on, the important issue here is the emotional tone of the encounter.

As such, emotion work cannot be realistically related to any rule structure or behavioural blueprint that is appropriate to the situation at hand, as is the case with practical consciousness. So although it operates primarily in a non-discursive sense, it is rather different in terms of its substantive content and its operational level. Thus it operates much closer to the borders of the unconscious and conscious awareness and is more prone to tacking back and forth between them than is practical consciousness. In effect we are talking of an intermediate form of awareness between the unconscious and practical consciousness as defined by Giddens. The emotional dimension of human action, therefore, should not be confused or conflated with the cognitive "aura" of practical consciousness. It has less to do with the possession of a kind of knowledge and more do with the predisposition to present oneself to others and to deal with them in a certain manner based on the kind of person one is.

The emotional dimension of self and its influence on encounters leads us to consider the question of whether the self is a unitary or multiple phenomenon. I think that J. Turner's (1988) view that there is a "core" self around which various "peripheral" selves orbit is the most adequate compromise between these positions since it allows us to speak of the self as both a coherent and continuous unity as well as fragmented, contradictory and conflicted. In other words, on the one hand, this formulation allows us to think of the person as a unique cluster of personality characteristics and typical behaviours that serve to distinguish them from other people. On the other, it is consonant with the views of Mead, Goffman, Garfinkel, Laing and others that stress that who a person "is" in terms of self-identity may vary according to the different "audiences" to their behaviour.

In Goffman's terms individuals may present different versions of themselves to audiences who are separated from each other in time and space. For example, a son or daughter may portray a well-mannered, "responsible" version of themselves to their parents while displaying a careless, anti-social persona in front of their peers. A career person may be meek and caring with spouse, partner, or children and become transformed into an ill-tempered tyrant when dealing with work colleagues. These examples do not simply point to a one-way influence from the person to the audience – as if individuals autocratically decided which aspect of themselves they were going to present to which audiences. The various witnesses and audiences to a person's behaviour will have their own demands and expectations of people they "know" and these serve as constraints on the "performance" aspects of a presentation of self. Parents, for example, have preconceptions of their children as certain kinds of people – the son who "could never" be involved in criminal activity, the daughter who has always been the "quiet dependable one". Peer groups assign special roles to particular people – "the joker", the "nutter", the "leader" and so on. So there is a two-way flow between the influence of individuals who wish to present a particular version of themselves and the expectations and demands made by various audiences that they be, or portray, a certain kind of self.

In this sense the self is not a fixed set of behaviours and personality characteristics, there is spread of potential behaviours and traits that are applicable to various aspects of the self that are being displayed at any one time. I say "aspects" here deliberately in order to avoid the imputation that I am adhering to a strong version of the "multiple selves" thesis. There is some ambiguity around this issue, although the very idea of different presentations of self lends itself to a relativism which implies that there are as many selves as there are relevant and significant audiences for the portrayal of different self-images and identities. Goffman's own work is no less equivocal since at different times it can be used to support both the idea that there is a "hidden manipulator" behind the mask of various performances or alternatively that "the person is a composite of multiple selves, each of which projects a set of claims" (Manning 1992: 47).

As I say, J. Turner's (1988) view that there is a "core" self around which various satellite selves orbit has a number of advantages in this respect. First, it allows for variation within tolerable limits – something that the extreme version of the "multiple selves" thesis strains hard to accommodate. Secondly, the idea of the simultaneous existence of a central core self plus a number of other subselves allows for an understanding of the person as possessing a continuity in time and space. This is both an essential precondition for ontological security in Laing's terms – as well as for an appreciation of the individual as a historically emergent emotional being who may, at various times, become estranged from her or his real self as in the case of various kinds of mental illness. However, the fact that periperal selves or aspects of self co-exist also means that there may be different "presentations" of the core self to different audiences.

Another advantage of this formulation is that while there is a coherent unity about the self it may be, none the less, the site of contradictory impulses, wishes, opinions and behaviour. Such contradictory aspects of self may arise from opposing tensions, deriving on the one hand from the unconscious with its unacknowledged desires, impulses and emotional "flooding" and, on the other, from the more reasoned, rational control of conscious awareness. This is particularly the case where elements of reflexivity and self-monitoring ensure that "flooding-out" (or losing control) in front of others will be a rare occurrence. Another source of contradictory tension within the "unity" of the self may arise from the difficulties of "managing" the felt disparities caused by staging performances to radically different audiences. That is, different "versions" of the self may imply quite contrary character qualities or personality traits, for example, the timid respectable parent who turns out to be a child abuser, or the extreme case of the serial murderer, who always seemed to his family, wife and friends to be a very normal, sensitive and caring individual (as was the case with the "Yorkshire Ripper": see Burn 1984).

The psychological contradictions involved in attempting to suppress or deny the less dramatic co-existence of contrary qualities revealed to different audiences (work, family, friends) have not been investigated by those interactionists influenced by the multiple selves thesis. This is because very often these sociologists are more interested in the consequences for the interaction itself rather than for questions of motivation and individual psychology. Goffman's work is a good example of this in so far as he eschewed the psychological level of analysis and concerned himself only with "the syntactical relations among acts of persons mutually present to one another" (1967: 2). Consequently Goffman was mainly concerned with the performance problems that occur when the normal spatial or temporal segregation of audiences has broken down and previously undisclosed aspects of a person's identity and behaviour are glimpsed for the first time. In this respect Goffman's primary interest is in how potentially discrediting information is controlled and managed by those with an interest in preserving the smoothness of the interaction. However, it is clear that this ignores some very interesting questions concerning the ways in which individuals manage psychologically to juggle with contradictory (and hence, potentially undermining) bits of information about themselves and the self-images that they routinely project to others.

A final advantage of the core and peripheral selves model is that the phenomenon of self-deception can be incorporated within its terms of reference. In a sense the model provides an explanation of the motivation for particular instances of self-deception as well as the means by which they may be achieved. In this case self-deception involves the psychological segregation of discrepant performances rather than simply the physical and social separation between audiences. Something of this order must occur in cases of multiple personality disorder, where a number of very different but complete personalities reside in the same person without any of the "personalities" being aware of the existence of the others. However, it is conceivable that a similar process may also occur in a less dramatic form as the manifestation of different aspects of behaviour and personality traits (rather than of complete personalities).

In the case of self-deception there is a requirement that the individual is both aware and unaware that they are deceiving themselves. That is, they actually have to bring off the self-deception by convincing themselves that they are not responsible for what they, in fact, have done. The existence of satellite selves or aspects of the core identity provides a ready-made means by which such psychological segregation can be accomplished. Thus the separation of performances and projections of self may serve to "buffer" potentially dissonant and self-discrediting effects of the discrepant behaviours or traits. This makes a form of denial possible whereby a person could claim that behaviour undertaken under the auspices of one sub-persona is not an authentic or relevant part of themselves. This might further involve the invocation of "real" as opposed to "false" selves – as with Laing's characterization of schizophrenia. Irrespective of whether we are dealing with pathological or normal behaviour, the notion of core and peripheral (aspects) of self does allow leeway for people to deal with dissonant aspects of self and social behaviour.

Decentring the subject: the role of discourse

Clearly, it is necessary to deal with contradictory elements of behaviour in order to come to terms with the critique of humanism and the subject made by structuralist and poststructuralist approaches to social analysis.

These schools of thought tend to view as superfluous all talk of individuals apart from the play of social forces, since it merely reaffirms the ideological myth of bourgeois individualism. The "myth" insists that individuals should be the centre of social analysis because they are the origin of meaning and social structure. Moreover this "ideology" insists that individuals (or human subjects) appear as unified, coherent subjects who are consciously in control of their behaviour. This removes attention from the fragmented or multiple nature of identity and the unconscious, irrational and contradictory nature of subjectivity.

To a certain extent this "individualistic" view is true of some schools of thought that centralize or focus on the role of individuals in social life. In this sense the approach I have outlined above draws on the important features of the humanist (or "modernist") subject such as conscious awareness, self-monitoring, reflexivity and a sense of unity and coherence around identity. However, at the same time it allows for the possibility of contradiction, self-deception, emotionality and the effects of factors beyond the reach of conscious awareness. So instead of abandoning the subject as many poststructuralists and postmodernists advocate, I believe that we should be reclaiming the subject (I prefer to say "individual") for social analysis in a reconstituted form. Certainly the subject must be "decentred" in social analysis if this simply means that individuals cannot be understood as the ultimate origin of meaning and social structure. However, individuals and their personal subjectivities are existential realities and not simply mythical creations of traditional philosophy or social science. Thus, the "subject" cannot be abandoned or pronounced dead as many poststructuralists and postmodernists insist, but must be reshaped and reconstituted.

Another facet of this critique is that humanist schools of thought (including the work of Goffman, Mead, Blumer, Garfinkel, among others), are engaged in a form of subjectivism because they do not recognize the constitutive role of social discourses, practices (and the power relations they are associated with) in the construction of individuals as subjectivities. That is, they neglect the influence of wider social forces other than those of face-to-face conduct in the construction of personal identity. It is certainly true that the influences of language, discourse and power are centrally important in the construction of personal identity and that these factors are often neglected by humanist schools of thought. But again this cannot mean the abandonment or purported disappearance of the human subject. As individuals, people are not solely constructed in and through discourses (or any other social, structural or systemic factors) any more than they are the exclusive products of intersubjective processes. Just as social processes cannot be reduced to the effects of individuals operating as if they were separate psychological atoms, so individuals must not be dissolved into social processes or reduced to their effects.

It has to be acknowledged that social activity, especially as it manifests itself in everyday life, cannot be properly understood if analysis is limited to the domain of interaction itself. Contextual factors much broader than this need to be addressed if we are to provide a truly adequate and comprehensive account of activity. Macro-structural features enter into and are thus an integral part of the fabric of daily social life, just as the seemingly fleeting and insignificant details of interaction are directly implicated in the reproduction of the macro-structural features (Giddens 1984, Layder 1993,1994). The micro-world of everyday life cannot be viewed as an irrelevant foreground to social-structural factors of real importance (as it is in the work of structuralists such as Althusser and Lévi-Strauss and poststructuralists such as Foucault). Conversely, the macro-world cannot be written off, or underestimated as an incidental backdrop to social activity (as it is in the work of many interactionists and ethnomethodologists).

One of the distinctive features of the theory of social domains, however, is that it suggests that although macro and micro factors are "deeply implicated" in each other, as Giddens phrases it, they also remain domains in their own right with their own independent characteristics. Unlike in structuration theory, therefore, they are understood as in part separately constituted domains that interlock, overlap and interweave with each other. I shall reserve a more detailed exploration of these matters for later chapters, although it needs to be noted here that only by preserving their coherence and integrity as domains in their own right is it possible to avoid according an unwarranted priority to one or the other in shaping activity. In the case of structuration theory priority tends to be given to the domain of activity, or social practices because Giddens explicitly denies that macro-structural features have an existence beyond actors' memory traces, activities and the motivations and reasons they give for their behaviour. Thus the macro-structural domain is effectively undercut as a partly independent realm of social reality.

There are two main sorts of macro-features that need to be registered as important in structuring self-identities, emotion and subjectivities in general. These are first those concerning positional and hierarchical (including distributional) features of social structure reflected in categories such as class, gender and race. Thus an individual's location within these hierarchies confers advantages and disadvantages of a material, cultural and status kind according to one's exact position (subordinate or superordinate) and the particular hierarchy in question. Other factors that significantly influence the relationship between these hierarchies, such as the family, the economy and the state (Seve 1978, Leonard 1984) also interrelate with them to solidify and cross-cut the social divisions they engender. The position of individuals within different conjunctions of these structural conditions will imbue them with a particular sense of themselves (their identities and psychological predispositions). Thus occupancy of lower positions in any of the hierarchies will produce feelings of inferiority, lack of confidence, and so on.

The economy affects individual personalities in so far as the ability or inability to purchase consumer goods and to command status and prestige in the community will produce either positive or negative emotions and feelings of pride and shame. Standards of living also induce particular forms of feeling, and condition access to various kinds of skills such as writing and public speaking that affect a person's self-confidence. The family is the site of the establishment of parental control over children, and as Bernstein (1973) has shown when analyzed in relation to the class structure and the use of different speech codes, it produces different capacities to cope with and manipulate the middle-class culture and modes of communication that predominate in the educational system. The family also introduces individuals to the gender and age hierarchies that pervade society as whole and that induce certain sensitivities, orientations and behavioural styles in males and females.

Secondly, other "macro-structural" features play a considerable role in the construction of personal identities and behaviour and concern the inter-connections between power, discourse and practice to which Foucault in particular has drawn our attention. I hesitate to call this nexus of overlapping influences "macro-structural" since Foucault (and other poststructuralists) would have been reluctant to so describe them. There is certainly a sense in which they refer to phenomena different from the positional and distributional forms I have already mentioned, although there are also considerable overlaps. Discourse refers to what is known and can be talked about in relation to a particular topic or area – anything from modern medicine, to sports car engines and thus there can be discourses encompassing any particular body of knowledge. Typically discourses display some internal consistency and coherence; for example, discourse concerning the efficiency of car engines is related and limited to what is known or is possible to know about the mechanics of car engines. It has nothing to say, for example, about socially acceptable forms of sexual intercourse for instance – this is a separate discourse and has its own cluster of relevant problems and possible solutions.

Defined in this way, discourse is formed out of the combined influence of language and special areas of knowledge. Foucault's contention is that those who use particular forms of discourse acquire various powers as a result. Thus knowing about the law or various diseases allows a person to intervene in issues concerning the legal or medical professions. The acquisition of various discourses creates capacities in people and specific psychological dispositions – in short, discourses affect and construct subjectivities in various ways. Thus discourses about sex and gender issues are influential in shaping self-attitudes such as how to behave as a woman or a man of a certain age, as well as what is appropriate sexual conduct in different settings or historical periods and so on. Clearly the positional and distributional factors overlap with discursive influences since they represent the sites in which particular discourses operate – for example, age and gender hierarchies. The great virtue of Foucault's formulation is that he conceives of discourses as very general and pervasive in their influence. They create power relations and forms of resistance based around access to particular discourses throughout society in terms of status groups and including marginalized and stigmatized groups in society, such as gays, mentally ill people, prostitutes, old-age pensioners, and so on. Thus power, and resistance to it, infiltrates and circulates around the whole social body and into everyday life in a very general and pervasive manner. In this sense discourses are not restricted to the main institutional aspects of society; their influence strays into non-legitimate, "deviant" or marginal areas and groups.

There is an intrinsic link between discourse and subjectivities and the very notion of discourse has a flexibility that allows it to reach the parts of society that other concepts and frameworks cannot reach. However, the influence of discourse is also limited in a way that is infrequently recognized by some of those who are its strongest advocates. Thus, there are definite limitations to its capacity to construct identities. Typically this kind of Foucauldian analysis is coupled with a rejection of the subject (or the individual) and hence cannot easily register the identity and personality-forming influences of human agency in the arena of face-to-face interaction as they are in Mead's and Goffman's analyses. The importance of the interaction order for the construction and maintenance of individual self-identities and behaviour cannot be underestimated, as I have tried to show. So although this kind of discourse analysis has a contribution to make, when it is coupled with a rejection of humanism and the individual subject, its very severe limitations have also to be acknowledged.

Psychobiography: subjective careers

We must also understand the self as a historical emergent and have some means of tracing and registering its ever developing nature. The notion of "psychobiography" points to the development of the self as a linked series of evolutionary transitions, or transformations in identity and personality at various significant junctures in the lives of individuals. In this sense psychobiography traces the life "career" of an individual and ties together both the subjective and the objective facets of an individual's experience (Hughes 1937). Although the idea of career is conventionally associated with occupations, various writers (like Hughes) have freed it from this limited application and have used it to denote "any strand of any person's course through life" (Goffman 1961b: 119). Goffman suggests that the focus of interest should be on those things that are basic and common to those sharing the same career. This emphasis is very useful for certain sociological problems in which there is a common set of stages or processes that a group or category of people goes through, such as mentally ill people (of whom Goffman spoke of a "moral career"), married couples, addicts or those experiencing specific kinds of physical illness such as polio (Davis 1963). However, for present purposes, while wishing to retain the idea that there may be shared or common elements in people's careers, we do not want to focus on them to the exclusion of important unique configurations of experience.

I am suggesting that it is possible to identify two main types of events or processes in careers. First, there are those phases or stages that are common to all those who undergo the career such as those identified by Becker (1953) in his analysis of how people become habitual marihuana users (learning how to smoke the drug, learning how to get high, and getting to know how to enjoy the effects). Secondly, there are those things that happen to particular individuals by virtue of the unique circumstances and bonds with others that surround their experience of the career. So, for example, the three stages identified by Becker will be experienced differently by each individual who undergoes them. This will be the result of varying factors, such as associating with particular people in the community of drug users, personality differences affecting receptiveness to drug experiences, particular problems encountered in the process of acquiring the habit, for example, ability to tolerate loss of control or disorientation.

The same is true of any career – individuals will experience it from the standpoint of their own idiosyncrasies of personality, their distinct set of friends and acquaintances and the specific combination of events that attend their passage through the career stages. It is necessary to give some attention to this more subjective side of the career in order to understand how the psychological elements of identity are formed – and it is precisely this that the term "psychobiography" is meant to convey. The other aspect of this is that instead of focusing on a socially defined set of career processes and stages, one is focusing on the life-careers of specific individuals. One is trying to establish the sequence of important life-events and the accompanying changes in self-identity and psychological reorientation that have constituted the person's life-career thus far.

By focusing on the common features of the social context of careers, sociologists have neglected the psychological dimension and individual life-careers. This has proceeded hand in hand with an overemphasis on the socially constructed nature of the self as it unfolds over time. Becker's analysis of the social process of becoming a marihuana user stresses this by underlining the changes in self-conception of the individual from non-user to habitual user of the drug. Certainly these are important facets of self-identity and this links up with the general proposition that the self is in large part a social construction and therefore it is liable to be transformed or altered according to the changing circumstances encountered by the individual. However, it would be a mistake to think that the self is simply a social construct and that it has only an outer texture that is moulded and shaped by external social forces. There is a general need for sociological conceptions of the self to take account of the way in which individual psychology and personality factors interact with the changing personal and social circumstances of the life-career as they unfold over time and affect self identity. Stebbins (1970) has usefully drawn attention to the notion of a "subjective career" that he contrasts with more objective elements such as "career pattern" or "career line". While Stebbins's approach is still intimately linked with a social construct perspective, it does contain relevant elements for the notion of psychobiography as I am using it.

In particular it highlights the importance of critical junctures in careers (such as a promotion blockage at work or a serious argument in a marriage or partnership) for triggering the subjective career. Stebbins defines the subjective career as the prospective and retrospective valuation of the career by the individual that results in a review of self-identity as it is bound up with the current career situation. In other words, individuals will review their present standing in their career and judge whether this is where they intended to be at this point in time, and moreover they will anticipate what kind of future beckons them when they look forward from this vantage point. At critical junctures people ask questions about who they are, what they have become, what they want to achieve and so on. The decisions they arrive at by such introspection will coagulate to form a "plan of action" (a loose strategy rather than a strictly coherent blueprint) based on their perceptions and interpretations of their progress and prospects. In Stebbins's terms their attitudes and opinions regarding the strand of activity in question will be reformulated in a manner that will predispose them to behave and act in accord with their resulting career plan.

A shortcoming of Stebbins's formulation, however, is that it tends to reproduce the same limitations as other interactionist views on career. Specifically, it tends to concentrate upon the construction of self and social behaviour as a response to the immediate environment, rather than as an individual's response based on psychological or personality factors acquired some time before the current situation. Also, there is no explicit recognition of emotional rather than cognitive factors at work in the introspective review of the career, nor is there any allowance for factors beyond conscious awareness and control. As a consequence there is no sense of contradictory tensions and pulls in the psyche of the individual. If these elements are incorporated into the notion of the "subjective career" then it dovetails more with the notion of psychobiography and thus becomes more serviceable for present purposes.

However, it must be borne in mind that the whole point behind the notion of psychobiography is that it maps the changing contours of self and behaviour over time from the point of view of the intersection of psychological and sociological factors. Thus it stresses how the person is individuated within a social context. In this respect it links up with Durkheim's (1964) work which suggests that in modern industrial societies characterized by a highly complex division of labour, individuality becomes more pronounced. In earlier, less complex societies there is a greater emphasis on the importance of like-mindedness of people for social solidarity (which Durkheim called "mechanical solidarity"). As societies develop greater complexity based on specialized roles and functions (such as occupations and governmental institutions), solidarity depends more upon the complementarity of the thoughts and actions of others rather than sameness (which he called "organic solidarity"). Thus there is greater leeway for the differences between individuals to be emphasized.

Durkheim's ideas suggest that modern societies provide the social conditions under which individuation flourishes. The notion of psychobiography complements this by adding a psychological dimension. It stresses that individuality is not only a matter of social pressure towards specialization and the expression of differences. It indicates that over their life-careers, individuals have quite different social experiences and are entangled in webs of social relationships that are unique both in terms of their quality and in terms of the personalities and behavioural patterns of those involved in them. In particular the early experiences of children with their parents, guardians or carers provides a forum for the psycho-emotional development of individuals as they develop into adulthood. Primary relationships in which there is a high degree of intimacy are also important at all stages of the life-career as far as personality formation and emotional predisposition are concerned. The notion of psychobiography therefore stresses that from the point of view of the individual, all social experiences are in an important sense unique. It is only the outer form of social relationships that is "standardized" in any manner, the actual people who constitute the social relation are unique personalities. Similarly, the configurations of people who surround the focal individual (at varying distances and degrees of relatedness) are "unique" to that individual.

If, as sociologists, we want to understand people as real, fully rounded human beings, we must understand them in their unique individualities – only in this way will we avoid viewing them as mere reflections of social influences. Thus we must look to the reverse side of the social arena to understand the specific configurations of real people that populate the "back regions" (to use Goffman's phrase – admittedly slightly out of context) of social life. It is this "other" side of social life that sociologists are loath to recognize for fear of slipping into a form of psychological reductionism. But this is simply a chimera if one constantly bears in mind that we are focusing on one side of a duality and that therefore the psychological and social are different sides of the same coin. By identifying psychobiographies as a unit of analysis, we are concentrating on the intersection or join between two fundamental features of the human social world.

That they represent a duality – two different aspects fused together – alerts us to the usefulness of the dualism on which they are based in social analysis. Distinguishing between objective and subjective aspects of social life underlines the characteristic features of each as long as we do not imagine that they are somehow separate or unrelated. Keeping the duality in mind also prevents us from falling into what could be called the "social constructionist" fallacy. This refers to the tendency for sociologists to avoid examining the psychology of individuals for fear of producing explanations that are inappropriate or couched at the wrong level. This may involve an aversion to reducing social phenomena to the effects of individual psychology – expressed by many writers despite different backgrounds and overall approaches (for example Elias 1978 and Durkheim 1982). Alternatively, others go to great pains to avoid underscoring the "bourgeois" myth of the individual subject, which is the typical response of structuralists, poststructuralists and postmodernists alike.

Although both of these anxieties have some substance in particular contexts, and while it is important not to repeat the errors of reductionism or subjectivism, this should not lead us into another error – that of "sociologism" or extreme "social constructionism" whereby the individual and individual psychology are virtually wiped off the map of social analysis. By focusing on psychobiographies we are keeping in sight the duality of subjective and objective aspects of social phenomena and their interrelation. In so doing we are also reaffirming the importance of what I previously termed the dialectic of separateness and relatedness. It may not be obvious that the tension between the intrinsic social involvements of individuals and their constant assertions of independence from these very same social influences and constraints is also present in the duality of subjective and objective features of social life.

This is so because each presupposes that there is an inner experience of social life that is counterposed (as well as related) to an outer social reality – that is a reality external (as well as internal, as inner experience) to individuals and particular groups in society. This also alerts us to the inherent connection between social power and pressure to respond to social constraints. That is, in some cases, the tension between involvement and independence is governed by the extent to which individuals are in control of their circumstances. As such this dialectic is related to another – what Giddens calls the "dialectic of control" – to which I shall return in Chapter 4.

Face-to-face conduct: the actor's perspective

Goffman's work is pivotal in understanding the nature of face-to-face conduct from the viewpoint of the acting individual, although it is accurate to point out that what Goffman has to say on emotion and psychology is generally limited to their implications for the interaction order. Manning (1992) has usefully identified some of Goffman's key general concerns. The first of these is what Goffman calls "situational propriety" and refers to "the practical knowledge of how to carry on in social situations" (Manning 1992: 79). We have come across this in relation to the notion of practical awareness, although situational propriety focuses on the actual details of behaviour that are appropriate and demanded by particular situations. For example, we are constrained to adopt a certain bodily posture and attend to the requirements of social space (not too close and not too far away from others), indulge in appropriate small (or more "serious") talk as the situation demands as well as conform to the requirements of manners and etiquette and so on. In other words we are required to "fit in" with any social gathering or encounter by adhering to a host of detailed rules and expectations that are unstated but mandatory in particular contexts. By "fitting in", or rather, by "not standing out" or "standing apart" we are demonstrating a practical grasp of the nature and importance of these rules. More importantly we are affirming our "normality" by conforming to them and this is more clear when such rules are broken or breached in some way. Occasional lapses in this regard can be explained away by reference to tiredness or clumsiness and so on, but if these excuses are not enough to explain consistent breaches, then "mental illness" may be attributed as the cause. The point is that there are certain obligations placed upon anyone to act in conformity with the demands of the situation – that is to behave in a manner appropriate to the particular context.

Goffman suggests that another key assumption that underlies all face-to-face interaction is the idea of "involvement". This refers to the capacity of a person to give the right amount of attention to a particular activity. There is a requirement that the individual displays an appropriate level of engagement and commitment to a social encounter and the other participants since this contributes to the general sense of ease that is felt in the encounter. In this sense there are involvement obligations such that there is pressure not only to be involved in what is going on, but to be involved at a level appropriate to the situation at hand. Every encounter requires a certain level of involvement and our daily activities follow an "involvement contour" of greater or lesser involvement as we move from one activity to another (Manning 1992: 12).

For example a situation in which someone is making romantic overtures requires that his or her partner be suitably engrossed and not be distracted by the football or lottery results on the radio. Other situations by contrast allow people some opportunity for engaging in "side involvements" while they have a main or dominant involvement. Thus people typically read magazines and so forth while waiting for an appointment with a doctor or a dentist. Of course, these side involvements are permissible only up to the point where the other person becomes available, then the main purpose must take precedence. Sometimes we are required not to be involved, as in listening to someone else's conversation, and often in these cases a "shield", such as a newspaper will disguise our involvement. In other cases shields protect us from the pressures of involvement as is often the case on public transport.

"Civil inattention" is another key assumption that underlies behaviour. This refers to behaviour in public places and points to the fact that although such areas are open generally to everyone, there are certain behaviours that are appropriate in such areas. Non-acquainted people offer each other "civil inattention" which refers to a willingness to see others and to be seen, while at the same time displaying a studied lack of interest so as not to express particular curiosity. It indicates that there is no intention of aggression or intrusion and that the other person's presence is respected and owed deference. This creates and preserves a sense of anonymity in public situations that is the result of collective effort on the part of those involved and is not an automatic or naturally occurring state of affairs. A good example of civil inattention is displayed by strangers in lifts who deliberately avoid eye contact by staring at their feet or the floor numbers as they ascend or descend. Momentary eye contact is a key feature because it signals recognition of the other but its fleeting nature means that it is non-threatening and non-intrusive. The "hate stares" directed at blacks in the USA is a good example of what happens when civil inattention is absent, and indicates that its presence demonstrates a sense of sharedness of a social reality and particular circumstances.

"Accessibility" is the opposite of civil inattention in that it refers to our readiness to be available to others – particularly to friends and acquaintances, but also to certain strangers who have been "ratified" by us in some way. It is difficult to say what distinguishes ratified from non-ratified strangers but it is certainly the case, for example, that we extend to some the right to ask for the time, for directions or to give change, while expecting to exercise the right ourselves. The extent to which we make ourselves available to others is a skilled accomplishment, sometimes involving quite tricky balancing acts. For instance, often during hectic daily routines we manage to limit mutual accessibility to a brief smile or eye contact with those we know or with whom we are acquainted, sometimes in passing on a busy street or in a corridor.

Goffman (1974) was also interested in what he called "frame analysis". This refers to the fact that we perceive the social world by putting particular "frames" around our observations of behaviour – such as deciding that a kiss that we witnessed was a perfunctory peck on the cheek rather than one with sexual implications. Frames provide ways of organizing our experience that would otherwise be an overwhelming chaos of facts and events (Manning 1992: 118–19). Lawyers often create frames in an endeavour to show that their client's behaviour has been misconstrued by the prosecution witnesses. For instance a convincing lawyer might claim that a woman accused of shoplifting is, in fact, not a criminal but merely absent-minded. Frames are often superimposed on each other so that there are frames-within-frames so to speak, and Goffman concerned himself with the ways in which we identify and make transitions between frames. One of the overall themes of this work, as Manning has shown, is that the ways in which we persuade others of the realness or genuineness of what they see are exactly the same procedures that we use to "cheat, deceive or manipulate them" (1992: 120). This, in a sense, repeats a theme that Goffman had originally offered in his earliest book the *Presentation of self in everyday life* (1959), in which he portrays the individual as staging performances that hide a cynical and manipulative self. In *Frame analysis* there is less emphasis on the theatrical analogy of the earlier work, but a similar attempt to show at least how it is possible for people to manipulate situations for their own ends.

However, as several commentators have observed (Collins 1983, Manning 1992, Giddens 1987, Rawls 1987) it would be a mistake to understand Goffman's work entirely in this light since there is definite evidence of other emphases in his work. The influence of Durkheim's (1965) writing on religion is of no little importance here with its stress on the sacred character of society. Goffman takes from this the importance of ritual honour and care in social life and this introduces a moral dimension to the notion of the interaction order. In this sense, individuals are not viewed simply as cynical manipulators but rather as protectors of situations and others. People attempt to save face for others so that situations themselves can be rescued and they employ tact and trust in order to protect others' and their own selves. So it is clear that Goffman also views the individual as something like a sacred object that needs to be constantly honoured and thus overall, the individual in social life is Janus-faced, capable of being both calculative and courteous (Manning 1992: 60). Therefore, the interaction order and the individuals who populate it, at one and the same time, protect and exploit, as well as manipulate and trust the selves involved in social situations.

I think it can be appreciated that this duality is associated with all the themes and assumptions underlying social encounters as Goffman envisages them. Civil inattention, accessibility, situational propriety and involvement can all be brought to bear upon situations of trust or exploitation from the point of view of particular individuals. Even though civil inattention may be thought to be primarily in the service of generalized trust in modern societies (Giddens 1987, 1990), it would be an exaggeration to imply that it always is so. Thus it is that con-men, robbers and pickpockets are intimately aware of the implicit procedures and expectations associated with civil inattention and as a consequence manipulate them for their own ends. Also, in an even more generalized sense civil inattention can be used as a protective buffer against all manner of potential social involvements – it is never simply and solely in the service of trust, ritual honour and respect for strangers.

In short, the duality in Goffman's emphases mirrors the double-edged nature of social life, its cynical, manipulative side and its co-operative, moral side with an emphasis on trust. This is also reflected in Goffman's assumption that social life is what in Schelling's (1960) terms is a "mixed-motive game" which contains different combinations of manipulation and trust according to the circumstances. This relates in a rather complicated and diffuse way to what I have termed the dialectic of separateness and relatedness. The question of why some people are manipulative in certain situations and trusting in others, or why some circumstances elicit different levels of both of these qualities, is a vexed question, and although I would not presume to offer any cut-and-dried answers it may be that the cross-cutting pulls and tensions between the forces of separateness and relatedness provide at least some clues. One way of understanding this is to focus on the nature of the social bonding of the individual, and in particular whether it tends towards close involvement in the social world or reflects more of a pull towards independence.

For instance the impulse to manipulate others may result from a species of independence based on alienation, disaffiliation, rivalry or competitiveness. In such circumstances the inclination towards trust may be thwarted by the need to be constantly "on guard" against threats to self and self-image. If not leading directly to forms of active manipulation of others these sorts of bonds would certainly give rise to a cynical attitude towards them and hence undercut any sense of a trusting feeling. Two examples from a wide range of possibilities can be mentioned here. The first concerns the idea that men (rather than women) are more prone to taking up an independent stance vis-à-vis others. Both feminist and other scholars (notably Tannen 1987, 1992) have argued that the typically male mode of orientation to the social world tends towards status rivalry and competitiveness, whereas women are geared more towards forms of involvement and seeking rapport with others.

Now it is possible, as Tannen herself mentions, that seeking to manipulate others by promoting solidarity and trust (involvement with others) is no less manipulation because of it. That is, women can be as manipulative as males but they tend to use other channels rather than power plays (independence), hence the possibilities are complicated and by no means clear-cut, one way or the other. Nevertheless, it is clear that the duality of separateness and relatedness threads through the issues of manipulation and trust. The second example concerns the behaviour of people suffering from serious forms of mental illness such as schizophrenia. As Laing (1969) has observed, such people often feel threatened by close relationships with others and suggests that withdrawal from social life may be a means by which they can "control" the behaviour of others whom they consider to be a threat. The issue of lack of trust in others is paramount here. Schizophrenics may stand apart, or even isolate themselves in an effort to preserve their own identity, which is under threat from anyone who gets too close.

Scheff on emotion and social interaction

As the previous examples show, Goffman touches on topics germane to a social-psychological perspective on everyday life, but it has often been asserted that he does not readily engage with issues of motivation or the psychology of individuals. This is typified by his analysis of emotion, particularly that of embarrassment, which he views as an intrinsic aspect of the interaction order. Goffman is quite explicit that "the proper study of interaction is not the individual and his psychology, but rather syntactical relations among the acts of different persons mutually present to one another . . . Not, then, men and their moments, rather moments and their men" (1967: 2–3). If we take this to be a statement expressing the major thrust of Goffman's work we must understand it as an attempt to delineate an area or topic of study proper to sociology (or social analysis) alone – which is akin to Durkheim's (1982) attempt to identify a realm of social facts only amenable to "scientific" sociological analysis.

However, while there is some point to identifying a domain of social reality in its own right, this should not be taken to exclude the analysis of areas that clearly interpenetrate with it as the focal domain. From the point of view of the theory of social domains, Goffman's dismissal of individual psychology is quite unsatisfactory. As with the other elements of face-to-face conduct identified by him, we must acknowledge that although they are intrinsic features of the interaction order they should not and cannot be explained exclusively in terms of this order. We shall see later on, that Goffman does, in fact, distinguish between the interaction order and other social orders (or domains) and this allows him at least to sketch some of the interrelations between them. However, it is in respect of the realm of individual psychology that Goffman is most remiss.

To a very great extent this neglect by Goffman is rectified by Scheff's (1990) work on the emotions in social life in which he draws on Goffman's analysis of embarrassment. This not only involves supplementing Goffman's work with that of Lewis's (1971) on shame, but also involves showing how Goffman's analysis implies a theory of motivation. Scheff points out that Goffman established the importance of face-saving, and deference and demeanour in social life. People are extremely sensitive to the gestures of respect and disrespect they receive in any social encounter. That is, the exact amount of deference they receive through verbal or non-verbal gestures during a face-to-face encounter is a "comment on, an affirmation or denial, of momentary social status in the encounter" and thus "social status is not permanent but continuously reviewed and contested" (Scheff 1990: 28).

Scheff goes on to point out that Goffman's (1967) analysis of embarrassment implies a theory of motivation that Goffman himself would have denied. That is, people's preoccupation with face-saving has to do with avoiding the emotion of embarrassment both for themselves and for others. Thus, "fending off embarrassment is a crucial motive in all social encounters in the sense of being the most pressing of the participants' immediate concerns" (1990: 29). Every time we present ourselves to others we risk rejection either directly or more subtly. If rejection does occur then, depending on its intensity, we will experience embarrassment, shame or humiliation (Scheff includes guilt and anxiety as well as embarrassment and humiliation under the label "shame"). It is this emotion that Goffman emphasizes, as an adjunct to impression-management and face-saving and, as Scheff observes, this is associated with a social bond that is threatened in some way.

However, Scheff suggests that impression-management and "cutting a good figure" (what he calls the "bella figura" syndrome) are not the only preoccupations in social life. Equally, when we are valued and accepted as we are, or as we present ourselves to others in encounters, we experience a pleasant emotion of pride and fellow-feeling (Scheff 1990: 75). Pride and shame then are the "primary social emotions" (1990: 15) and coupled with the amount and form of deference received in routine encounters they constitute what Scheff terms "a subtle system of social sanctions" (1990: 75). Thus for Scheff this system provides an answer to the question of why and how social control is so compelling. That is, it provides a fuller account of the nature of social constraint than Durkheim was able to give when he posited that conformity is encouraged by a system of formal sanctions in which we are rewarded when we conform and punished when we do not.

Scheff points out that conformity occurs even when there are no obvious sanctions and also notes that formal sanctions are "slow unwieldy and expensive". Therefore, he suggests that "there must be a highly efficient system of control of informal sanctions, a system which is almost invisible" (1990: 74). This is the emotion-deference system and it functions as a very compelling form of social control because we experience the pleasure of the emotion of pride and fellow-feeling or the punishment of embarrassment, humiliation or shame. Unlike formal rewards and punishments that are infrequent, the deference-emotion system "functions virtually continuously, even when we are alone, since we can imagine and anticipate its movements in vivid detail". Moreover, so far this system has been missed by social research because it is too subtle to be traced by social surveys or experimental methods. Field workers have also failed to register its existence because "it often functions outside the awareness of interactants". In short, "unlike the system of formal sanctions the deference-emotion system is virtually instantaneous and invisible, and cheap as dirt" (Scheff 1990: 75).

Scheff insists that emotions exist within individuals as well as between interactants and thus he distances himself from Goffman's self-imposed limitations. Goffman's analysis of embarrassment, for instance, relies on the idea (dealt with in a previous section) of the breakdown of normally segregated audiences in which selves are revealed that are incompatible with those presented on other occasions. In this kind of situation embarrassment occurs and Goffman insists that this "clearly shows itself to be located not in the individual but in the social system wherein he has several selves" (Goffman 1967: 108). Scheff is quite adamant that a full account of emotion must include some reference to inner feelings and I am in full agreement since this is consistent with the wider implications of domain theory.

As a complement to Goffman's analysis that focuses only on emotion as an aspect of outer behaviour or, in other words as part of the interaction order, Scheff draws on the work of Helen Lewis (1971), a research psychoanalyst, on shame. By contrast with Goffman's, her work focuses only on the inner processes involved, so Scheff is keen to marry the two analyses. From her examination of clinical sessions Lewis identifies two types of shame, overt (or undifferentiated) shame and bypassed shame. In the sessions most of the shame episodes she examined were "invisible" – that is, they remained unacknowledged either by the therapist or the patient. In overt shame the patient obviously feels painful feelings but these are not identified as shame. Rather they are referred to by a variety of terms that serve to disguise the shame experience, such as "feeling foolish, stupid, ridiculous, inadequate, defective, incompetent, low self-esteem, awkward, exposed, vulnerable, insecure, and so on" (Scheff 1990: 86).

All these terms were regarded as shame markers by Lewis because they occurred in conjunction with two other features. First, the patient perceived the self as negatively evaluated either by self or others, and secondly, there was a change in the patient's manner. This latter involved such things as stammering and repetition of words, lowered or averted gaze, blushing, and a marked drop in loudness of speech, sometimes becoming almost inaudible. Scheff notes that both the verbal and non-verbal markers of overt shame are forms of "hiding" behaviour. Using disguising labels is a form of hiding, as is the averting of gaze to avoid eye contact with others, or speaking softly so as to "hide" one's thoughts (Scheff 1990: 86). Bypassed shame also begins with a negative evaluation of the self, but unlike the overt type its markers are subtle and covert in which the patient's thought and speech take on a speeded-up and repetitive quality.

Whereas in the overt type the patient feels pain but tries to hide it from self as well as others, in bypassed shame the person seems to try to avoid pain before it can be fully experienced by engaging in rapid thought, speech and actions. Scheff comments that both kinds of shame "are equally hidden since one is misnamed, the other avoided. These two basic patterns explain how shame might be ubiquitous yet usually escape notice" (Scheff 1990: 87). Lewis suggests that once started (say by a comment perceived as critical of self), the shame experienced may be the start of a long sequence whereby the person beomes ashamed of being ashamed in a never-ending loop. Lewis terms these "feeling traps" in so far as they are contagious within a shame-prone person and therefore such persons may be "in a more or less chronic shame state" (Scheff 1990: 18).

Lewis's analysis of shame provides a very neat counterpoint to Goffman's analysis of embarrassment. Goffman posits the idea of the contagion of embarrassment between interactants in so far as one becomes embarrassed that the other is embarrassed, who in turn becomes embarrassed, which increases the first person's embarrassment, and so on. This constitutes an interpersonal feeling trap that complements Lewis's idea of an inner, intrapersonal feeling trap and Scheff is very keen to join the two kinds of analysis so that one can "convey the extraordinary force of the deference-emotion system. This system occurs both between and within interactants" (Scheff 1990: 76). On two counts, though, Goffman was unable to convey the "explosive force" of the deference-emotion system. First, his omission of the psychological dimension meant that he did not attempt to describe the interaction between the inner and outer processes, and secondly, he did not appreciate the link between shame and anger that Lewis noted.

Scheff believes this link to be an extremely important one and may account for chain reactions of shame and anger. Lewis observed that shame was usually followed by anger and could become involved in a continuous loop. Lewis analyzed this in relation to individuals, but as Scheff notes if we connect her analysis to Goffman's we can begin to appreciate the potential volatility of the deference-emotion system. Normally it produces an alignment of the thoughts, feelings and actions of people. That is, mutual conformity and respect lead to pride and fellow-feeling and further conformity, and so on. But where there is a real or imagined rejection in the form of criticism or insult on either side, the system may produce "a chain-reaction of shame and anger between and within the interactants. This explosion is usually very brief, perhaps a few seconds. But it can also take the form of a bitter hatred lasting a lifetime" (Scheff 1990: 76).

Scheff's overall thesis is rather diffuse and pursues a number of different directions, many of which are not directly relevant to the present discussion. However, there are two other comments made by Scheff that I would like to mention here. First, he suggests that if we look closely at ordinary conversations we find that deception and self-deception are commonly practised and that, in turn, they are related to unacknowledged shame. This clearly connects with the issues raised in an earlier section where I pointed to the link between practical consciousness, self-deception and emotionality. Secondly, Scheff centres his attention on what he calls attunement, which refers to the achievement of joint feeling and attention between people in interaction. Of course this is in line with Scheff's main stress on the emotional as well as the cognitive component of social bonds.

He makes the point that if we consider attunement and its ramifications, we are forced to rethink some of the basic assumptions that are associated with the dominant models of social interaction. In particular Mead's and Schutz's ideas about role-taking and intersubjectivity have to be qualified and refined if they are to take account of the variable states of attunement. Mead's and Schutz's models of interaction depend upon fairly abstract notions of co-operative activity and reflective intelligence and they give the impression that interactants are in a state of continuous attunement. However, says Scheff, if we examine concrete instances of conversations and encounters we find that people actually experience encounters as "a fast moving blur of misunderstanding, error, folly, and alienation, with only rare and all too brief moments of attunement" (Scheff 1990: 50). In part this is because we operate in social encounters on at least two levels. At one level we attend to and respond to each other's spoken words and this may give the impression that there is a fair degree of understanding (even agreement) being manifest in the encounter. However, simultaneously, and at a deeper level, we harbour unstated feelings and thoughts, which, in essence, may mean that we are really worlds apart from the other(s) in the encounter. I think that this notion of attunement and the implications just outlined are extremely important for any theory of social activity. In effect they add to our understanding of the complexity of everyday conduct by identifying different levels and modes of communication and focusing on the possibility of contradictory tensions and pulls in the individual's inner world.

All in all Scheff's highly original contribution based on the integration of a number of different theories and disciplines is a crucial step forward for a sociological theory of the micro-world of social encounters. In this regard it recognizes two absolutely central features that I believe are entirely compatible with the theory of social domains as I have so far outlined it. First, it recognizes that human consciousness is a combination of several levels of awareness and acknowledgement by the actor during the course of any encounter. Thus the emotional dimension infiltrates thought and action at every opportunity – sometimes displacing the cognitive elements, sometimes lying low behind them, at other times coalescing with them with an explosive intensity. Secondly, and in conjunction with this, Scheff's framework recognizes the need for a rapprochement between psychological and sociological levels of analysis. Scheff's is one of the very few sociological approaches to the study of face-to-face conduct that seriously attends to the problem of the individual's contribution to the workings of the interaction order. Most sociologists, like Goffman (and Durkheim before him), tend to assume that the social domain is largely autonomous from the psychological domain. Now, while it is important to understand that the social domain cannot be analytically reduced to individual psychology, it is equally important to recognize the connections between subjectivity and the dynamics of face-to-face conduct.

Encounters and trust

There has been much written about trust in modern social life particularly in relation to the increasing risks (of nuclear war, ecological disaster, environmental pollution and so on) that characterize much of modern daily life. Giddens (1984, 1990, 1991) in particular has pointed to and examined the relation between trust and risk, and trust and ontological security in modernity. I do not want to repeat his arguments here, but I do want to make some comments on the general nature of trust in social life and how this fits in with the model of the social agent that I have attempted to portray in this chapter. Giddens makes the point that in modernity we are required to trust in "expert systems" of specialist (professional) knowledge or competence. For instance when travelling by air we assume that the aircraft we fly on has been properly assembled and serviced by a whole host of experts whose competence we do not question, but simply "trust" in as a matter of course. Similarly we put our trust in those who operate the airports and control the flow of air traffic.

All around us in modern society there are expert systems based on specialized technical knowledge that require our trust. The same is true of our use of symbolic tokens like money in which we express confidence that our transactions with another will be honoured irrespective of whether we have trust in the other people involved. Giddens (1990) makes a distinction between trust in persons that involves face-to-face commitments and trust in expert systems or symbolic tokens that involves "faceless" commitments, but he generally seems to view trust itself as a unitary phenomenon – as if all kinds of trust were the same. Thus he defines trust as "confidence in the reliability of a person or system . . . where that confidence expresses a faith in the probity or love of another, or in the correctness of abstract principles (technical knowledge)" (1990: 34).

While I agree that trust is a crucially important element in modern social life I want to suggest that it is a much more variegated and complex phenomenon than Giddens implies. Even his distinction between trust in people and expert systems requires us to say that these are such different things that it is misleading to call both forms of trust. Craib (1992: 170–71) has made a similar point in saying that the trust "I have or do not have in my insurance company is not the same thing as the trust I have or do not have in my wife, or my friends or my ability to do things". Craib points out that Giddens tends to see a continuity between these two types of trust, the ability to trust in others in an intimate sense (especially as it is learned as a child) being a precondition of being able to trust in expert systems or symbolic tokens. However, Craib notes that the two types of trust can exist separately and without connection. The example of someone who is very successful in a worldly sense requires trust in money and expert systems generally, but this may be accompanied by a "failure of trust in personal relationships and an inner emptiness" (Craib 1992: 171). Conversely a "loving old couple who keep their money in a mattress" have plenty of trust in their personal relationship but very little in expert systems like banks, accountants, or financial institutions in general. I agree with Craib that by lumping these different types together, there is a danger of confusing fundamentally different things. Even Giddens's own definition of trust seems to suggest this since it seems unwise to suggest that faith in the probity of another is equivalent to faith in the love of another and/or faith in the correctness of abstract principles. While there is a superficial similarity in the sense that they all involve confidence (in them) on behalf of those doing the trusting, beyond this there would appear to be vast differences in the nature of the psychological commitment and investment involved.

For example, to trust in the love of someone is a very different proposition from trusting that a solicitor is above board and working in one's best interests as a client. In turn, these examples appear to be different from trusting that the fuselage of an aeroplane has been assembled according to correct structural principles. Without going into this in great detail at this juncture, it seems that trust in expert systems (the law and aeronautical engineering in this case) is predicated on the lack of viable alternatives for those who "have" to trust in them. It is the layperson's lack of expert knowledge that places them in a situation of dependence on the expert and thus their trust is not truly volitional since they have no real choice in the matter. By contrast, trust in the love of another is something that is, in principle, controllable in the sense that one decides to make an emotional commitment to another on the basis of experience and feelings about the quality of the relationship. The emotional tone of the psychological invest-ment is also a quality that distinguishes it from confidence or faith in experts or the knowledge they possess.

Even this small indication of some of the subtleties and complexities involved when we examine instances in detail lead to the conclusion that it is difficult to generalize with confidence about the notion of trust. None the less, it is important to be aware of the range of phenomena that are covered by the term trust used in a generic manner. Not only is there a difference between trust in the probity of a person as compared to trust in the love of another, but also the notion of trust as a generalized feature of interaction is very different from trust that develops out of sustained per-sonal knowledge of, and involvement with, another such as in friendship, colleagueship or courtship. Trust as a generalized feature of face-to-face conduct is apparent in Goffman's discussion of civil inattention. When people acknowledge the presence of others by briefly making eye-contact and then looking away almost immediately, the message that is sent out is, as Giddens suggests, "you may trust me to be without hostile intent" (Giddens 1990: 82). In this sense civil inattention is a continuous backdrop to all encounters with strangers. Giddens goes on to make the point that trust also features in encounters with acquaintances since the very ini-tiation of an encounter requires an elementary sense of trust as a basic building block. Furthermore, says Giddens, "trust and tact are more fun-damental and binding features of social interaction than is the cynical manipulation of appearances" (Giddens 1987: 113).

It is surely correct to say that there is a moral dimension to social encounters – and that this feature of Goffman's work has often been overlooked by commentators. However, to insist that trust and tact are more fundamental and binding than manipulation in social interaction is rather questionable. Certainly, much of the basic interchange of information and the orderliness in which the "business" of encounters is conducted rests on the predictable "trustworthiness" of others. But this is a minimal sense of trust in so far as it represents a background assumption that one can "count on others" to follow an orderly sequence and employ recognizable social skills to produce a certain outcome and so on. This is much the same as saying that we generally "trust" that others are competent social actors who are capable of bringing off the encounter. But to say that we generally impute to others the best of intentions or that we ourselves mostly act out of selfless or altruistic motives would be a vast overgeneralization.

As I said in a previous section, civil inattention can be displayed for reasons relating to the manipulation of others. For example, thieves may employ it to create an illusion of "normality" and that there is nothing untoward afoot – which in turn creates favourable conditions for the commission of a crime. The fact that civil inattention is widespread and common does not guarantee that it occurs in the context of tact or trust. As Goffman observes, even the seemingly "moral" motive of saving others from potential embarrassment may flow from the more selfish reason that this would be expected of others in return – a sort of conditional altruism. It is surely more accurate to understand manipulation and trust to be two sides of the same coin of encounters that manifest themselves according to differing circumstances and the personalities of those involved. In this respect I have to agree with Craib (1992: 169) that Giddens often tends to speak of encounters as if people always want things to go smoothly for the best of intentions. However, as Craib observes, motives relating to the fear of punishment and instrumental self-interests are just as important as trust and tact when it comes to maintaining social order in encounters.

This also has to do with the question of whether one is speaking generally of trust as a background element of face-to-face conduct or as an upfront, integral feature of the action, or even some combination of the two. The point is again that once we begin to scrutinize particular instances of trust, its generalized nature falls away. An example of this concerns Vaitkus's (1991) reworking of Schutz's notion of the practical attitude. Vaitkus points out that we do not relate to each other in encounters simply in terms of what Schutz calls the "practical attitude" that assumes the sharedness of a practical problem that has to be solved. Rather, we encounter others in terms of what he calls a personal "fiduciary" attitude (or in other words, what we have been calling trust, or faith and confidence) that takes precedence over the practical implications of what we are doing. This attitude assumes the sharedness of an "offering" or "gift" to another that is accepted by them. These social offerings are not restricted to material objects, and Vaitkus has in mind such things as offering someone a place to sit, opening up a conversation, telling them secrets and so on. The point about these things and the fiduciary attitude is that their meaning for the people involved has primarily to do with the act of giving and receiving and in the way these are performed rather than with any practical considerations. Thus, for example, when we ask others round for dinner, the practical problem of hunger is entirely subordinate to the social context of dining in which the main point is to share food and converse with the guests. Importantly, Vaitkus includes what he terms the impractical currents of social activities as reflected in moods, emotions and attitudes such as depression, excitement and fear, since these things have to do with the nature of our social bonding with others. Similarly, according to Vaitkus such things as flattery, teasing, sarcasm and rivalry are bound up with the attiude of basic trust since they have to do with giving and receiving social offerings, or the rejecting and withdrawing of them (1991: 167).

This latter observation about rejection or withdrawal is very important because as Vaitkus indicates, although there may be a general predisposition towards basic trust in others in modern society, this does not mean that this is invariably the case in particular encounters. After all we choose to offer "social gifts" to certain people rather than others and whether we withdraw or reject offerings depends upon the current state of our relationships with them. This is where the importance of moods and emotions comes to the fore since the existence of such personality or behavioural traits reinforces the individualized nature of trust as it actually manifests itself in the social world. In this sense an attitude of basic trust is only a background condition, a potential shaped by the cultural context. *Actual* trust is always something of an interpersonal negotiation that mobilizes the personalities of those involved. In this sense particular manifestations of trust have to be understood as partly psychological phenomena.

Trust, self and ontological security

The previous point shifts the focus of discussion to the foreground of social activity in which the psychological make-up of individuals plays a crucial role. Thus, again trust reveals itself to be manifold. In this case it is important to emphasize its psychological rather than social anchoring. This is not to deny in any sense the social context of trust and its diffuse importance in all facets of social life. My point is, rather, to suggest that the individual psychological dimension is a crucially important supplement to the social aspects of trust (particularly those associated with the interaction order). There is an intimate connection here between trust and feelings of basic security, self-esteem and social anxiety. In this sense, trust is not concerned primarily with the way in which we have faith and confidence in other people, but rather, in the way we trust in ourselves. That is, this sense of trust is concerned with a fundamental belief in self-identity a sense of the integrity of the self.

Existential psychology and psychiatry have frequently focused on these aspects of the self, particularly in the context of the example of mental illness of either a neurotic or psychotic kind. Laing (1969) argues that schizophrenia is linked to the experience of ontological insecurity and this has much to do with basic trust and confidence in the self. Someone who experiences ontological insecurity does not feel substantial or real, or as possessing value, worth or genuineness as a person. In short, this person's own sense of identity is constantly in question and forever teetering on the brink of collapse. Very often this leads to an inability to cope either with being on one's own or being with other people since both of these situations could pose a severe threat to an already impoverished self. On the one hand, other people threaten the ontologically insecure person by the potential for "absorbing" them and so obliterating the fragile sense of identity. On the other hand, such a rudimentary notion of self is constantly in need of support and recognition by other people. Both situations are unfeasible for the insecure individual, who therefore is likely to oscillate between the two extremes "of complete isolation and or complete merging of identity" (Laing 1969: 53).

I shall return to the implications of this for what I have termed the dialectic of separateness and relatedness in a moment, but let us first consider the implications for so called "normal" or "healthy" people. It is clear that serious mental disturbance may occur in individuals who cannot count on, or be confident about, their own autonomous identity. But those who

approach the world with a firm a sense of security (those who feel themselves to be real, genuine and worthwhile) never do so in a complete and
unproblematic manner. As Craib (1992) has pointed out, ontological security is not something that is simply there or not there, it is always a matter
of feeling more or less secure so that everyone, not simply those who are
seriously disturbed, may be affected by some feelings of insecurity in this
sense. Thus, clearly a sense of trust or confidence in oneself, and a feeling
of one's own efficacy as a separate and independent person, are crucial to
an individual's ability to operate successfully in social life.

This relates to the previous discussion on awareness and emotion where
I indicated that the work of Collins (1983) and Turner (1988) was of direct
relevance. The issue there was that the continuity and smoothness of
encounters is to some extent dependent upon feelings of self-esteem and
self-worth in the interactants. As Turner observes, people with low self-
esteem will work harder to avoid anxiety and to sustain a sense of self in
encounters, especially where others seem to be undermining it. If this is
the case then such individuals may seek to change or leave the situation.
Conversely, to the extent that identities and self-worth are being confirmed and supported by others then the encounter will tend to be prolonged and will more likely be repeated. More generally, says Turner,
people need to feel included, to feel that they are really part of the activity
and in touch with the flow of events (1988: 204). Crucially, this involves the
need to trust others and to sense that their responses are predictable. This
feeds into a sense of security about identity and of feeling right about their
dealings with others, for without these basic elements of trust people
become anxious and confused. In this respect Turner cites Garfinkel's
(1967) work, which suggests that when routine situations are disrupted,
people are at pains to repair a sense of the factual nature of a shared world
in order to control anxiety levels. In this sense Turner's observations link
the psychological dimension of trust and its emphasis on emotional security, identity needs and feelings of bondedness with others, with work on
the nature of the interaction order that is reflected in Garfinkel's concern
with the dynamics of face-to-face conduct and local practices.

Moving further into the realm of individual personality the same themes
are reinforced in the literature on psychotherapy and self-transformation.
For instance, Jampolsky (1994) stresses the need for individuals to adopt a
trust-based approach to social life in order to produce self-esteem and self-
worth and thus to break from the paralysing effects of acting from the basis
of fear and anxiety. In short it seems that much of the psychotherapeutic

literature stresses that the attempt to find a neurosis-free mode of being in the world is predicated on the ability to acquire the personal character-isitics of tolerance, generosity, patience, open-mindedness and gentleness and so on (Jampolsky 1994: 125–217). This of course complements Laing's work on ontological insecurity, which indicates the kind of self-defeating strategies that are adopted by those who lack such personal char-acteristics for whatever reason.

All this material then points to the fact that typically people move between different levels of security (trust, confidence, self-esteem, anxiety) according to both the dynamics of situations themselves and the general cultural emphasis on trusting responses, as well as with regard to the per-sonality characteristics of the individuals involved. In tacking between these different emotional energy levels, people are caught between the demands of the interaction order and their own psychological responses to particular situations.

At this point we can usefully refer back to Laing's work on ontological insecurity in order to throw light on the dialectic of separateness and relatedness. The dialectic is applicable to experience in general, not just to those who are obviously suffering from neurotic or psychotic symptoms. Indeed Laing's discussion of the plight of those suffering from chronic ontological insecurity also reveals a great deal about the way in which trust and confidence in oneself operate in the normal circumstances of day-to-day life. As Laing describes it, the problem for chronically insecure indi-viduals is how to maintain their hold on an already precarious sense of identity. For reasons that do not concern us here such individuals have not developed a strong sense of their own self identities as separate and inde-pendent people; as a result they often feel less real and alive than others and are constantly uncertain about their worth and integrity. The main issue for these people concerns their sense of personal autonomy. As Laing points out, there is not only a failure to sustain a sense of self alone, but also a failure to sustain it in the company of others. Lacking in a true sense of their own autonomy, such individuals experience aloneness as extreme isolation and a threat to their sense of self since they need others to supply them with, and thus confirm their identities. On the other hand, for the insecure person being with others also constitutes a threat since they are unclear and confused about their own autonomous identities. Thus, other people simply add to this lack of clarity because insecure individuals feel as though their self-identity is being merged or engulfed by them. Instead of experiencing the usual separateness from, or relatedness to, others such individuals constantly oscillate between the two unfeasible alternatives of isolation and merging of identity.

By suggesting that the experience of separateness and relatedness is the "usual" or "normal" form, we can appreciate that even when an autonomous identity is not seriously in question, there are similar existential problems to be faced in the normal circumstances of everyday life. In this sense we constantly steer a course between the attractions and repulsions of one side of the duality and the other. That is, one of the inherent and enduring features of social life involves maintaining a sense of our self-identity as distinct from others, while at the same time attempting to merge and achieve maximum rapport with those with whom we are currently involved. Tannen (1987) describes this as a duality between involvement and independence that she says "reflects the human condition" and I am inclined to agree. We are constantly trying to balance the needs for involvement and independence since "we need to get close to each other to have a sense of community, to feel we're not alone in the world. But we need to keep our distance from each other to preserve our independence so others don't impose on us or engulf us" (Tannen 1987: 15).

Tannen goes on to argue that cultures as well as individuals place different values on the importance of these needs and this is often reflected in forms of communication. For example, Western men place more emphasis on their need for independence while women tend to emphasize social involvement. Tannen is careful to point out that this is a matter of emphasis; it does not mean that Western men never express involvement or that women never assert their independence. However, as a matter of emphasis this difference in valuation is reflected in women's tendency to attend to the "metamessages" of talk – the part that comments on relationships and encourages rapport – whereas men tend to attend more to the informational content of talk. This tendency to focus on "factual" information supplied through talk rather than on conversation as a means of establishing connectedness or "keeping in touch" often disadvantages men in terms of maintaining personal relationships.

However, Tannen goes on to make the more general point that irrespective of whether we place value on involvement or independence we are always balancing the conflicting needs for both. The problem is that we generally require both at the same time and this places us in a double-bind situation in our relations with others. Tannen focuses mainly on the communication problems raised by this, but what she says is equally applicable to other facets of social activity. The problem is that anything we say to demonstrate our solidarity or involvement with others can be conceived of as a threat to our own, and to their individuality. Conversely, anything we do to indicate that we are keeping our distance from others threatens our own and their need for rapport and involvement (Tannen 1987: 16–17). We cannot satisfy both needs at the same time, so anything we do or say will always pull against one of these fundamental needs, even if in only a minor and trivial way. I have previously referred to the tension between these contradictory aspects of social existence as the dialectic of separateness and relatedness, and both Laing's and Tannen's work confirms its importance both in understanding some facets of mental illness as well as the more routine "normal" aspects of daily life. The core of the dilemma for the individual concerns what Tannen refers to as a balancing act between the need for involvement and independence. Although the individual is constantly attempting to rectify an existing tilt to one side or the other, it is never something that can be finally resolved, since as Tannen observes, a move in one direction directly compromises the opposing tendency. In any encounter all we can do is arrive at a "working arrangement" that is necessarily less than perfect.

As with other dilemmas associated with the dialectic of separateness and relatedness – such as the need to maintain emotional composure while displaying emotional sensitivity – what lies at the heart of them is the confrontation with the nature of reality and human existence. This is, perhaps, the most basic of existential contradictions and concerns the fact that in the final analysis, as individuals we are alone in a fundamental sense. Many philosophers and existential psychiatrists (including Sartre and Laing) have noted this, but sociologists have been rather more resistant to acknowledge it – perhaps in their zeal to emphasize the importance of the social context of human existence. While not denying the pivotal importance of the social realm and the impossibility of stepping outside its influence in one sense, it is also of the utmost importance to recognize the fact of existential aloneness as a simultaneous (and opposing) dimension of social life.

The main consequence of refusing to recognize this is that we are likely to overlook an important facet of human subjectivity – the contradictory tensions that afflict the human psyche consciously and unconsciously and in routine and unconventional situations alike. The felt sense of existential aloneness is a realization that every competent member of society has to confront and embrace since the experience and acquisition of a fully formed and autonomous identity is conditional upon it. One has to realize that one is a separate person from everyone else and, as Laing notes, "no matter how deeply I am committed in joy or suffering to someone else, he is not me, and I am not him. However lonely or sad one may be, one can exist alone" (Laing 1969: 52). Jampolsky mirrors these sentiments when he says (in relation to the question of personal growth) "I am the only one who can journey within myself; no one else can experience my inner life in place of me" (1994: 121).

Indeed it has been argued that such a realization is also a precondition for establishing non-dependent and non-manipulative ("healthy") relations with others. Whatever the merits of this particular argument it is clearly of the utmost importance for individuals to have a full appreciation of themselves as separate, integral beings before they can "take on" the social world in any efficacious sense. Set against the fact of existential aloneness is the equally pressing fact of our social involvements and connectedness with others. Apart from our dependence on others for our material well-being (to provide food, shelter, transportation and so on), we also forge social ties of various degrees of intimacy and emotional openness. Our attachments to others always imprint themselves on our own self-identities, becoming part of us, and joining us irrevocably to others. Thus it is that our existential aloneness co-exists with our intrinsic enmeshment in social ties of mutual dependence.

It is in the context of this dialectic that the psychological issues surrounding trust, security and self-identity work themselves out. The contradictory pulls of these two dimensions of existence are reflected in the psychological conflict, tension and energy required to control and manage the constant listing between the two sides of the duality. How specific individuals deal with these tensions and conflicts will to some extent vary across cultures and situations and in relation to their own and other's personality characteristics. However, there is no doubt that the more "permanent" or at least more durable resolutions of such tensions and conflicts indicate something about the general psychological well-being of individuals. For within the terms of the dialectic a wide variety of psychological responses are possible, ranging from "normal" adjustments to the demands of social life while preserving an independent sense of identity, to the pathological response of complete withdrawal, social isolation, paralysis and fear.

Conclusion: the person and social encounters

In this chapter I have not attempted to give anything like an overall account of the psychology of the person since this would anyway be beyond the bounds of the present study. However, I have attempted to give a broad overview of this topic in so far as it fits in with the general framework of domain theory. In this respect I have given an indication of the complexity of the psychology of humans as social beings without attempting to develop an inclusive theoretical framework, or to work out the detailed ramifications. In particular I have tried to point to the richness of the psychic interior of individuals as seen from the point of view of their individuality – their uniqueness as personalities. As such, individuals are complex and contradictory beings capable of self-deception to varying degrees and intensities as well as consciously formulated intentional behaviour. Also as we have seen, people constantly veer between manipulative and altruistic modes of relating to others, sometimes managing to combine both in the same sequence or episode of face-to-face conduct. I have also emphasized the emotional depth of the human being as it is reflected in social life. The contradictory tensions and pulls of emotional exchanges and the energies emanating from particular personalities all combine to create an individual who is far from a coherent unity acting in a uniformly rational manner. I have argued that although trust is of great importance in social life in general, this cannot mean that the individual is always and everywhere a creature cut entirely from moral cloth. Caring for other's feelings and cynical manipulation are not alternatives, they are equally important potentials of social life, and whether one prevails over the other in any particular situation will depend upon the actual circumstances and the personalities of those involved.

As Dennis Wrong (1967) suggested some time ago, individuals are never completely socialized in the sense that they always display conduct that is fitting and proper to the situation. The human psyche is imperfectly socialized in this respect – the force of unconscious and "selfish" energies always struggle for recognition and effectivity in even the most routine of encounters. Although it is true to say that the human being is prey to self-interest as much as to altruism, it is, perhaps, more accurate to suggest that much behaviour falls somewhere between the two extremes. It is the fact of a person's individuality – their unique personality – that imposes a demand upon them to attend to their own feelings, emotions and needs in any encounter irrespective of the insistence of others' demands. In this sense the individual never achieves a full and continuous sense of ontological security – it is always a tenuous affair that needs to be constantly achieved and reaccomplished from moment to moment from within situated encounters.

Thus it is that varying levels of anxiety surround issues of self-identity, esteem and security for the individual. Such anxiety is a constant feature of the investment of psychic energy expended in face-to-face conduct. I have referred to this energy variously as emotional "work" or as an aspect of primary awareness that operates between the wishes, desires and drives of the unconscious and the practical awareness of (and the capacity to carry through with) the requirements of routine social life. Clearly then, the person is not simply a creature defined by reflexivity, and practical or rational consciousness. Such a cognitive emphasis must be balanced by an appreciation of the sense in which the human being continuously operates at the edges of the requirements of the social world. The individual is constantly embroiled in a struggle to attend to social and situational constraints while responding to the often invisible structure of emotional expression in encounters with others. The outcome of this problematic balancing act again depends crucially upon the personalities and psychic dispositions of individuals as well as the nature of the situations in which they find themselves.

This simply underlines the importance of finding a place for the analysis of the psychological interior individuals within the broader framework of sociological analysis. The dialectic of separateness and relatedness – which to some extent expresses the double-edged bond between individuals and their social environment – is a "fact" that must be addressed in any social analysis. This dialectic stresses that the individual is, at one and the same time, intrinsically psychological and social in nature. For the purposes of sociological analysis the interior of the person cannot be simply understood as an internalization of the rules and skills necessary for social participation and impressed on the individual by the social environment. The individual is also psychologically predisposed in the sense that their uniquely formed personality imprints itself with equal force on their social behaviour. Thus I have highlighted the importance of the individual's psychobiography as a means of tracing the interaction between social and psychological predispositions as they are acquired over time and space.

The dual psychological and social nature of the person's "interior" is also reflected in another aspect of social existence. That is, there is a sense in which society exists within individuals (as internalized norms and behavioural dispositions), but also a very real sense in which it has an exterior nature. Society, therefore is also a force operating outside individuals and their motivations and cannot be reduced to them. In this sense both Durkheim and later Goffman were right to stress the independence and exteriority of the respective social domains in which they were most interested. However, they were remiss in failing to see this in relative terms and thus to overlook the important and subtle linkages between the social and the psychological realms. Chapter 3 takes seriously the sense in which society and social organization in general has a life somewhat independent of individual's reasons, motivations and local practices. Thus the thrust of Chapter 3 will be on documenting some of these connections. However, I shall proceed from the vantage point of the macro-social world rather than from the point of view of the individual and face-to-face conduct as has been the case in this chapter.

3

The social fabric examined

Although Chapter 2 examined the link between the subjective world of the person and the person's more immediate social context, it did so decidedly from the point of view of the experiencing individual. In this chapter I want to reverse the emphasis by bracketing issues of self-identity, subjective experience, and so on, while I focus on the elements of the social fabric itself. I must stress, of course, that this is merely a matter of emphasis that is necessary for the analytic purposes at hand. In this regard we must be careful to bear in mind that issues of subjectivity, identity and human agency are closely entangled with the more encompassing aspects of social organization in the sense that it is human social activity that gives life and continuity to social organization. The discussion will proceed along the following route. First, I shall give a preliminary overview of the arguments, concepts and definitions that are contained in my characterization of the social fabric. I shall then offer a series of definitions of the principal terms and concepts that arise in the ensuing discussion. The aim is to provide the reader with a more general vantage point on domain theory before encountering some of its key elements in detail.

Preview of concepts and issues

First, let me clarify the issue of the domains themselves. What are they and how do they interconnect? There are four principal social domains that are of concern here and Chapter 2 has already dealt in some detail with one of them – that of *psychobiography* (including self-identity) and has also

76

raised issues concerning another domain, that of *situated activity*. The other two domains are *social setting* (including fields) and *contextual resources*. These four can themselves be subdivided into smaller "domains" or even understood as component elements of larger "domains". I shall go into these complexities in due course but for present purposes and to avoid undue confusion, these four will be regarded as the core domains. In essence they are ontological features of the social world.

By approaching the matter in this way I am not suggesting that such concerns are prior to, or more important than, epistemological matters (that is, claims about the validity or adequacy of knowledge) as some writers have argued (see Bhaskar 1979, Giddens 1984). In my opinion epistemological questions (how we know things) and ontological claims (about the nature of the things we know) cannot be completely separated from each other because they are intrinsically related (see Layder 1985, 1990). In this respect my claim that these domains are basic ontological features of social reality has to be seen in the more embracing context of domain theory in general. That is, I would argue that specific claims like this have to be evaluated from the point of view of the theoretical framework as a whole and its overall aims and objectives. Thus one of the central objectives of domain theory – to attempt to weld both the subjective and objective sides of social life into a comprehensive theory that accounts for the production and reproduction of social life through human activity – sets the terms under which more specific claims about the nature of social reality can be judged. (Similarly its aim – outlined in Chapter 1 – to incorporate a moderate form of "objectivism" has to be viewed in this light.)

The domains are completely interdependent. No particular domain is the prime mover in terms of influence and in this respect the mutual influences are represented as a circuit as depicted in Figure 3.1. Although it is not possible to represent this properly in diagrammatic form, it is more accurate to envision the domains as more or less completely overlapping with one another as people's social behaviour moves through the dimensions of time and space. Nevertheless as Figure 3.1 indicates, the ligatures that draw together the domains and constitute their connective tissue, as it were, are social relations and practices, which, in turn, are inscribed by forms of discourse, power and control that flow in both directions through these practices and relations. These clusterings of relations, practices, discourses and power are the common factors that thread through all the domains and draw them together in various configurations.

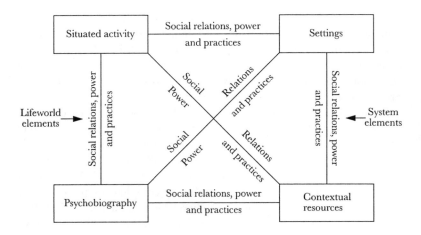

Figure 3.1   The social domains.

Figure 3.1 also introduces the notions of *lifeworld* and *system* as the underlying elements of a basic duality in modern societies. This pairing of terms is taken from Habermas (1984, 1987) who conceives of them as referring to fundamentally different features of social reality. My own usage is similar to Habermas's although there are also significant differences as I shall go on to show. In so far as "lifeworld" and "system" point to an ontological difference in societies, I am in agreement with Habermas, and hence they can be understood in my terms as more "inclusive" or "meta" domains. In this sense the lifeworld refers primarily (although not exclusively) to aspects of social life that have to do with the lived experience of human beings as they go about their everyday business. Thus lifeworld elements appear more pronounced when we focus on the social domains of psychobiography and situated activity. System elements have to do with the reproduced, institutionalized features of society such as economic markets and bureaucratic organizations that mediate relations of power and "relations of ruling" (Smith 1988). System elements therefore appear more pronounced when the analytic focus is on social settings, fields and contextual resources.

A crucial difference between my own and Habermas's employment of these terms concerns the manner in which these two features of social reality intersect. Habermas seems to understand system elements as if they were naturally "uncoupled" from those of the lifeworld – as if the two domains had independent "lives" of their own. According to Habermas, one of the pathological features of modern societies is that their system elements have to some extent re-established themselves in the "lifeworld" through a process of "colonization" and thus have "sullied" its natural state. From the standpoint of critical theory Habermas's view is that efforts to reform or transform society should aim to stave off or remove altogether the colonizing tendencies of the system. From this perspective lifeworld and system are understood as naturally discrete entities, each of which is integrated according to very different principles (see later discussion).

Contrary to this, I understand the relation between system and lifeworld to be one of mutual interdependence, imbrication and complementarity. That is, although settings and contextual resources are the main sites or locations for the influence of system elements, they never exist in a "pure" state – they are always interfused with lifeworld elements. Conversely, although the influence of the lifeworld is strongest in the areas of situated activity and psychobiography, system elements always intrude into these areas although not *always* in a pathological manner as Habermas believes. The point is that lifeworld and system elements are deeply interconnected with each other through the medium of social practices and activities. The relatively independent influence of lifeworld and system elements is registered in the predominance of system influences in settings and contextual resources, while lifeworld elements predominate in the areas of situated activity and self-identity.

The question of how the interchange between elements of lifeworld and system are "carried" in social activities is crucial in understanding the links between lived experience and the institutionalized features of social systems. This returns us to the question of the connections between the social domains generally. As I said before, the common threads that bind the domains to each other are clusterings of social relations and practices along with the discourses and forms of power that they "enclose". Of great importance for the question of interchanges between lifeworld and system domains is the emphasis on particular characteristics of social relations. The *reproduced* aspects of social relations that are aggregated to form the social settings in which social activities and practices are played out (and the diffusion of their effects) are of critical significance here.

I shall discuss this (and many of the other issues dealt with in this section) in more detail later in this and subsequent chapters. Here I merely wish to flag two aspects of the problem. The first is that social relations have a dual nature and that their reproduced aspects come to play a significant role in "carrying" the respective influences of lifeworld and system elements into social practices and activities and into the personal lives of particular people. Secondly, there is a further connection between forms of power and control and the social relations and practices in which they are grounded. Although this will be the subject of Chapter 4, it is worth mentioning at this juncture that I distinguish between different types of power and control relations and their consequences for practice as they relate to the social domains.

Having given something of the broad picture let me now indicate how the discussion of the chapter will unfold. After providing some definitions of key concepts and ideas the chapter proceeds by outlining the nature of the principal social domains and their empirical characteristics. In a sense Chapter 2 has already begun this task by suggesting some of the connections between self-identity, agency and situated activity. Thus I take up the story from this point and turn to a discussion of situated activity that takes as its subject matter the analysis of specific aspects of face-to-face conduct, or what Goffman (1961a) has referred to as "focused gatherings". As I have have already pointed out at various junctures, Goffman also uses the term "interaction order" to define a province of concerns that constitute a level of social analysis in its own right. While there is a great deal that is interesting and worthwhile in Goffman's vision of the "interaction order" and which meshes with the perspective I am currently employing, it needs to be made clear that what I refer to as "situated activity" is not synonymous with the "interaction order" in Goffman's terms. I define the significant differences in the following section on key terms and concepts, although here I should point out that the interaction order is a more inclusive concept than that of situated activity which has a fairly specific focus.

From here the discussion moves to a consideration of social settings. As I intimated above, the connections between situated activity and settings are such that there is significant overlapping of influences and effects between them and in this sense activities and settings can be understood as contiguous. However, settings are distinguishable in that they serve as local holding points for aggregations of *reproduced* social relations and practices. Thus they are important junctions in the two-way traffic of effects between contextual resources and the face-to-face encounters that occur in local settings. As a result, social settings are key areas for the study of the reproductive effects of activities on wider (macro) system features. Finally, attention turns to "contextual resources" that refer to social resources that are drawn upon by social actors in order to "produce" their social behaviour. I distinguish between three types: first, "material resources" such as money, property, or ownership of any (material) substances that can be exchanged for money or credit. Secondly, "dominative resources" having to do with the securing of power, authority and control over others (which also implies that the absence of such resources creates vulnerability to control by others). Finally, there are "cultural/discursive resources" these include a diversity of phenomena (including practical, technical and interpersonal knowledge and skills) required for competent membership and meaningful activity in the social world. The important feature of such phenomena is that they typically take on a discursive (written and/or spoken) form as is the case with, for example, norms, ideas, ideologies and commonsense.

A preliminary way of understanding contextual resources is to conceptualize them in terms of two distinct modes of existence (I shall later distinguish a third mode). First, they must be understood from a "macro" vantage point as a "distributive pattern" that reflects their allocation on a society-wide basis. Thus, material, dominative and cultural/discursive resources are unevenly spread throughout any social system and hence differentially available to various groups of a class, gender and racialized nature. On the other hand, from the point of view of ongoing activity itself, such phenomena have to be thought of as local aggregations of interactional resources that actors draw upon to make their activities happen. In this latter sense contextual resources must be conceptualized as localized activity lubricants that connect with subjectivities and have a cognitive –emotive reality embedded in actors' experiences of the social world. This dimension of their existence is quite unlike that associated with their distributive mode, which has no necessary counterpart in the mental states of individuals.

In both their distributive and interactional modes, resources are closely implicated in psychobiography, situated activity and settings, although they also constitute a partly independent domain. It is important to understand the intrinsic connection between human activity and the contoured forms of the institutionalized features of social life and in this respect there is a significant overlapping between lifeworld and system elements. However, it is also important to recognize that there are differences between the domains themselves in terms of their characteristics (internal properties) and the manner in which they are related to each other – thus they are not reducible to one another. Similarly, in speaking of domains we must be careful not to think of them as static things or entities – for they are intrinsically social processes whose dynamism derives from the productive and reproductive effects of social activities. Since these processes involve unfolding and evolution over time, it is necessary to come to grips with the different senses of time and history that are pertinent to the different domains. Likewise, as I mentioned briefly before, the theme of power runs through all the domains, but it is crucial to note that the form of power varies in relation to particular domains.

Some key terms and concepts

I now want to introduce a group of related concepts and defintions that will help to clarify the subsequent discussion. These concepts are closely interrelated and partly overlap with and depend on each other. The definitions and concepts relate to the first part of the chapter, which attempts to identify the nature of situated activity and its links with social settings. Since the focal point of reference is situated activity itself, it is necessary to specify its nature by distinguishing it from several other closely connected terms and concepts. These are: "social relations", "reproduced social practices", "discourses", "situated activity", "the interaction order", "the lifeworld" and "social settings". I shall introduce the working definitions in an order that makes most sense in respect of illuminating the nature of situated activity.

Social relations

These differ from situated activity in terms of their inclusiveness – social relations stretch beyond the confines of particular instances of situated activity. They refer to the generalized social connections and bonds between people in terms of social positions and the practices associated with them. (The positions and practices themselves may vary in terms of the degree of their "formality" and specificity.) In principle, situated activity does not require that the participants have any specific social connections beyond those fortuitously "created" through mutual presence, although in many instances such bonds will exist. Thus, strangers and the unacquainted may become involved in situated activity despite having no formally defined social bonds beyond the immediate encounter.

Social relations endure beyond the presence or absence of those involved whereas situated activity does not. In this sense social relations are intrinsically more general in scope and may "draw together" a number of instances of situated activity. For example, social relations between workmates or colleagues bound by a formal contractual tie to the workplace none the less regularly engage in situated activities patterned around the work task. Parent–offspring relationships provide another illustration of enduring bonds that are socially defined in terms of formal expectations and obligations, patterns of deference and so on. However, actual contact and the quality of relations between parent and offspring will depend on the "state" of the relationship. Typically though, the two will come together in specific episodes of face-to-face interaction, and each instance will have a small life and history of its own in which the social relationship is reproduced in various ways.

In this sense situated activity is about the existential availability ("thereness") of the people concerned as well as the living, emergent nature of social activities. Conversely, social relations are about the trans-situational ties that join together particular episodes of situated activity. Of course situated activity very commonly incorporates the inputs of social relations as in the above examples. The crucial point is that they are not identical. Social relations have a persistent enduring quality about them that situated activities lack – since they are located in instances in time and space limited by the mutual presence of those concerned. In saying this, however, it is important to recognize that situated activities play a crucial role in reproducing social relations. That is, they play a role in creating the persistent and enduring qualities of social relations while they themselves are characterized primarily by their evanescent quality. This derives from their link with reproduced practices.

Reproduced social practices

Like social relations, reproduced social practices have a generality that carries them beyond specific instances of activity. For example, the socially defined practices general throughout a social community may sustain innumerable instances of situated activity. As such actors draw upon reproduced practices in their situated encounters with others in order to inform and "construct" their ongoing conduct. However, situated conduct is more than the sum of reproduced practices incorporated in the action – it has an innovative quality produced from the creative interplay between the unique personalities involved in the face-to-face encounter. Thus reproduced practices are drawn on (as models for behaviour) but reach beyond situated encounters. Thus social practices are continually reproduced in situated activity at the same time as the participants also depart from them during the unfolding of the encounter. In this sense face-to-face activity creates aspects of practice that are unique to the encounter itself, but which are meaningful to the participants only in the wider context of a recognizable body of reproduced social practices.

Discourses

As Foucault has demonstrated, discourses, practices and power are closely tied together. Discourse refers to all that can be discussed, spoken or written about a specific topic or subject area. Thus the discourse of medicine refers to the body of knowledge and expertise associated with the health and illness of the human body. The practices associated with this discourse are all those to do with the diagnosis, treatment and care of the physical and mental disorders of the human body. That discourses and practices are intrinsically linked to power is exemplified in the capabilities they confer on those who deploy them as well as those who are "subjected" to their deployment. Discourses feed into the subjectivities of individuals who fall within the orbit of their influence, by providing markers of normality and behavioural guidelines, as well as giving a sense of identity by placing and positioning the person within a cultural milieu and a set of social relationships. In this sense discourses are the means through which the social relations between positions and practices are articulated and diffused throughout the social body.

This poststructuralist usage of the notion of discourse is of no little importance, but as I pointed out in Chapter 2, it would be a mistake to think of identity and social agency entirely in these terms. A sense of the independent contribution of psychobiography is no less pivotal for a rounded understanding of the constitution of self-identity. Similarly, the partly independent effects of situated activity (and the interaction order in general) on the presentation of self has to be registered in order to leaven the over-inflated role that discourse has assumed in poststructuralist (and postmodernist) analyses. These latter schools of thought tend to imply that discourses float in social space in some anonymous, quasi-objective manner, and this view should be resisted. Likewise the idea that discourses are mechanically attached to individual personalities must be similarly rejected.

Like social practices, discourses are drawn upon by social actors in face-to-face encounters in order to formulate their behaviour and to make the encounter "happen", so to speak. Thus discourses are one important element in situated activity and as with social practices and social relations they are simultaneously reproduced and transformed by the very social practices they help to form. People and their activities are not simply resultants of the play of discourses and social positions, for individuals are capable of rejecting, choosing, reformulating and manipulating the discourses that they have at their disposal. This is indeed what happens in social encounters – the activity itself provides a force field that produces emergent effects which transform the discursive inputs that derive from the cultural milieu. Discourses, then, are elements of a more general cultural context of resources that both enable and constrain the behaviours of those within their sphere of influence. At the same time within situated encounters people transmute, transform and refashion these resources by the very act of utilizing them and making them work in real-life contexts.

Situated activity

This involves face-to face conduct between two or more people who are in each other's "response presence" (Goffman 1983). This latter is important since it refers to the ability of each person to monitor the behaviour of the others present and to modify their own behaviour in the light of the other's responses. Goffman's notion of "ratified involvement" is also of paramount importance here in that such encounters are centred around a particular set of participants with a common focus of interest. As Goffman points out (1967), the question of who is rightfully thought of as "included" (a ratified member) and who, as a consequence, is excluded, is important in delineating the boundaries of the encounter. Similarly, the level of involvement in the proceedings is important in facilitating the ebb and flow of face-to-face business. The "situated" part of the term points to the evanescent quality of such encounters – their tendency to fade away as those involved (and who literally make the encounter happen) disperse in time and space. That is to say, situated activity exists only by virtue of the presence of particular people at specific times and places – thus it is "situated" because it is integrally tied to local circumstances and practices.

Situated activity produces "emergent effects" that are specific to those local circumstances and practices. That is, the coalescence of a number of different personalities and their behavioural inputs creates a social effect that is more than the sum of its constituent parts. Collective agreements and shared understandings are created during the encounter that influence the subsequent proceedings. Several people meeting up (in whatever sort of context or circumstances) will, as Goffman phrases it, create a small, localized "social system" whose membrane sets them slightly apart from the wider social environment for the duration of the encounter. Each person will be significantly influenced by the collective atmosphere of the group that itself will be influenced by such things as the personalities and moods of specific individuals, the emotional tenor of the proceedings, the gender and "racialized" mix and other power and status attributes of those involved, how well they know each other and on what basis, and so on. Furthermore, as Garfinkel (1967), Austin (1971) and Wittgenstein (1972) have shown, the meaning and sense of what transpires in the form of conversation, gestures, facial expression, tone of voice and so forth will be closely tied to their situated character – that is, their use and function in those specific circumstances.

Situated activity is not entirely "cut adrift" from the general continuity of activity because every instance of a situated encounter will be intertwined with the reproduction of general social practices, relations and discourses as they are drawn upon by the actors during the encounter. So in a very real sense the notion of unique encounters set within strict temporal (or spatial) limits – and that appear and disappear along with the participants – emerges as a possibility only in the context of its linkage with the general continuity of social reproduction. Another way in which situated activity ties in with the more general continuity of social life is through routine connections between people. Thus, although situated activity is characteristically punctuated by the arrivals and departures of particular people and a common focus of interest, in another way the careers and daily pathways of individuals often intersect repeatedly at different times and places and as a result produce "carry-over" influences that serve to link encounters. When the same people (or even only some of them) meet up again, typically they will couch their behaviour in terms of what has gone before. Over time these sorts of re-assemblies begin to have little histories of shared experience attached to them (rather like those inscribed in individual biographies) and hence the successive encounters will trade upon the spill-overs and knock-on effects of these accumulated experiences. None the less, at the same time, each reconstitution of the group, or part thereof, produces a unique situation in its own right.

The interaction order

The interaction order is a term coined by Erving Goffman and has a wider reference than that indicated by situated activity. Situated activity is an important element of the interaction order since much face-to-face behaviour conforms to its requirements and functions. However, the interaction order denotes a distinct set of concerns (care of social selves, commitment to a minimal sense of trust, the production of meaning and so on) that are specific to that order, are general features of it, and distinguish it from other social orders. To talk of an interaction order involves delineating broad dimensions and ingredients that all face-to-face social interaction possesses and the boundaries and intersections these make with other social orders. Situated activity has a much more specific reference and concerns real, describable actors and their activities. Situated activities are expressive of the interaction order but do not in themselves constitute this order.

The lifeworld

The concept of the lifeworld has a wider reference than situated activity and the interaction order, but presupposes both of them. Habermas's description of the lifeworld as an "intersubjectively shared world" (1987: 225) that brackets together personality, action (what Habermas calls "communicative action"), society and culture is apt here. In this sense it is the wider socio-cultural backdrop to situated activity and the interaction order and informs and underpins them both. It focuses on the possibilities of lived experience in the context of a shared world.

Social settings

Settings are the proximate locations of social activities and specific social practices. Although they are primarily composed of reproduced relations and practices, they also include some reference to a geographic region as well as the physical "housing" (such as a building or a street area) in which particular forms of activity or practices are to be found. These, though, are subsidiary to the reproduced relations and practices that define the social contours of settings and that range from highly formalized organizational environments to the more informal settings of personal or family life. It is very important to stress that social settings are not simply empty backdrops to social activity. In a basic way they enter into, and are constituted by, the routine practices of people. However, it is equally crucial to acknowledge that they also exist relatively independently of specific people and practices. In so far as they are *reproduced* they are elements of social systems and are thereby linked to other social system features such as money, property, power and discourses.

The nature and modes of situated activity

Moving on from the formal presentation of concepts, I now examine some of the internal dynamics of situated activity. In this sense I want to place on hold questions associated with the intersections between the psychological, interactional and macro-structural domains in order to make the specific characteristics of situated activity stand out in relief. In this respect I shall draw on the work of some authors who might dispute my more encompassing arguments and presuppositions about the nature, existence and interrelationships between social domains. Mead and Blumer are examples of such authors and I shall begin with them because they exemplify the usefulness of the perspective of symbolic interactionism as a means of coming to terms with some of the central characteristics of situated activity.

As both Mead (1967) and later Blumer (1969) stress, face-to-face interaction has its own emergent dynamics that force us to direct attention to the exchange of symbols and gestures in human encounters. For these authors the importance of meaning in human behaviour is paramount, since humans organize their activities around it. Thus, the meanings that individuals impute to the behaviour of others, to conversational exchanges, or to social and physical objects, influence the way in which they formulate and express their own behaviour. Meaning in this sense emerges out of the give and take of communicative interchanges within the parameters of the situations in which they occur. That is, meaning is not something given in a particular object – the meaning of a drug for the drug user is not contained in the drug itself, the meaning of an embrace is not an intrinsic feature of its physical manifestation.

Meaning derives from the responses of others to particular social events or objects and from the "negotiations" between people that circle around them. Thus a person becomes dependent on a drug as the result of a social process of learning how to use it in order to experience pleasurable effects. This involves interaction with other drug users and some level of participation in a drug subculture, even if this extends only to making contacts with pushers (Becker 1953). Similarly, if a person hugs another, the recipient's response will be crucial in forming an agreed definition of what the embrace means for both people. If the initiator intends it as a prelude to more intimate relations with the other, and the recipient responds positively, then this will be the "meaning" of the embrace. Conversely, if the recipient rejects the "opening" offered in the gesture then some other meaning (such as "embarrassing *faux pas*") will impress itself on both participants. In these examples people do not bestow meaning as a reflection of their prior attitudes, say to drugs or to embracing in general. Nor does meaning reside in the object itself – a reflection of a characteristic that all embraces (or drugs) possess. Instead, meaning grows out of the social exchanges between the people in the encounter (Blumer 1969).

This approach has much in common with the ethnomethodological emphasis on the indexicality (or contextual specificity) of meaning (Garfinkel 1967). Philosophers such as Austin and Wittgenstein have also noted a similar phenomenon in that the meanings of words or utterances actually used in everyday communication are significantly influenced by elements "internal" to the situations of their use. Factors such as tone of voice and facial gestures contribute to the way in which people "hear" or interpret what others are saying. So the sentence "I will come at 5 o'clock" when uttered with a certain intonation and accompanied by a particular facial expression (and possibily other bodily gestures) can be understood variously as a promise, a threat or an appeal (Wootton 1975). Similarly, the use of pronominal expressions ("he", "she", "they" and "it") require detailed contextual knowledge about exactly who or what such expressions are referring to, before a listener has access to their meanings. The notion of indexicality extends to even more subtle and qualitative aspects of face-to-face conduct. The collective mood emanating from a gathering or encounter will significantly affect the emotional tone of what transpires between the participants, as will the emergent agreements, compromises or unresolved arguments that are a feature of the events and transactions among them. In short, what is apparently said or "seems" to be going on in an encounter to an outside observer may be highly misleading or plainly inaccurate without access to "inside" knowledge of the dynamics of the group. It is possible to understand the meaning of utterances or behaviour as, Garfinkel (1967) puts it, only "from within" situations; we cannot read off what is going on from knowledge gleaned from external appearances.

There is certainly a lot in this contention: much behaviour and talk can be understood only with reference to contextual particulars. Moreover, this argument can be extended to make a point about social analysis in general to the effect that those approaches that tend to view social activity from an external and/or macro-perspective (like functionalism, structuralism and versions of role theory) will have difficulty in giving accurate or adequate accounts since by definition they are unable to adopt an analytic vantage point that takes account of the inner dynamics of situations. Indeed, this is the kind of radical argument that ethnomethodologists have levelled at what they call "conventional" sociology. On this argument, approaches like functionalism simply construct artificial theoretical edifices that reflect an external analyst's point of view rather than coming anywhere near to a faithful rendering of the actual reality of social situations.

Some ethnomethodologists have claimed that the subject matter of sociology should be based solely on the study of people's artful production of local practices in concrete situations rather than on any notion of a macro (or even micro) reality or structure. In fact some have suggested that ethnomethodology is indifferent to any kind of "structure" at any level and suspends belief in persons, individuals, subjective content, interaction patterns and so on (Hilbert 1990). The net effect of such a strategy is arbitrarily to restrict social analysis to a narrow province of concerns surrounding the construction and accomplishment of local versions of social reality. This is thus a conscious effort to deny the influence of both psychological and macro-structural dimensions for sociological analysis and in my view represents a rather blinkered attempt to close down areas of inquiry and to restrict the boundaries of knowledge – both of which must be resisted at all costs.

Perhaps a less dogmatic version of this is also contained in Blumer's vision of symbolic interactionism in so far as he is less prone to making such sweeping claims although the overall effect is similar. Blumer's argument is that in order not to falsify the data or the "facts of the matter" as far as social interaction is concerned, we must concentrate our attention on the analysis of meaning and its situated nature. In this respect psychological analyses incorrectly view social behaviour as the result of fixed traits of the individual (such as personality factors or inner drives) being projected into the social arena. Blumer contends that social interaction and the meanings that give it coherence and shape are constructed almost entirely by, and within the give and take of, face-to-face conduct. Established sociological approaches (in particular functionalism) are macro-structural in orientation and take a contrary position, tending to view social behaviour as the outcome of macro-structural factors such as role expectations or status positions. For Blumer this simply overlooks the way in which people conduct and orient themselves in terms of the meanings that things have for them in social life, rather than according to the dictates of external factors and analytic "variables".

It is clear that Blumer's argument arrives at much the same conclusion as many ethnomethodologists – that the study of everyday behaviour requires concentrated (not to say blinkered) attention on the internal dynamics of situated activity, to the exclusion of other dimensions. Now while I am in agreement that situated activity is a domain in its own right and that this means that we must treat its properties and characterisitics as distinctive, this should not lead us to view it as cocooned and hermetically sealed from the influence of other social orders or domains. In this sense we must part company from those who wish to see it as the most important or exclusive area of social analysis. The problem is to try to depict the distinctive character of the interaction order without denying the significance or influence of other domains. A point in question here is the issue of indexicality. Although much social behaviour is understandable only in terms of its situated context, it does not necessarily follow that it is neatly and fully separated from the realm of individual psychology or from an institutional realm.

In fact I want to convey the contrary impression – that there are no separations between social domains since they are interconnected and interdependent with each other. As Giddens (1984) puts it, activities and structures are "deeply implicated" in each other, and I would certainly endorse this point in relation to my present argument since Giddens is highlighting the fact that structures are produced and reproduced by people in their daily activities and that activities in turn are facilitated by the enabling resources provided by structures. However, in saying this I am not suggesting that their distinctive features are lost or minimized in the process. This is important because Giddens strongly implies that there is no real distinction between the realms of activity and structure – their distinct properties dissolve into the singular composite form of practices. However, I am arguing that practices are formed out of the intersection of distinct domains that are both strongly bonded and inextricably interwoven with each other. Secondly, although I believe that social production and reproduction are related to each other through activity, I also believe that it is very important to be clear about what is meant by this deceptively "transparent" formulation. I think the generic phrase "the production and reproduction of social life" is in dire need of both elaboration and qualification, otherwise it becomes something of a slogan that is unthinkingly applied. Exactly which aspects of social life are being referred to in this phrase? What is their precise nature and what is the extent of their influence? I shall argue in Chapter 5 that there are different types and forms of production and reproduction applicable to different domains and these need to be unpacked and examined in detail. Generic phrases about the simultaneous production and reproduction of social life do not do justice to the complexity of the issues involved.

Having outlined some of its distinctive characteristics, I want now to turn to the relationship between situated activity and the other domains that are implicated in it. There are two points to bear in mind here. The first is that it is only in analytic terms that it is possible to separate out the influences of the different domains. In reality they are so closely interwoven that it is virtually impossible to discern their respective strands of influence. Secondly, the very fact of this interrelatedness does not in any way undermine the indexical (or situation-dependent) nature of some aspects of such activity. That is, there is no contradiction implied in saying that while other domains significantly affect the form of situated activity, there is still room for the unique features of the situation to impress themselves on the face-to-face conduct occurring within it.

In this sense the influences of the various domains meld into one another to produce emergent effects that overlay the (primary) emergent effects within each domain itself. This gives us a rather complicated model of the working relationships implied in the interdependencies between domains. I shall briefly try to indicate what this entails in the case of situated activity, but I shall refrain from giving a detailed general account at this point since it would drag us away from my main purpose, which is to pinpoint the main characteristics of situated activity. As I attempted to show in the previous section, a number of authors have demonstrated that the meaning and the dynamics of face-to-face conduct (its tempo, its atmosphere – based on who is doing what to whom and why) result from its situated character. This is accurate *but only in so far* as some core aspects of situated activity will result from the internal ingredients of specific situations. This "core" constitutes the primary emergent feature of situated activity.

However, not all aspects of activity can be understood from within situations (or even more broadly in terms of the interaction order, as Goffman defines it). Elements of psychobiography, setting and contextual resources will also play a role in structuring the activity. In so doing they will overlay and inter-mix with elements of the other domains to produce new dynamic properties in the activities themselves (including the meanings that serve to "lubricate" the behavioural exchanges in the encounter). This overlaying and interfusion creates secondary emergent effects that often refashion and reformulate the primary ones – sometimes to such an extent that they are unrecognizable and cannot be "recovered" for analytic purposes. So the establishment of secondary effects may involve the partial "withering away" of the primary ones or their incorporation into the new (secondary) forms. This clearly happens in the case of the intrusion of aspects of the settings of activity into actual episodes of behaviour. It is the influence of different kinds of settings as they reflect the wider availability of resources that creates typical variations in the form of situated activity itself. These combine with other effects of a psychological or psychobiographical kind to produce complex, textured overlayerings that manifest themselves in actual instances of face-to-face conduct.

Before considering some of these variations I shall adopt Goffman's definition of social interaction as "environments in which two or more individuals are physically in one another's response presence" (Goffman 1983: 4). He goes on to add that "presumably the telephone and the mails provide reduced versions of the primordial real thing". The point about Goffman's definition is that it limits interest to those situations in which people are able to monitor the behaviour of relevant others and can therefore respond to the unfolding action in a reflective manner. Thus the spotlight is on "focused interaction" and does not stray into the area of larger social gatherings such as crowds or audiences. If this serves as our definition of situated activity, let me now turn to some of the variations indicated above. First, I shall consider variability in relation to two sets of general, abstract qualities that pertain to all forms of situated activity. These are continuity in time and space, and the degree of relatedness or connectedness of the people involved. The notion of connectedness can be understood in terms of three subdimensions: (a) how well the people know each other, (b) the "purpose" of their social ties, and (c) the specific circumstances of their contacts.

Transient encounters

By definition transient or one-off encounters have an impersonal quality to them. That is, they occur fundamentally between "strangers", or perhaps more accurately, between the "unacquainted" since they differ in terms of whether the context of the encounter is formal or informal. However, such incidents also vary in terms of their duration because it is by no means the case that they are inevitably fleeting. In this sense a one-off encounter may be exceedingly brief, as in a momentary exchange of words between passers-by in the street or some other public thoroughfare, but it may also be more prolonged as in the case of two travellers sharing the same compartment, or occupying adjacent seats on a train, bus or aircraft.

The issue of duration is very important since by its very nature a fleeting contact reduces the potential for information exchange and the further development of the relationship beyond superficial communication or ritualized gestures. The more prolonged the encounter, the greater the probability that it will move beyond its initial impersonal basis. This is exemplified in the case of two air-travellers meeting for the first time on a long-haul flight and who strike-up a "relationship". The length of time together (say 15–20 hours) provides them with the chance to become quite intimate in the sense of being able to share personal information – perhaps about the state of their respective marriages or partnerships, or about some career "problem" that they are both currently experiencing – even though they have no intention of continuing the relationship beyond the time shared on the current trip. (Of course, they may decide to take it further by swapping addresses or arranging to meet.) The achievement of levels of intimacy in such situations is commonly thought to result from the very lack of background personal knowledge of the other that is an intrinsic feature of temporary "in transit" situations. This lack of information in fact may serve to reduce barriers to communication that would otherwise have prevented such rapport. Ironically, the history of shared intimacy and experience upon which "familiarity" rests may also be a history of tensions and conflicts around unresolved personal issues that re-emerge from time to time, and thus hinders the free flow of communication – as frequently happens in long-standing relationships.

More fleeting or transitory one-off encounters are marked by the consistency of their "impersonal" character and the reduced amount of facework involved, although there are differences that hinge on the nature of the ties between the participants. For instance, as Goffman has noted, our general relationships with others in public places are characterized by the observance of "civil inattention" (see Ch. 2). This allows people the chance to communicate minimal but essential information about their intentions at the same time as it preserves their own and other's rights to privacy and anonymity. Thus people on the street or in elevators sustain only the briefest of eye-contact to acknowledge the presence of others, and then avert their gaze so as not to intrude into others' personal space. Staring in such circumstances would be a threatening gesture. Civil inattention suggests an expression of mutual trust, but as I pointed out in Chapter 2, it would be a mistake to think of this as the only motive.

Perhaps, just as often the ritual enactment of civil inattention is deployed in an effort to minimize contact with (particular) others, as in the case of

someone not wishing to allow another to "waste" their time, by responding to them curtly and "on the move" and so preserve the "anonymity" of
the situation. (This phenomenon has been noted between doctors and
pseudo-patients in the context of a mental hospital: see Rosenhan 1973).
Also, as Goffman has pointed out, the use of "involvement shields" like
newspapers or books can be used to protect oneself from unwanted contact, just as they can disguise actual interest with an apparent lack of
involvement. In both these cases, anonymity is preserved in spite of efforts
to break it down, whereas as a general rule, civil inattention sustains social
distance in order to subserve a mutually agreed upon objective of maintaining peaceful co-existence.

Of course not all transitory, one-off encounters occur in anonymous
public (or "open") contexts like the ones just mentioned that lend a certain
informal atmosphere to the encounter. Neither do all such relationships
have the rather diffuse character of those that typify relations in public.
Some encounters of this type take place against a more formal, even
bureaucratic, background in which there is a definite purpose to be served
by a specific social contact between two people. For example, encounters
between customers and store assistants are frequently of this type, as are
those between ticket collectors (or sellers) and passengers on public transport. Encounters in even more bureaucratic settings (involving hierarchical authority), such as when a member of the public is summoned to meet
with an official to explain taxation irregularities, are also of this formal
and very specific type.

In Parsons's (1951) terminology one-off encounters are ranged along a
continuum in terms of the inclusiveness of the relationships involved. On
the one hand, there are those that are "open" and dependent on the give
and take or general willingness of the participants to enter into diffuse and
intimate (affective) relations. However, this of course depends (apart from
the readiness to enter in to such relations) on the duration of the encounter
and the kinds of circumstances that prevail such as whether people are
"thrown together" (as in the occupancy of adjacent aircraft seats), or
whether it is a combination of luck, accident and choice that people
become involved in a relationship (as may happen in a crowd at a sporting
fixture or a street festival). On the other hand, the more closely defined
impersonal encounters tend to centre around a common point of interest
("functional specificity" in Parsons's terms). They also tend to exclude
emotional considerations ("affective neutrality" for Parsons), in so far as,
for example, the excuse that one was feeling too depressed to pay one's

taxes would prove inappropriate mitigating circumstances. Similarly, it is unlikely that a customer in a store would be allowed to take home an expensive watch without paying for it on the grounds that they "liked it very much and promised to take good care of it".

Intermittent encounters

Turning away from transient one-off encounters between those who are strangers and the unacquainted, let us now consider those that have a "history" of prior contact. Although these encounters will be fuelled by the residue of previous shared experiences, it is also clear that such relationships will not necessarily be continuous or spatially close. For example, children often grow up, marry and leave the geographical area of the family home but still maintain intermittent contact with their parents and friends. Also, mobility resulting from educational and work commitments may produce such a spatial spread of involvements. These can also differ in terms of the "closeness" of the relations between participants. For instance kin relations with family of origin and family of marriage or partnership frequently involve diffuse emotional attachments and obligations and sometimes economic support, although this is by no means always the case.

Although ties of friendship often involve high degrees of intimacy and emotional sharing, there is less of an "obligatory" nature about expectations of economic (and other material forms of) support and frequency of contact ("visiting") than there is with kin. However, sometimes the actual emphasis is reversed in practice, with friends providing greater emotional as well as economic support and more frequent face-to-face contact. Beyond close friends there are people with whom one is "acquainted" and in certain cases such people will perform much the same services and provide comparable levels of support as friends or kin. However, the very fact that they are classifiable as "acquaintances" (at least at certain points in time) indicates that there are no reciprocal expectations about emotional or material support. In this sense such acquaintances are a step or two away from close friendship, but not too remote to be considered as possible friends at some future (but indeterminate) time. Much depends on the exact circumstances and intermittency of contact and the nature of their shared experiences. There is no doubt that the likelihood of intermittency of contact is increased the more one moves towards the "acquaintances" end of the continuum. This also underscores the fact that acquaintances are a highly varied category in themselves and are associated with a wide spectrum of possible settings. Leisure or sporting activities, night-school classes, bars, night clubs, and so on, can be the source of many such acquaintances whom one sees on a "casual" basis (if they happen to "be there" on the day or evening in question).

Such intermittency also has a significant effect on the form that encounters take. The more this is linked with the kinds of acquaintances just mentioned, the more the substance of the interaction will settle on spurious levels of intimacy and guarded forms of "openness" because the punctuated nature of the relationships prevents the development of a shared history and the exchange of valued intimacies. However, when close friends, partners or spouses are considered in the context of intermittent contacts (for reasons such as geographic mobility, dual-careers, separations, arguments and so forth), encounters are qualitatively different. It is the break in continuity of a previously shared history that becomes the focus of exchanges and thus a central objective of the interactants becomes the reparation and restoration of the continuity. As Goffman has observed, a participant in such an encounter is constrained to demonstrate that they have kept fresh in mind "bits of the other's biography" and to make inquiries about "the other's significant others, recent trips, illness if any, career outcomes, and sundry other matters that speak to the questioner's aliveness to the world of the person greeted" (Goffman 1983: 13). Thus, a ritual of mutual updating on a "lost" past forms the motif of the encounter.

Regularized encounters

Although relations between kin, friends and acquaintances afford various kinds of material support, primarily they are vehicles that provide for the expression of affect in human relations. They become the main switch points through which the discharge of emotion and the reciprocity of feelings flow. Apart from this expression and exchange of affect, the other common element that groups kin, partners, friends and acquaintances together is the degree of "choice" exercised over maintaining contact and managing the quality of the relationship. Clearly what is meant by "choice" may vary according to the extent of felt obligations – often most fiercely experienced in the context of kin relations – none the less it is not something that is externally enforced. In this sense, the defining feature of these relations is their volitional quality, the fact that contacts between participants are initiated, sustained and terminated at will according to how well or badly the relationship is faring. The underlying basis of affection, love or feeling that predominates in these relationships may also account for the volatility that frequently characterizes them, and the swiftness with which they are sometimes broken-off or subsequently rekindled.

These common features distinguish them from other kinds of regularized relations that derive from externally imposed ties like those of work, educational institutions or legal sanction – as in probation orders or compulsory admission to mental hospitals or prisons. In these cases there is a low degree of choice or control over whom one shares social and physical space. Regular work colleagues are imposed upon us by the setting of some kinds of work – such as a factory assembly-line or a suite of company offices, even though we normally do have some say concerning the question of with whom we choose to socialize during "breaks". Clearly, in such cases the influence of the setting heavily insinuates itself on activity that takes place within its environment and offers an illustration that conforms to the "model" of the overlayering of domains that I referred to earlier. I shall return to this example when considering the influence of both the setting and the wider socio-economic context on situated activity, although it needs to be noted here that differences in setting and the extent of their impingement upon situated activity itself are variable factors. More generally the particular forms of control inherent in different kinds of settings play a decisive role in shaping the tenor, style and substance of social activity within their orbit of influence. Forms of control range from the extremely coercive and disciplined organizations found in the armed forces, prisons and maximum security hospitals, to the formal, but less authoritarian work settings of some factories, and through to the largely informal (but none the less, still controlled) environment of many service settings like restaurants or stores.

A pervasive effect of such settings on situated activity derives from the externally imposed contractual tie that characterizes such work situations and the typical forms of authority and control over the labour process that go with it. Such configurations give rise to the predominance and recurrence of certain themes in worker behaviour. This is most obviously expressed in the differing ways in which workers engaged in monotonous jobs attempt to structure the working day as a means of making the time pass more quickly and hence, exercising some control in the situation (see Roy 1973, Burawoy 1979). This and other means of wresting power and control figure prominently in workers' lives and perhaps represent the establishment of small areas of autonomy and discretion in environments that by and large eliminate or minimize freedom and choice.

As Habermas (1971) has pointed out, it is exactly in the area of the labour process that motives of a strategic variety are likely to be found. That is, the external constraint of the contractual tie and the associated forms of control that police it serve to draw workers into the adoption of "instrumental" and "strategic" atittudes and motives in their behaviour. In short the work is seen solely as a means of gaining money in order to eke out an existence. Everything they do, including talking and generally associating with other workers serves this end, and as a result, fully rounded human relationships are suppressed. However, Habermas tends to over-stress the influence of instrumental motives in the area of work and hence underplays the importance of "genuine" relationships and involvements with other workers that are based on the intrinsic satisfactions derived simply from communicating with friends and colleagues. As long as we do not repeat Habermas's excesses here, there is surely something in the view that instrumental motives surrounding the acquisition of money play a pre-dominant role in these kinds of situations. It is clearly an example of what Habermas (1987) refers to as the "colonisation of the lifeworld" by system elements (principally money and power).

This brings us back to questions and issues concerning the nature of the interrelationships between situated activity and what I have termed (fol-lowing Habermas) "system" elements of society. Here I want to pursue these matters in terms of a more formal discussion of the concepts involved and how they are related to each other, taking up the argument from where I began in the opening sections of this chapter. So let me leave the issues of the nature and modes of situated activity at this juncture and return to them in the context of a more general discussion. Let me simply emphasize that the previous discussion has focused on the forms of situ-ated activity produced by variations in time and space, and the intimacy, purpose and immediate circumstances of ties between people. In the following sections I want to deal with system elements (settings and con-textual resources) as they intermingle with the lifeworld elements (psycho-biography and situated activity).

Habermas's lifeworld–system distinction

Although, as I have previously noted, there are number of important dif-ferences from Habermas in the way I define and use the terms "lifeworld" and "system", they none the less usefully indicate an ontological division that penetrates to the heart of social reality. It is in this sense that there is an overlap between Habermas's thinking and the theory of social domains. Habermas insists that system elements refer to the wider functional processes of society (for example, the way in which the economy and polity are co-ordinated and integrated) and these can only be understood from "the standpoint of an objective observer who objectivates the lifeworld . . . as a system" (Habermas 1987: 232). That is, in order to understand society as a system we have to make a methodological switch from the perspective of participants in the lifeworld to that of an observer who views society as an objective system. This methodological switch reflects not simply a theoretical point of view but "an actual distinction within the social organisation of societies" (Honneth 1993: 292).

However, my vision of how this distinction should be employed, and what it entails for our understanding of social life, is quite different from Habermas's. To clarify this let me first say what I mean by the terms in some more detail and then follow with an attempt to distinguish my own position from Habermas's. In my view the distinction between lifeworld and system points to a fundamental division in social reality. On the one hand, lifeworld elements refer to the lived experience of people and groups as they engage in, and are engaged by, the social processes that constitute society. System elements by contrast refer to the reproduced relations and practices that contribute both to the structural continuity and integrity of whole societies and to the ongoing activities of people. In this respect the system elements represent the historical outcome of the previous activities, conflicts and struggles of various individuals and groups in attempting to secure forms of domination and control. System elements therefore represent the standing social conditions that appear as a macro-reality confronting social actors in their everyday activities.

As Marx pointed out, people "make their own history, but they do not make it just as they please; they do not make it under circumstances chosen by themselves, but under circumstances directly encountered, given and transmitted from the past. The tradition of all the dead generations weighs like a nightmare on the brain of the living" (Marx & Engels 1968: 96). In short, the extant social fabric represents the historically formed social conditions under which people act and that provides the constraints and enablements for these activities. It is important to understand system elements as phenomena that are not identical with activity but that are deeply implicated in it all the same. Activity always involves actual participants in situated encounters whereas "circumstances inherited from the past" are not in themselves social actors, nor must they be confused with the activities that brought them into being in the first place.

Furthermore, although circumstances inherited from the past are ultimately transmitted through living actors in the present, they have a reality different from human actors and behaviour – they are the social conditions under which human behaviour takes place. These standing conditions are embodied in the discourses, practices, powers and relations that are simultaneously the resultants of past activities and the continual accomplishments of present behaviour. System elements then represent the inherited resultants of previous activities – what they came to, as social-structural residues – and lifeworld elements reflect the existential "thereness" or actuality of contemporaneous encounters. This ontological division is also underlined by the conjuncture of two very different frames and dimensions of time and their diffusion into present activity as it continually unfolds and projects itself into the future.

Let me now indicate some of my departures from Habermas's views on lifeworld and system. I share part of Habermas's concern to say that to some extent system elements co-ordinate people's behaviour through functional interconnections that are not intended by them – capitalist markets being prime examples of this type of co-ordination. However, I do not want to say as he does that systems are norm-free regulators of co-operation, or that action is formed solely through consensus and the search for understanding. In short I reject Habermas's definitions of social and system integration whereby the former is thought to be achieved "through consensus, whether normatively guaranteed or communicatively achieved" whereas system integration is accomplished "through the nonnormative steering of individual decisions not subjectively coordinated" (Habermas 1987: 150).

Only part of this definition would be useful for the argument I am presently putting forward – that is, the effects of system elements on action cannot be understood primarily as the result of subjective decision-making. As Habermas says in connection with the example of the market, such systemic mechanisms "stabilize nonintended interconnections of action by way of functionally intermeshing action consequences" whereas lifeworld elements are driven by the attempt to communicate and achieve consensus and understanding between people. In this respect, unlike the system's concern with the unintended consequences of action, activity in the lifeworld is concerned with harmonizing the "action orientations of participants" in order to achieve mutual understanding (Habermas 1987:

150). Again there are aspects of this construal of the distinction between lifeworld and system that are perceptive and useful. Unfortunately, Habermas often depicts the two in an extreme way and consequently goes too far in implying the "purity" of the distinctions (see Layder 1994).

Several authors, notably Giddens (1987) and Mouzelis (1991, 1992) have pointed to this problem in Habermas's work. However, there are two aspects of their critique that need to be separated. The first, with which I am much less sympathetic, concerns the distinction between lifeworld and system itself. According to Giddens and Mouzelis, Habermas confuses a methodological distinction with a substantive one. In other words, they suggest that the distinction should be reserved exclusively for analytic purposes – it is not (and never was) meant to indicate a real distinction in social organization. In this respect both Giddens and Mouzelis argue that Habermas has misused Lockwood's (1964) distinction between social and system integration which he intended simply as an aid to the analysis of features of social life that are related in a complex manner. Moreover, the authors insist that there is no real substantive distinction in social life to which it corresponds.

I find this claim quite unconvincing. First, the idea of a wholly "analytic" distinction makes little sense if one is at pains to argue that there is something more than rhetoric to social analysis, and I presume that both Giddens and Mouzelis would generally be concerned to uphold such a position. Surely to argue for the usefulness of an analytic or methodological distinction (such as that of social and system integration) is to suggest that there is something intrinsic to the substance of that which is being analyzed that makes it necessary in the first place – otherwise the distinction is indeed spurious! That is, if the distinction is not about something substantive in the social world then its status is merely rhetorical. In this sense it would seem both possible and sensible to make distinctions that do have some actual basis in the social world. In this case Lockwood's distinction gains appreciably in strength by attaching itself to claims about its substantive basis. Thus Lockwood's distinction is both analytic and real and it is indeed a comparably real division in social reality to which Habermas is drawing attention and trading on in his theoretical discussion of the lifeworld and system distinction.

In this respect to suggest that lifeworld and system (or social and system integration) are not factually distinguishable, would seem to be a wholly artificial line to pursue. Thus the idea that Habermas is confusing analytic with substantive distinctions is somewhat incidental to the main concerns of Giddens and Mouzelis. The point these authors are actually making is not an argument against "real" distinctions *per se*, but rather against the idea that social systems have an existential status different from that of social activity and its various forms. Now I want to agree with Giddens and Mouzelis that Habermas has a tendency to reify the notion of system by defining and generally speaking of it in overly pure and extreme terms, but I would argue that this is quite separate from the question of whether there exist discernable ontological differences between social domains.

In this sense my own view is even more radical than Habermas's. That is, in so far as I posit the existence of more "ontological domains" than Habermas, then I am suggesting a more complex ontology than that implied in the lifeworld–system distinction. However, I do want to uphold a *version* of this distinction along with Habermas, without accepting the whole baggage of his theoretical assumptions and implications. In a basic sense I would agree with Habermas that by focusing on this distinction he is pinpointing a fundamental theoretical problem to do with the agency–structure and macro–micro dualisms in sociology. I thus have no hesitation in endorsing his view that "the fundamental problem of social theory is how to connect in a satisfactory way the two conceptual strategies indicated by the notions of 'system' and 'lifeworld'" (Habermas 1987: 151). It is exactly this attempt to forge a link between vastly different approaches to social analysis (which have proven to be immensely fruitful in their own terms) that constitutes Habermas's great theoretical achievement. Such advancements in understanding are underestimated if one simply concentrates on whatever problems remain in the wake of Habermas's attempted *rapprochement*.

Habermas's overall objective is sound enough, it is the manner in which he attempts to achieve it, and the results of his endeavours to do so, that present basic weaknesses. The most problematic issue concerns the manner in which he attempts to forge the connections between lifeworld and system. In this respect his definitions of the two terms are most definitely overdrawn and unrealistically "pure". As a result his attempt to describe the relations between the two domains sometimes creates the impression of a yawning gap between them rather than a mutual intertwining. The crux of my unease about Habermas's formulations is contained in his own words when he says:

> . . . the social . . . is split up into spheres of action constituted as the lifeworld and spheres neutralised against the lifeworld. The former are

communicatively structured, the latter formally organised. They do not stand in any *hierarchical* relationship between levels of interaction and organisation; rather they stand *opposite* one another as socially and systematically integrated spheres of action. (Habermas 1987: 309)

This modelling of the relationship between the two orders seems to imply a radical separation between them. Indeed, at times, Habermas speaks of elements of the lifeworld (mutual understanding, communicative action, the exchange of validity claims and symbolic forms and so on) being "shoved out" or being "withdrawn" from different areas of society as system elements (power, money, formal-rational actions) take over ever larger spheres of social life. The great danger of this construal of the two domains, as Honneth (1993: 298) has observed, is that it creates "two complementary fictions". On the one hand, we have the idea that there exist norm-free organizations of action (system elements), and on the other, we have the notion of the existence of power-free spheres of communication.

Empirical research has exposed the questionable assumptions underlying both of these positions. For example, in formal organizations such as in industry or government bureaucracies, where, according to Habermas, system imperatives are supposed to dominate, the practices and political strategies undertaken by management and administration are never completely severed from normative issues. In fact they are the result of communicative processes among the participants (or members) concerned. In this sense system integration does not take place "behind the backs" of the ordinary members (those less powerful) of the organizations. Similarly, questions of power and domination can never be separated from the arena of communicative action and consensus. As Honneth (1993: 300) puts it, Habermas implies that "whereas purposive-rational domains of action seem to be separated out from all processes of the integration of the lifeworld, the social lifeworld is represented as freed from all forms of the exercise of power". The "isolation" or restriction of power to a certain domain that follows from this sort of approach is particularly debilitating for Habermas's theory as a whole.

As a result power can be dealt with only as an aspect of systems and thus the effects of power and domination in everyday life (particularly those connected with the reproduction of society) are either ignored or downgraded in importance. This weakness in Habermas's framework will become more relevant in the context of the more rounded discussion of the nature of power in Chapter 4. However, it must be noted that

Habermas's insistence that, in effect, power is an aspect of systemic functioning, precludes the much more subtle notion of power that Foucault has emphasized and which he sees as implicated in the micro-practices of everyday life. In short, Habermas's view of power, limited as it is to the systems sphere, tends to repeat the traditional "sovereign" conception of power from which Foucault was at great pains to escape. This conception of power views it as a "top-down" phenomenon that spreads from an essential source or centre – in this case the system domain (and its requirements for material reproduction and functional integration). For the purposes of my own arguments I want generally to go along with what I regard as Foucault's more sophisticated appreciation of the ubiquitousness of power in modern societies, although as I shall go on to argue, there are also limitations and deficiencies in Foucault's position.

Social domains and lifeworld–system interlocks

Having made this critique of Habermas I think that it is also fair to say that at times he is more than a little ambiguous on some of these fundamental issues, with a tendency to vascillate between a "radical separation" argument and one that is more inclined to understand the lifeworld–system distinction in muddier terms (see, for example, Habermas 1987: 309–12). On balance, though Habermas's position always shades towards the radical separation position and it is this that I want to reject, while simultaneously endorsing an argument for ontological difference. I want to argue that all the social domains I have identified are implicated in both lifeworld and systems – that the latter represents a duality that runs through all the domains. Further, I want to say that empirically, the effects of the different elements vary – as do their implications for social reproduction. However, this empirical variability is not simply an effect of the contingency inherent in the "empirical world", although this is undoubtedly a relevant factor. There are also empirical variations in the weighting of the "presence" of lifeworld and system elements that are produced through the intrinsic effects of the (ontological) relationship between them.

Let me try to unpack these differences. First, considered strictly from the point of view of individuals who move between involvements in, and the influence of various settings and fields of activity, the variations produced through what I have termed empirical contingency are a direct consequence of the fundamentally *ad hoc* and additive character of the distribution of social locations in time and space. That is, social settings and fields of activity are the core sites of the truncated participation of individuals in so far as their sequence of involvements (as measured by the daily round say) meshes serially with an "unprincipled" though connected sequence of system characteristics (resources and position-practices) as they are spread out in time-space. People's practices and activities weave in, out and between these settings as they move through the time-space paths of their routine daily round. Considered over longer periods of time this produces a "contouring" effect reflecting the routinized pattern of visitations that not only indicate the volitional nature of social action but also represent some of the mandatory circuits and "obligatory passage points" (Clegg 1989) that are at the heart of the workings of power.

In more concrete terms it is plain that this patterning includes several sources of diversity. First, each person or group will vary in terms of the actual spread of their involvements in a multiplicity of social settings. Secondly, social settings themselves are variably situated in geographical and social space and time. As Goffman (1983: 2) reminds us, the settings of interaction cover a very broad range, including: village and city life, domestic and public settings, crowded kitchens as well as crowded streets, courtrooms, supermarkets and bedrooms to name but a few from a potentially endless list. Thirdly, these settings vary greatly in terms of how strongly they are affected by system factors as against lifeworld elements. However, I think that we can assume with Habermas that in at least a rough and ready way, social encounters in formal organizations (such as those in government and industry) in general terms will be more heavily influenced by the steering media of money and market power, for example, than will those of the breakfast-time kitchen or the bedroom. This is not to say that these latter encounters are not in themselves significantly influenced by money and power in other guises – we are talking about a matter of emphasis and degree.

This variation of settings according to their degree of connectedness with system and lifeworld elements is related to the empirical variations produced through what I have called the intrinsic relationship between lifeworld and system elements. To go back a little, the basic assumption of my argument is that lifeworld and system elements never exist in a pure state, they are always mutually interfused with each other. However, their influence, weighting and presence varies empirically according to their position in relation to the social domains. The majority of lifeworld elements are "driven" from the emergent nature of situated activity – that is, they subsist in the give and take of actual (contemporaneous) face-to-face encounters. We must be careful not to include all lifeworld elements in this respect since many of them function as background assumptions which serve "as a source of situation definitions that are presupposed by participants as unproblematic" (Habermas 1984: 70). In this guise, as cultural and discursive products that delineate a background store "of interpretive work of previous generations" against which situated activity takes place, they more closely approximate to the "system" end of the continuum. In this diffuse, cultural-discursive sense, lifeworld elements bind the constituent energies of personality, action and cultural subsystems together, as Habermas himself observes (1987: 225). But the driving force, the energy that constantly produces and reproduces this embracing scaffold is the continuity of situated activity.

Systemic elements on the other hand are driven from, and by, a different (onto) logic. They represent a set of already established "templates" of action based on the inherited circumstances of the past that are continually reproduced in the present. In Habermas's terms this is to do with the stabilization of unintended links between people's activities as they centre around socially functional tasks. This requires us to endorse a distinction between social and system integration wherein different *levels* of social activity and organization are understood to produce rather different consequences for social reproduction. This must be based on Lockwood's (1964) classic distinction in which system elements are defined as having to do with "core institutional features". The question of exactly what these features are in different kinds of society does not concern us here. What is important is that Lockwood distinguishes between relations between social actors and relations between system parts (core institutional features). As I said before, there is some controversy as to whether Lockwood's distinction is "purely" analytic or whether it has some substantive basis, but as I also argued, I find the idea of a distinction made for purely analytic purposes to be logically suspect – not to say theoretically and empirically unsound. Not withstanding this controversy the important point is that Lockwood's distinction picks out significant differences in levels of social organization that (as he argues) have very different implications for (understanding) social change. I want to draw attention to the converse of this – the different implications that follow for the process of social reproduction.

Interestingly, Lockwood's main examples of core institutional features are the economy and the polity and their interlocks (although equally, we could include here Parsons's classification of the functional subsystems of modern societies – including those to do with the dissemination of values such as religious organizations and institutions of socialization such as the family and school, and so on). The crucial point is that the "systemic" nature of these institutions consists in their performance of functionally operational tasks that make a major contribution to macro-structural continuity as well as to the micro (face-to-face) encounters that reproduce them. Talk of "functional" tasks or "operational functioning" at the level of whole societies must not be confused with the wholesale adoption of a set of theoretical assumptions (for example, about "functional needs" or cultural determinism) that are associated with certain variants of traditional functionalist theory. I believe that it is perfectly possible to use terminology traditionally associated with functionalism without committing oneself to *any* of the more discredited axioms of this school of thought. In this respect my adoption of such terms as "functional tasks" or "operational functioning" has more in common with what has come to be what Alexander & Colomy (1985, 1990) have called called "neo-functionalism" which commits itself to a much looser and theoretically more inclusive version of functionalism.

In my terms system "parts", as Lockwood calls them, are constituted in a fundamental sense through a historical process. They are inherited circumstances that represent the accumulated emergents of the activities of previous generations of people, which, as Marx observes, "weighs like a nightmare on the brains of the living". These circumstances congeal to form social conditions that are relatively autonomous from people in their situated encounters. That is, they come to have something of a life of their own since they reflect macro-structural "solutions" to problems of social regulation and integration. Eisenstadt's (1985) work, for example, indicates this sort of social evolutionary outcome and suggests that historically there emerges a distributive dimension to society centring on the occupational and organizational division of labour and various regulative and integrative mechanisms such as economic, political, bureaucratic, legal and cultural institutions.

This approach, which endorses an understanding of societies in terms of a "depth ontology" has a pedigree that runs through the work not only of Marx but also of Durkheim and Parsons (as well as Lockwood, Eisenstadt and Habermas). However, this is a position that is also consonant with the work of the philosopher Karl Popper (1972) and his notion of a "third world" of social and cultural phenomena. All these writers indicate

the importance of an objectivist position in social analysis without implying that *all* social phenomena can be analyzed in these terms – particularly
human agency and social activity. Not all these writers present quite the
same view of objective social phenomena, but none the less they all support the efficacy of some form of objectivism in social analysis. The theory
of social domains sides with this tradition of thought in social theory and
rejects the subjectivist critique that only mental phenomena, constitutive
of the "knowing subject", are of importance for social analysis.

However, the moderate objectivism implied in domain theory does not
reject the importance of the knowing subject in social analysis but rather
accords human agency a *related* yet *distinct* role in the constitution of society
and social life. Thus at this point domain theory sharply distinguishes itself
from the sort of synthesis proposed by Giddens in which human reasons
and motivations are understood as the central constitutive features of
social life. In Giddens's view (1976, 1979, 1984) social systems or structures cannot be thought to be (in any sense) independent of actor's reasons
and motivations for their social behaviour. Contrary to this, my argument
suggests that there is a basic ontological distinction to be taken into
account between lifeworld and system elements and that their mutual
influence must be regarded as an *overlapping dualism* and not a unitary *duality* as Giddens argues.

That is, although there is a fusion and mutual implication of these ontological elements, they cannot be understood solely in terms of actors' reasons and motivations, even though the latter are important features of
social life. Thus to understand the exact nature of the "mutual implication" of lifeworld and system elements it is first of all essential to grasp the
nature of their *ontological difference*, because only this starting point allows us
to understand the manner in which they interfuse with each other. By
beginning with the assumption of their inherent duality (as in structuration theory) one arrives (prematurely) at the "conclusion" that they represent a state of fusion, thus missing out an appreciation of the exact manner
in which they are fused and perhaps, more importantly, one is unable to
register the discrete characteristics of the elements that have been combined. Thus one ends up with an image of a diffuse amalgam of influences
and ingredients. Moreover the premature "conclusion" of fusion prevents
us from recovering some sense of the properties and characteristics of the
elements initially involved in this process. It is very important therefore to
appreciate the contribution of actors' reasons and motivations in social
life, but equally, it is critical not to overstress their importance in a general

understanding of social ontology (as is the tendency in Giddens's scenario of the "duality of structure").

Settings and the duality of social relations

Social relations have a dual character in so far as they contain both "reproduced" and free-form aspects. Their reproduced features reflect the already established character of social systems – the inherited historical circumstances that form the standing conditions under which current activities and practices play themselves out. People work within the constraints and enablements of social relations as they draw upon the resources that flow from them and the positions, powers and practices in which they are implicated. Such reproduced aspects provide tried and tested solutions to actors' dilemmas (Parsons 1951) and define behavioural expectations that attach to certain socially defined situations and circumstances. They provide, in other words, models or templates for action that people take into account in initially formulating their behaviour and which must be understood as constituting part of their knowledgeability. However, as individuals proceed with testing out these preferred solutions they encounter the unpredictable or "tragic" nature of social action (Crespi 1992). That is, in encountering the emergent vicissitudes of face-to-face interaction the individual is required to extemporize and thus to create or "add-on" to the behavioural repertoire that they are predisposed to deploy.

Thus in each circumstance of everyday life the individual is both applying "routine" or established behavioural formulations to interactional problems at the very same time as creating new "solutions" or ways of dealing with the emergent unpredictability of face-to-face encounters. However, this creativity is not unfettered by social structures (and systems) and thus is not entirely free-form as some interactionists (Blumer and the Chicago school) and phenomenologists (Schutz, Garfinkel) have implied or suggested. The situation corresponds more closely to that described by writers who have favoured a more social-structural version of symbolic interactionism such as R. Turner (1962, 1985) and Stryker (1981). With regard to "role theory" these authors have stressed that the degree of freedom to extemporize in face-to-face conduct is strictly limited by the kind of social-structural context in which such encounters occur.

I would endorse the main thrust of this thesis although only in the context of the conceptual framework of domain theory, since both Stryker's and Turner's propositions have a restricted application to the area of social roles. However, an emphasis on the different forms of social organization that provide the environment for social behaviour is crucial to understanding the variation in the degree of constraint and freedom that various contexts and circumstances allow. In terms of the general propositions of domain theory the whole relation between lifeworld and system elements is essential to an adequate grasp of this phenomenon. Pivotal here is the extent to which social relations are already sedimented in time and space and thus become inscribed and enshrined in routinized practices, thus defining the contours of social settings and the macro-patterning of contextual resources. The more sedimented and established they are in certain settings and fields, the reproduced aspects of social relations and practices are more pronounced and "demanding". In settings and contexts in which "informal" organization predominates, the more "open-ended" aspects of face-to-face conduct have more chance of coming to the fore in these domains. An important qualification is contained in the phrase "coming to the fore" because it is patently not the case that the reproduced elements disappear altogether. They have a distinct and persistent formative influence on the proceedings in all cases but an important variation concerns whether in relative terms they occupy the foreground or whether they are "forced" into the background by a kind of displacement process. The crucial sorting mechanism here is the kind of setting that provides the immediate environment for the encounter.

Generally, the more the setting is socially organized in terms of a formalized set of objectives the more likely it is that the reproduced relations and practices that subserve them (such as a task structure) will permeate the substantive content (and outcomes) of specific encounters within its environment. The imposed objectives and purposes of the settings will define the character of much of the interaction and thus the situated and emergent features of encounters will be secondary to them. The bureaucratic rules and regulations that inform and shape the working practices in many employing organizations (see Edwards 1979) are good examples of the demanding or mandatory character of reproduced relations and practices. Workers *must* take account of established practices or risk censure (a reprimand), some kind of deprivation such as the withholding of certain rewards (such as promotion, a pay increase or better working conditions) or even a more serious penalty (such as being fired). In more positive terms anyone who flouts the established practices and social relations – and therefore challenges the discourses and powers that underpin them –

has to be willing to forgo the inclusive benefits that accrue from general (though not necessarily unquestioning) conformity.

This is not to say that informal factors do not operate at the same time or that the people involved are not creative and innovative in their behaviour. Rather it is to say that such factors will not be as decisive in shaping the outcome of episodes of interaction in those settings. This is most clearly exemplified in areas of social life where there are intermediary (mezzo) layers of social organization that interpose themselves between the "private life" of the individual and the society-wide cultural milieu in which the individual lives. The organization of work, careers and occupations in modern societies provide good examples in which a controlling layer of social organization is externally imposed upon the lives and daily routines of millions. These control elements are of decisive importance here because we have a conjuncture of power and the capacity to dominate the time of others (Adam 1990: 104–20). The existence of this kind of controlling force in people's lives is very much dependent upon the historical emergence of what Foucault (1977, 1980) calls "disciplinary power" and "bio-power" because such forms produce both docile minds and bodies. Foucault particularly emphasizes that disciplinary power depends upon the internalization by individuals of regimes of power since self-control becomes a positive means of responding to the forms of surveillance that are associated with these forms of power (see Ch. 4). Although this form of self-discipline is an integral feature of disciplinary power, it is important to stress that mezzo levels of social organization are "externally" imposed from the point of view of individual agents as well as from all those groupings of individuals who are subject to their influence.

This is something that Foucault is unwilling to acknowledge in any fundamental sense since the internal–external distinction apparently seems to resurrect the various dualisms (such as agency–structure and macro–micro) which Foucault wants to abandon and transcend (see Layder 1994). I shall take this up in greater detail in Chapter 4, but it needs to be noted here that from the standpoint of domain theory, Foucault's view that individual subjectivities are constituted simply through the effects of discourse (and their associated powers and practices) will not do. Such a position dissolves human agency and individual difference into a kind of group identity that neglects the constructive and transformative power of individuals as well as their psychobiographical differences (level and type of emotional expression and so on: see Ch. 2). So while I think that his historical analysis of the emergence of disciplinary power and bio-power is effective and feasible, I disagree fundamentally with Foucault's assumption that socal ontology is represented exclusively by, and in the contours of, discourses and practices. To understand the intricate workings of power within situated activity and face-to-face conduct we have to preserve some distinctions between the different but interlacing social domains in order to understand the fullness of their diverse and sometimes divergent effects.

By contrast with the formal and prescriptive environments, in the more diffuse and informal settings there is more chance of open-ended or innovative aspects of behaviour holding the balance of influence in particular encounters. Settings of family or leisure–friendship relationships are generally of this nature allowing people more latitude in the range of responses to others and in setting the agenda for joint action. (Although Blumer (1969) speaks of "joint action", he neglects to specify the wider social influences that determine the form of this jointness.) The purposes and objectives of such encounters are generated from "within" in the sense that it is the people directly involved who will be primarily responsible for laying out and implementing the interactional agenda. The time and skills of the participants are not "bought" (in a monetary sense although they may be in an emotional sense) and thus dominated by others (such as employers) who in many cases are socially related to the participants on an exclusively pecuniary basis.

Of course local considerations are not the only ones of moment here. Wider cultural issues are of paramount importance in influencing the "flavour" of the conduct in these more diffuse and informal settings, as are those events that constitute the history of previous encounters between the same participants. An example of the latter is when family members may refer back to "critical events" and to a corporate family identity that act as benchmarks for "allowed" or "tolerated" deviations from established conventions within these relationships. That is to say, there will be various forms of control that operate in such settings that impose constraints on those involved. The point of difference however, is that the arena of conduct is not "bought into" by control relations that bear no other intimate, emotional tie with those involved as it is in the case of paid employment, for example. Not withstanding the more pathological variants mentioned above, there is generally interactional space "reserved" in advance for spontaneity and intimacy in face-to-face conduct in such settings. This is afforded by the relative lack of an agenda specified in advance (the business to be dealt with during an encounter) that sets up behavioural expectations and targets such as those surrounding a work task and defined by some larger set of objectives and constraints such as a production schedule.

Thus this duality runs through all social relations and practices but in certain kinds of setting the reproduced elements play a stronger role in influencing behavioural outcomes. Of course settings themselves are intimately dovetailed with wider social circumstances that necessarily have an effect on them. The variation that I have described in the "presencing" of either reproduced or innnovative aspects of behaviour in particular settings has as much to do with these wider circumstances as with the inner dynamics of the settings themselves. In this respect, social relations and the practices and powers that they articulate, stretch through, and influence *all* domains. Thus, what I have termed contextual resources are as closely tied to the settings of social conduct as they are to situated activity and the psychobiographies of individuals and it would be a mistake to understand them as "cleanly" separated in any sense. The effects and influences that the domains have on each other are diffuse, overlapping and interpenetrating. In one sense their mutual effects are irretrievably dispersed.

As I suggested at the beginning of this chapter settings can be profitably thought of as local holding points for aggregations of reproduced relations and practices. In this sense I have already introduced some of the power dimensions involved by stressing an "outer" layer of control that obtains in many formalized settings. The notion of contextual resources completes the circuit of power relations involved here by drawing into the discussion the wider structures of power that give definition to specific social systems. It completes the circuit in the sense that the notion of power is connected via social system features such as resources and settings through to situated practices and the transformative capacities of individuals. In this sense the individual–collective dimensions and properties of power are expressed through, and carried in, the dual nature of social relations and practices.

Social systems, fields of activity and contextual resources

Face-to-face conduct is influenced by the widest and seemingly most remote features of society considered as a totality. This requires that I say something about the nature of modern societies as totalities or "structured social systems" in their own right. However, I do not intend to undertake anything like a detailed analysis of system features since this would take me too far from my primary concern with the nature of situated activity and practices as they are experienced by the actors involved. Further I want to concentrate upon the way in which material, dominative and cultural/discursive resources directly (and indirectly) impact upon specific episodes of activity. In this sense I am primarily interested in the point of view of social actors and the manner in which they are linked with these resources. From the actor's viewpoint there are two dimensions of resources that are of significance. First, the availability, accessibility, even absence of certain kinds of resources, and secondly, the manner in which a person's behaviour is shaped by them either by making things possible (enablement) or closing down possibilities (constraint). However, it is also necessary to view resources from an external vantage point that is independent of the perspectives or interests of particular actors or social groups in an attempt to discern the patterning created by the objective distribution of resources – in effect the patterning of inequalities – throughout society. Moreover the distribution of resources is affected by a number of other factors such as the existing forms of domination and control within modern societies. An interest in such macro-patterns and forms necessarily enjoins us to speak of the larger collectivities that constitute societies such as institutions, organizations, social movements and class, gender and "racialized" groupings directly implicated in the distribution and allocation of resources.

Traditionally sociologists have indicated these features of social systems by a variety of terms including those I have just used. Parsons (1951) among others has used the term "subsystem" to indicate the manner in which distinct areas of society associated with various "functional" tasks are differentiated from one another to form relatively autonomous spheres of activity but that are also interdependent with the others. As long as the term "subsystem" is separated from its more encompassing implications in Parsons's general theory, then it usefully distinguishes between institutional areas such as the economy, the polity, education, law, religion, morality and so on. In this sense the concept of subsystem points to the institutional specialization necessary in complex societies and in which each subsystem contributes to the overall continuity of the whole system through its interdependence with the others. While the notion of subsystem adequately expresses the institutional consequences of the division of labour in a complex society in the manner that Durkheim (1964) himself envisaged, it does not readily reflect the operations of power and sectional interest upon which much of the institutional structure is based.

In this respect I believe that Bourdieu's (1984) notion of social "fields" has a great deal to offer. There is much in the notion of field that is compatible with and complementary to the theory of domains. In particular Bourdieu upholds a version of objectivism without losing sight of the constructive activities of human subjects – although other aspects of Bourdieu's work tend to neglect subjectivity and intentionality. His concept of field points to the set of relations between the objective social positions that fall within particular fields, for example the fields of economic production, of art, of political power, intellectual life or of educational attainment. These relations exist apart from people's consciousness and their face-to-face dealings but none the less influence their intersubjective worlds. Internally the fields are hierarchically organized around individual and collective struggles for the acquisition of resources and the attainment of interests based on them. Externally, the fields intersect with and tend to reproduce each other. The two "master" fields are those of class and cultural relationships and these set the terms under which the hierarchies in other fields are organized. The positions of people within fields are determined by the amount and weight of the various kinds of capital (economic, cultural and symbolic) they possess, and the fields themselves are market-like in that there is a struggle and competition for resources as a result of the strategic deployment of forms of capital.

The idea of "fields" of activity or practices defined around the struggle for resources (economic and cultural capital) has the advantage of underscoring the importance of power and domination as it is reflected in the broader institutional or "systemic" nature of societies. At the same time, however, it also suggests that the different fields or institutional arenas are interdependent with the social system as a whole. Thus there is a complex intermeshing and mutual reinforcement of differing principles of hierarchy and domains of power. This said, it does seem that Bourdieu omits some central axes and principles on which forms of domination are based and through which they are actualized. In particular, gender and racialized categories of "difference" are important dimensions of power and inequality that are defining features of modern societies and must be incorporated into any view of social systems as totalities. In short, the notion of social system must be underpinned by the idea that it is a complex of hierarchies and fields of power (sometimes competing and sometimes mutually reinforcing) within which struggles over resources and sectional interests take place.

As Bourdieu makes clear, the occupational structure is also centrally involved in the notion of fields of struggle for resources and interests. Interestingly, this brings back into play the idea I mentioned in an earlier section, of work as "an outer layer" of control – and thus the notion of field complements those of "setting" and "system" as I have so far used them. First, fields are about objective networks of social relations and as such concur with the idea of settings and systems as sites of reproduced relations. Fields therefore are distal way-stations that relay more general contextual resources. If settings are local holding points or aggregations of reproduced relations and practices, then fields are the wider parameters that define the more general nature of the activities and struggles that go on within them. Thus fields are wider clusterings of resources, positions and relations that provide the society-wide backdrop to the localized encounters in specific settings. For example, in the field of arts various subfields exist such as painting, sculpture, the acting profession and so on. Each of these subfields takes place in the context of different kinds of localized settings. For example, acting takes place in the setting of live theatre, television (live or recorded), or film (itself spanning a diversity of environments). The field of "education" takes place in different kinds of schools (primary or secondary), universities, colleges, and other training and career development institutions.

Thus my own "appropriation" of Bourdieu's notion of field requires that it is understood as a level of the organization of specific social practices (across the whole range) that is at a further remove from the localized and crystallized settings in which much of the routine encounters of everyday life take place. As aggregations of reproduced relations, settings are contiguous with activity while fields set the broader organizational terms under which encounters are formed. The network of objective relations that Bourdieu speaks of as fields indicates the manner in which reproduced relations are stretched in time and space while at the same time these relations bind various layers of organization together as they are "dispersed" in time and space. Fields and settings and the contextual resources that underpin and feed into them represent different phases and modalities of the social relations that link them with each other and other social domains.

The problem of power and domination also raises related issues concerning legitimation, exploitation and ideology, all of which can be understood as important modes in which power structures and forms of domination are stabilized and buttressed. This returns us to the question of the nature of resources on a collective level and the way in which they are deployed by dominant groups in order to maintain their positions of power. As far as material (economic) and dominative resources are concerned, the situation is somewhat simpler with respect to their implication in the reinforcement and stabilization of forms of domination. Clearly, as both Marx and Weber have pointed out, economic and/or dominative resources (including legal authority) may be used as means of restricting access to others and thus forms of rule and domination may be predicated on their possession. As a consequence resistances or challenges to such power revolve around and depend upon acts of dispossession or appropriation by subordinate groups that may or may not command wider social support or legitimation.

There is a gulf here between the nature of economic and dominative resources as compared with what I have termed the cultural and discursive forms. The former represent the basis on which modes of domination are typically established (in terms of possession or exclusion), whereas the latter are primarily concerned with the manner in which social and cultural forms in general, and modes of domination in particular, are signified and symbolized – that is, given meaning and expression through language and other public forms of discourse (the press, books, advertising, television, interviews, debates and so on). Of course, all cultural phenomena are not only of this nature, but often involve forms of material embodiment such as art, cultural objects or the visual images that constitute the signs and symbols of adverts, fashion or company logos, but nevertheless they have a nature that is easily convertible and transferable to a discursive form, that is they can be written about or spoken of in relation to a field of knowledge or expertise about a particular area, topic or skill. Therefore, in so far as the property of discursivity has to do with the formulation, conveyance and communication of signs and symbols, then it is centrally involved in the constitution of forms of knowledge and, as Foucault has observed, such knowledge confers powers (capacities and identities) upon those who have access (such as professionals) to these domains of knowledge.

Culture, ideology and discourse

Cultural-discursive phenomena cover a vast range and include such things as values, norms and expectations, ideologies, commonsense, practical skills and knowledge, cultural rules, taste and fashion – among others.

Similarly, the diversity of social and psychological needs and functions served by cultural-discursive phenomena is quite remarkable. As might be imagined social commentators have focused on many of possibilities here – from seduction (Baudrillard), to the formation of subjectivity (Foucault and the poststructuralist movement in general), the organization of taste (Bourdieu), ontological security, the engineering of consent and the securing of hegemony (Gramsci). It would be quite impossible to summarize meaningfully such a diversity of phenomena and anyway this is not my immediate purpose. Rather, I am concerned with outlining the collective properties of social systems, especially their institutional configurations understood against the background of cross-cutting struggles over resources (including cultural and economic capital) between groups pursuing sectional interests. In this respect it is worth drawing attention to a distinction between the generic elements of signification that are a feature of all discourses and more specific aspects as found particularly in ideological forms and which are geared to the legitimation, justification and rationalization of forms of power, control and domination and the sectional interests that they protect.

I hasten to add that the distinction between ideological discourses and other types is not always a clear-cut matter either in empirical or analytical terms. In this sense there is a great deal to be said for Gramsci's (1971) view that discourses correspond to differing means and levels of making sense of the world and that they are variously related to, and "infected" by, ideology. For example, in Gramsci's view philosophy, science, economics, religion, commonsense and folklore represent different degrees of elaboration and coherence and since they are all open to the "influence" of ideology they may be harnessed to its service. This directly relates to Gramsci's conception of "hegemony" that refers to the manner in which consent is organized without recourse to violence and coercion. In this sense the consent and compliance of subordinate groups to the rule and domination of others is secured via the operation of bodies of ideas that are in some sense informed and "infected" by ideology. Gramsci emphasized the way in which ideology is linked to popular forms of consciousness (everyday understandings) and commonsense and therefore allows an incorporation and coincidence of the interests of ruling and ruled groups through popular knowledge and culture.

Gramsci's and later Laclau & Mouffe's (1985) conceptualizations of ideology paved the way for radical revisions of Marxist theory in this regard. These authors saw ideology not simply as a reflection of the economic basis of capitalist society – particularly the social relations of production – but rather as one among a number of other cultural discourses, albeit one that had a decisive role to play in the legitimation of class domination. This work provided the theoretical conditions in which the poststructuralist break with the Marxist theory of ideology came about (see Barrett 1991). Perhaps the most successful attempt to break the "totalizing" mould of Marxist theory is Foucault's rendition of the links between knowledge, power, discourse and practice. In this scenario the traditional Marxist conception of ideology is abandoned in favour of a plural notion of discourses but without the respective class reductionism of Gramsci and the discursive reductionism (the reduction of social processes and relations to the operation of discursive practices) of Laclau and Mouffe. In this respect Foucault's analysis allows for a more generalized interest in power relations other than those created by social class, as well as in the powers and practices generated by and through discourses rather than simply in the forms of knowledge contained within the discourses themselves.

I shall pursue at other junctures a more detailed exploration and critique of some of Foucault's central ideas (particularly the question of power), although here it is necessary to make some initial points in relation to the question of ideology. As I have suggested, Foucault distanced himself from some of the central axioms of Marxism and one of these was the concept of ideology itself. Foucault makes an epistemological point here in suggesting that the notion of ideology in Marxism is unnecessarily bound up with claims about true and false beliefs and ideas. That is, because ideology is thought to perform a "mystifying" function by disguising the real sources and relations of power in society, it creates in those who are subjected to it a form of "false consciousness" whereby they are unable to grasp the "truth" of their oppressive social situations. Foucault felt that this was an epistemological cul-de-sac that diverted attention away from the more important questions concerning the nature and consequences of various claims to truth.

In parallel with this Foucault rejects the "totalizing" impulse of forms of Marxism (particularly Althusser's structural Marxism) that suggest the predominance of a single major ideology related to the class structure of advanced capitalism (see Abercrombie et al. 1980). For Foucault the idea of a monolithic and all-powerful ideology based on class domination has to be replaced with an understanding of modern societies as possessing multiple sites of power and displaying cultural diversity in terms of the influence of different discourses, practices and powers. Thus Foucault focuses on the plurality of discourses, cultural practices and their power effects at many different points in the social arena. This is the crux of Foucault's dissatisfaction with the concept of ideology: it "seems" to centre attention on the question of whether particular forms of knowledge are true or false according to their function in ordering our understanding of social structure. Foucault favours the idea that there is no sharp and discernible contrast between truth (scientific truth in Althusser's terms) and falsity. Instead we must appreciate that different discourses contain their own truth claims that are "valid" in their own terms. Thus the point of social analysis becomes the investigation of the power effects of various discourses rather than with whether they are true or false as such.

There is certainly some merit in this view of discourse analysis, notwithstanding the criticisms I shall make later regarding Foucault's views on the nature of discourses and his analysis of power. In particular it allows us to view culture as a plurality of discourses containing various and sometimes divergent (even competing) truth claims and producing a variety of power effects and practices (including a variety of influences on subjectivity). While accepting Foucault's misgivings about the more rigid Marxist usages of the concept of ideology, I do not see any real reason to preclude its use in the context of a reworked understanding of discourses. In this respect ideology may be seen as a subtype of a range of discourses available within cultural and subcultural repertoires. However, the notion of ideology must retain a reference to the rationalization and facilitation of relations of power and control even if we understand these in the broader terms that Foucault sets out. That is, we do not have to view ideology as inherently linked with the issue of the truth or falsity of various bodies of knowledge in order to conceptualize its implication in the justification and rationalization of asymmetries of power. Neither do we have to accept an intrinsic connection between ideology and specific forms of domination (like class) or the overriding importance of one aspect of society such as the economy or the state. In short we can accept the general tenor of Foucault's critique of Marxism and his amendment of critical analysis in general without abandoning altogether the notion of ideology.

Defining ideology as a form of discourse concerned with the facilitation of relations of power and control, without any of the above-mentioned "restrictions", enables us to view it within the play of a diversity of cultural discourses. In addition, the idea of a plurality of discourses allows us to see them as variably related to ideology, such that some could be described as "purely" or "systematically" ideological while others could be conceived as *partly* ideological or as containing ideological elements. This is essential if we are to incorporate (albeit in modified form) some of Gramsci's insights on hegemony. This is so since the idea that cultural forms like commonsense or popular culture may be fused and aligned with modes of domination and control, or that discourses "infect" each other to varying degrees is possible only if we view ideology as *in principle* distinguishable from other cultural discourses and practices.

Resources, social activity and discourse

Having dealt with cultural-discursive resources as collective or social system properties, let me now shift focus to concentrate on the way in which resources impact upon social activity. As I said earlier my main concern is with the actor's point of view and the manner in which the actor's experience is influenced by resources. In order to do this I argue that we must understand resources in terms of three modalities, or dimensions of existence, which in turn must be viewed against the backdrop of a dualism between subjective (internal) and objective (external) aspects of society. Another way of saying this is that resources enter into social life at three junctures or levels. First, they exist as an asymmetrical distributive pattern within social systems (bracketing together resources, fields and settings). That is, the manner and extent to which certain kinds and quantities of resources (money, property, education and so on) are objectively "available" to different groupings in society (of a class, gender and "racialized" nature for example). Of course, this objective distribution is also related to, and significantly influences, the local "allocation" at the level of fields and social settings. Secondly, on the subjective side, resources are deployed by individuals who exercise some degree of control over those that are available to them. That is, given the inherent limitations imposed by the distributive pattern and as they are filtered by fields and settings, individuals exercise choice about the deployment of resources on the basis of their preferences and predispositions. Thirdly, resources are intrinsically involved with situated activity in so far as they are selectively drawn upon by individuals (or groups) according to the emergent circumstances of social interaction – that is, as ongoing adjustments to the behaviour and responses of others. Thus we have the following triad of modalities of resources:

Individual		**Interaction**		**Distributive pattern**
(Predisposition)		(Selective uptake)		(System availability)

In this scenario it can be seen that interaction mediates between the objective limits on the availability of resources to individuals (considered singly, as well as members of a diversity of social groups) and the subjective predispositions of individuals themselves. It is in the encounters of everyday life that resources are deployed by specific individuals according to the contingencies of the immediate circumstances in which they find themselves. In preceding sections I have concentrated on the collective properties of resources – the macro-distribution that determines local availability to specific individuals and on which society-wide asymmetries of consumption, education, social influence, and so on, are based.

This may be contrasted with a more subjective sense of "availability" and consequent variability of "take-up" of resources. That is, resources also play an integral part in the immediate constituting of encounters. They exist as a kind of interactional currency that individuals draw upon and expend in the ongoing flow of social life to allow encounters and social activities to happen in a very general sense. For example, objectively people's class background influences whether they can benefit from the educational system in the form of what Bourdieu has called "cultural capital" and this, in some sense, will directly affect a person's life-chances and lifestyle. However, from the subjective point of view of an individual the actual deployment of aspects of this cultural capital in particular instances of face-to-face conduct will depend upon a host of personality and situation-specific factors.

Let us consider for the moment some of the personality factors involved. To recap, I am speaking of personality in the sense of those attributes of self-identity that are part of the psychic make-up of individuals as it has developed over time throughout their unique biographies. In this respect it is the conjunction of social and psychological influences that determines the attitudes, preferences, personal and behavioural styles that an individual may adopt. Accordingly I use "predisposition" as a blanket term to stand for all these components of subjectivity. In talking about individual "variations in the take-up" of resources I am drawing attention to two specific aspects of subjectivity that are of moment here. The first relates to the concept of "internalization" that signals an individual's psychic registration of the existence and hence potential deployability of particular resources (such as language, cultural capital, subcultural "know-how", like style of speech, fashion and so on). It is necessary to remember that there is a world of difference between recognizing the existence and availability of a particular resource and regarding it as something to be used in the appropriate circumstances. For instance, an individual might be able to adopt a certain speech style but prefer not to, or even definitely decide against it. Such behavioural decisions are influenced by attitudes, tastes, preferences and opinions that are clearly dispositional phenomena and are significant aspects of an individual's personality or general psychic make-up. They are formed in and through a person's psychobiographical development and operate to some extent independently of the appropriateness of behavioural responses or the availability or absence of skills upon which they are based.

The second aspect of subjectivity that bears upon the issue of variation in take-up is the question of choice and intentionality. This has more to do with judgements about the appropriateness and effectiveness of forms and styles of behaviour that are, in turn, bound up with the ongoing dynamic and emergent nature of face-to-face encounters. Thus for example a person may normally resist the use of a speech style or idiomatic form of communication (including non-verbal varieties) but in the presence of certain others or delicate situations may decide to do so in order to "blend in" more with a group or to make the other(s) feel "at home" (at ease) say, in a fraught or unusually demanding situation. This nudges us towards a consideration of the interactive dimension of resources. In this the subjective dimension meets up and combines with the external characteristics of resources as a pattern of distribution in the wider society and fields and settings as local sites of availability. It is in the arena of social activity that questions about the availability, access, inclination and recognition of resources become dispersed into the behavioural solutions demanded by particular situations. The interactive dimension mediates the external availability of (material, cultural-discursive or dominative) resources and the individual's willingness or reluctance to deploy those that are at hand. In this sense activity itself is the area in which there is a shuttling back and forth between subjective and objective dimensions.

For example, an individual may play down educational achievements and academic knowledge to gain or maintain acceptance in some subcultural grouping such as a sports team or a street gang. Conversely, the same individual may refuse to draw upon his or her memory "stock" of cultural capital in order to avoid deterring or embarrassing a friend, or a potential ally in certain "sensitive" situations. Likewise individuals may refrain from deploying cultural capital in situations where this might demean their boss, especially if they value their jobs. In all these cases the importance of retaining the status quo in the relationship – that is remaining mutual friends, convenient allies, or in a superior and subordinate relationship – takes precedence over any supposed advantages gained from the deployment of cultural capital. Thus it is that the form that resources take as components of subjective attitude and behavioural disposition is rather different from the distributive pattern of availability of resources determined historically by collective struggles and reflected in current group membership and the social organization of the field or setting in which the relevant activity takes place.

The three dimensions of resources are interdependent for they "create" each other's reality and in that sense each exists only in relation to the others. Therefore, it is not enough to opt for a single-dimensional ontology on the question of resources as is the case with Giddens's insistence that social phenomena have no existence beyond actor's reasons and motivations – or that power resides only in activity. Certainly, it is true to say that resources are *connected* to activity (and people's reasons and motivations) but it is not true to say that they have no form that is quite distinct from, and partly independent of, activity. It is necessary to envisage a tripartite ontology of modes of resources that "contain" or possess different properties and characteristics as in Table 3.1, which interact with each other. Unless this is envisaged the very different contributions, effects and influences of various domains of social life may be overlooked.

I have already pointed out that the triad of resource modes exist within the broader context of an internal (subjective) and external (objective) dualism. This issue is particularly important in attempting to understand the influence of cultural-discursive resources in social life since they affect the predispositions of human beings in a broadly encompassing manner. The central issue here concerns the question of what model of social ontology is most adequate for social analysis. The theory of social domains

Table 3.1 Resources: dimensions and properties.

Individual	Interaction	Distributive pattern
Internalization	[Social agency]	
Predisposition	Appropriateness	Availability
	Effectiveness	Access
Decision/choice/ intention	[Ability to "go on" and to get things done]	

asserts the importance of dualisms in social analysis in general along with the idea of a "depth" or "differentiated" model of social ontology. This is in contradistinction to other schemas that advocate one-dimensional views of social life. For example this is the implication of Giddens's ontology in which human social activity is thought to be the only domain in which resources "have a life".

Also Foucault's work (and the poststructuralist analyses that have resulted from it) reflects a constricted ontology although what it includes in its terms of reference is different from that found in Giddens's formulation. In Foucault's work discourses (and practices) are thought to be the exclusive media/medium of social life and thus as "resources" they are collapsed into the very same ontological space as discourses and practices (and the powers they confer). Thus in one fell swoop the contributions of human agency and social interaction are lost to the analysis since they have no legitimate place in Foucault's social "scheme of things". In order to underline the implications and distinctiveness of my own position here, let me spend some time describing how my view of discourses differs from those of Giddens and Foucault.

The nature and analysis of discourse

The theory of social domains views discourses in terms of the three modalities in which resources are manifested in social life, which I have already described. This position is different from Giddens's in the sense that it presupposes that in formulating their behaviour, social actors *draw upon* discourses which (as Foucault insists) have an existence above and beyond the consciousness and intentionalities of people. However, I do not go along with Foucault in denying the importance of consciousness and intentionality as components of human agency. So although Giddens is right to say that operationally, discourses are carried (internally) in actors' reasons and motivations, he is wrong to assume that they have no (external) existence as well. Previously I have simply spoken of this externality as an objective and asymmetric distribution of resources at different levels of society. With specific reference to discourse, this idea can be unpacked to reveal three senses in which their "externality" may be understood.

(a) The first sense of externality is connected with Foucault's notion of discourses as "epistemes" or domains of knowledge that etch the parameters of available meaning and that subsequently influence practice by incorporation into the subjectivities of social actors. (This is also consistent with a "network" conception of theory: see Hesse 1974, Layder 1990.) In a Foucauldian sense domains of knowledge (and the practices and powers they give rise to) are distributed unevenly throughout the social body in the same sense that other resources exhibit a macro-level pattern of distribution and a localized allocation in specific fields and settings.

(b) In so far as they represent the manner in which economic, cultural and dominative (authoritative) resources are signified, legitimized and symbolized, discourses inform and are enshrined in the rules specifying the rights, expectations and obligations associated with social positions. In fact, this is consistent with Giddens's own assumptions about the nature of social positions (1984: 89), although the "autonomy" of discourses is explicitly denied by his insistence that social reality does not have an existence independent of actors' reasons and motivations. In my terms the notion of "practice" must be reserved to connote the actual behaviours associated with the enactment of these positions and thus there is a partial disengagement between positions and practices. In this sense (although for very different theoretical reasons), neither Giddens nor Foucault properly distinguishes between the properties of practice as against those of discourse.

(c) Discourses have an externality in Popper's (1972) sense of a "third world" of "objective knowledge" – of art, science, language, ethics, institutions and culture in general. In Popper's vision these are obviously human creations but because they are capable of expression as ideas through language they possess a certain autonomy *vis-à-vis* human endeavour. They are collective, historical emergents and residues of past activities (and this is also consistent with Marx's idea that people create their own history but only by directly engaging with circumstances "inherited from the past"). In this sense discourses are more detached and autonomous from activity and practices than in Foucault's formulation. This ontological severance needs to be recognized in order to distinguish discourses from practices. Importantly such a recognition enables us to view them both as potentially separable and not simply and exclusively intertwined with each other – although, of course, they may often be so.

There are other characteristics associated with objective knowledge in Popper's view and they are directly applicable to the understanding of discourse in the wider context of domain theory. First, the word "objective" in the phrase "objective knowledge" should not be confused with the (positivist) idea that such knowledge cannot be doubted because it expresses a scientifically verifiable truth. "Objective" here is not meant to express a claim about truth as against falsity but is, rather, a claim about the relation between knowledge-in-general and the human beings who generate it. The linguistic form in which knowledge is signified and expressed is pivotal since it allows us to "stand apart" from our perceptual present and examine experience in relation to a past and an imagined future. Furthermore "objective" should not be taken to imply that such knowledge is unchanging, eternal and beyond the grasp of human intervention. In fact, the very "objectivity" of social and cultural knowledge ensures its malleability since this characteristic allows us to examine and critically evaluate it with a view to its elaboration, extension or transformation.

Although Popper has no intellectual affinity with structuralist and poststructuralist schools of thought, his conception of a "third world" of objective knowledge (world 1 being that of objective material things and world 2 being the subjective world of minds), there are some striking echoes of their views on the human subject and agency. First, in this respect is the notion that objective knowledge in the form of ideas, science, art, social institutions and so on may exist independently of any knowing subject as long as it is encoded in the form of world 1 objects such as books, computers, films and documentary records of all kinds. As Magee (1973: 61) notes, this highlights the "crucial difference between the knowledge in people's heads and the knowledge in libraries, the latter being far and away the most important". In this sense objective knowledge inhabits the public domain of world 3 and is not in the private states of mind of individuals (world 2). Further, "in this private, individual sense most human knowledge is not 'known' by anyone at all. It exists only on paper" (Magee (1973: 72). It is worth quoting Magee at a bit more length on the nature of world 3 phenomena:

> The libraries and record systems of the world consist of world 3 material most of which is likewise not in anybody's head but is nevertheless knowledge of a more or less valuable and useful kind. It is indeed most of the knowledge we have. Its status as knowledge and its value and usefulness are independent of whether there is anyone who "knows" it in the subjective sense. Knowledge in the objective sense is knowledge without a knower: it is knowledge without a knowing subject. (Magee 1973: 72)

I would argue that discourses have the same nature and characteristics of objective knowledge since they would be part of world 3 in Popper's terms. Although there is a similarity between Popper's notion of knowledge without a knowing subject and structuralist and poststructuralist ideas about the abandonment of the subject, I would not want to press the comparison too far since Popper is not concerned with general issues in social analysis such as the nature of social practices and power or of face-to-face conduct. However, given the importance of subjective minds as constitutive of world 2 phenomena, there is no hint in Popper's formulation of a complete abandonment of the knowing subject. Rather, Popper's views open up the possibility that discourse can be undertood *both* as an objective external phenomenon (a sort of cultural storehouse) and as part of an individual's subjective interior that feeds into their social conduct. It is this possibility that I wish to reserve for a reworked understanding of discourse as Foucault defines it. With regard to Giddens's work the problem is quite the opposite. He acknowledges that mental states (motivations and reasons) are important in social analysis but denies the externality and relative autonomy of social phenomena.

A further problem with Giddens's construal of discourse and resources in general concerns what Goffman calls "the interaction order". Giddens is keen to deny the autonomy that Goffman wants to accord to this order since the idea of different orders implies a separation of effects and mutual influences whereas they should be understood as invisibly and indissolubly tied together. In Giddens's view individual motivations and reasons are directly connected to institutional phenomena in social interaction. Social interaction itself has no *independent* formative effects or influences on activity. I shall deal in detail with the problems of analysis that arise from this issue in Chapter 5, so here I shall restrict my comments to the absolute minimum. I think Goffman's vision and understanding of the workings of the interaction order provide a more adequate basis for understanding the macro–micro links involved in the organization of society in general. This is because there is no reason to suppose that the idea of an interaction order in its own right severs the connections between institutions and face-to-face conduct. On the contrary, the implication is that the integral relations between them are understood in a fuller and more complex way.

Thus viewing resources (in this case discourses) as possessing three ontological dimensions (as discussed in the previous section) utilizes Goffman's notion of a relatively independent interaction order by suggesting that the domain of social interaction mediates between the subjective predispositions of individuals and the influence of system patterns. A crucial difference from Goffman here is that the individual and individual psychology are also given a relatively independent role to play whereas Goffman himself was more concerned with emphasizing the effects of interactional dynamics. Now seemingly, Goffman would be content with the idea that there is a dualism of orders here (micro and macro). Giddens, on the other hand, wants to opt for a single-dimensional view of social life wherein individual reasons and motivations meet up with institutional requirements through the idea of a duality of structure. However, although in a sense Giddens wants to "rescue" the human subject from the rampages of structuralist and poststructuralist thought and preserve its importance for social analysis (all of which is laudable as a set of aims and objectives), the unfortunate consequence of Giddens's framework is that the individual loses a measure of independence from social influences by absorption into the "duality of structure".

Let me now turn to a consideration of how my view of discourse and discourse analysis differs from that of Foucault. I think the main lines of cleavage concern Foucault's understanding of the relation between discourse and practice. In my opinion Foucault's construal of this relationship is unnecessarily constricted because he assumes the following:

  (a) that discourses are translated into practices via the category of subjectivity (alone), and

  (b) that subjectivity itself is constituted exclusively (or filled-up) by discourses, and

  (c) that discourses, practices (and power) are inseparably welded together such that they cannot be understood as partly independent of each other.

Assumptions (a) and (b) are related and centre on Foucault's attempt to abandon the subject and a concern with human agency and thus to avoid the subjectivism and humanism that he believes result from such a preoccupation. As part of the abandonment of the subject the attributes of intentionality and transformative power are erased from Foucault's notion of human subjectivity. These are exactly the sorts of attributes that Giddens believes to be essential to the notion of human agency, and here I must agree. People are not simply "processing units" who imbibe and regurgitate discourses (knowledge, beliefs, attitudes) as a result of their social positions and social locations and the powers that these confer. There is implicit in Foucault's notion of subjectivity the idea that people are *simply* nodal points in the intersection of various discourses. Such a view reflects an attachment to the idea that human beings are nothing but ciphers of social influences and determinations – a residuum of some of the worst excesses of structuralism.

Such a stark and lifeless model of the human being will surely not do, and while I want to acknowledge the kernel of truth contained in the idea of people as nodal points in the intersection of discourses (that is, that their lives are necessarily bound up with the limits that discourses place around forms of activity), I want to reject the idea that human subjectivity can be defined exclusively in these terms. Humanist and interactionist schools have conclusively demonstrated that human consciousness and agency involves the capacities of intentionality and transformative power – even if these capacities themselves are predicated on exposure to certain dis- coursive influences in the first place (such as forms of reasoning and so on). Clearly human beings have no real control of the cultural array of dis- courses available to them as a consequence of their social locations and positions – these are in a sense "enforced" by the distributive patterning that they must confront and deal with in their daily lives as an ongoing feature of social systems. However, it is also clear that from the discourses that are available to them, people are able to select and edit their influ- ences and as a consequence, decide between various courses of action on the basis of their relevance to the circumstances in which they find them- selves.

This involves the capacity to reshape or reconfigure discursive knowl- edge (and the "practical knowledge" and consciousness that it feeds into) in order to serve a person's wishes and requirements. However, to recog- nize this is not to suggest that the transformative elements involved should be understood as constant "reformulations" or complete reconfigurations of the form and content of discourses. In this sense the creative and transformative skills employed by social actors are often more closely asso- ciated with social reproduction in so far as they serve to shore up or pre- serve the interactional status quo and the moral fabric of the interaction order – as in the face-saving devices and strategies observed by Goffman (1967). Also, discursive elements may be used in a transformative manner while themselves remaining unchanged. For example, the use of specific pieces of knowledge, forms of language and linguistic style are often the result of clear decisions to alter the meaning of a situation by defining it in a certain manner (as in the example of someone calling a person by their first name, having previously addressed them more formally). In this sense it is the "appropriateness" of, or the productive effects that flow from, the deployment of certain social skills that results in the transformation of the social circumstances. Of course the intentions and transformative powers of human agents are not the only matters of relevance in the mediation and transmission of discourses to social activities – elements of the "interaction order" also play a crucial role.

In this respect Foucault does not distinguish between practices and situated activity and thus any influence deriving from the emergent dynamics of face-to-face conduct escape his analytic grasp. As a result of this omission Foucault does not understand the pivotal mediating role that situated activity plays in the transmission and relaying of discourses to and from the practices and activities that they help to shape. Neither does Foucault make any real attempt to distinguish between the production and reproduction of social life in his definition of practices – and this takes us back to the point about his rather mechanistic views on subjectivity. For Foucault, practices seem only to be implicated in the process of social reproduction – the manner in which the social fabric is replicated over time and space. He omits any account of social production in the sense of the continual creative work that goes on in social interaction as a result of the give and take of encounters and the moral order associated with face-to-face interaction.

Finally this is also related to the discussion about Popper's conception of objective knowledge and world 3 phenomena. As I pointed out, such a view overlaps to some extent with poststructuralist calls to abandon the subject, although in other respects the implications of Popper's position are quite at odds with Foucauldian analyses. Foucault's vision is that discourses are carried in practices and the powers that are inscribed in (or are an effect of) them both. Thus they are inseparable although neither are reducible to the intentions, consciousness or subjectivities of people. Discourse, practices and powers tend to float in some objective, impersonal realm beyond the grasp and intentions of people. Thus as with his neglect of the independent importance of situated activity, Foucault does not appreciate the way in which the relationship between discourses and practice is fractured and mediated by situated activity and the psychological dispositions of individuals. While registering this critique of Foucault it is also necessary to point out that discourses themselves as aspects of world 3 have an "encoded" life of their own that enables them to exist independently of specific forms of practice.

Situated activity and social systems

Let me now return to some of the issues raised earlier regarding the nature of situated activity. Having teased out some of the dynamics of social systems (settings, fields and resources) at a rather formal level I shall now spend some time illustrating the manner in which these formal elements coalesce in specific empirical examples of social activity. Therefore at this point I shall rejoin my account of the nature and modes of situated activity. To recap briefly on this, I suggested that in a preliminary manner we can discern some important features of situated activity in terms of its duration and continuity in time and space. Thus I discussed the way in which three types of encounter – transient, intermittent and regularized – could be understood to have different effects and implications for those involved in terms of the intimacy and purpose of episodes of behaviour. Although I noted that situated activity only takes place against the background of social influences, the implication of the discussion was that these time-space features could in a sense be abstracted from a more encompassing discussion of the effects of other factors. This is true, but only up to a point. As I also noted earlier, although situated activity produces its own emergent effects – its own unique contribution to the flow of conduct – it only does so in the context of its position in a complex overlayering and feathering of domains.

In this respect the discussion of transient, intermittent and regularized encounters needs to be put into perspective since such features can only be fully understood with reference to the contributory influence of other domains (psychobiographies, settings, fields and resources). For example, as I pointed out in my discussion of them, regularized encounters of an instrumental kind are more typical in the context of certain types of settings (such as a factory or an educational establishment) whereas transient encounters are more likely in the more diffuse areas of everyday life (like shopping or public transport). Similarly the field of activities concerned (arts, politics, work, leisure) and the availability of resources will also filter into the equation (through the medium of the setting) to exert an effect on the nature of specific episodes of social activity. Also, we must not overlook the contributions that individuals make to encounters in the face of such seemingly overwhelming social forces.It is to some examples of this texturing or imbrication of domains and influences that I now wish to turn.

As I have just mentioned, it is important not to lose sight of the individual as such since subjectivity must not be thought of as a kind of "summation" of discursive influences as they impinge upon the individual, nor must the person be pared down to such an extent that the person is regarded simply as a cipher of system demands or constraints (although these are undoubtedly crucial in their own right). Thus I shall begin with the issue of subjectivity and try to show that in addition to (perhaps in spite of), the formative influence of general cultural and social discourses, elements of psychobiography (in the form of personality predispositions) are drawn into the flow of conduct in specific situations and make their mark on them. Moreover, this is the case even in those circumstances where there is a predominant presencing of system characteristics – as in the following example of a factory work setting.

Subjectivity and situated activity

Situated activity clearly varies according to the extent to which particular personalities impose themselves upon the encounter in question and how the emergent characteristics of the interaction intertwine with these personal imprints to produce a textured effect. This obtains irrespectively of the social setting or environment in which the activity is taking place. Thus the realm of self and psychobiography may have an independent effect even where there is an overlayering of the effects of different domains. The importance of making such an observation has to do with understanding how the emergent effects of situated interaction are formed in the first place. The point here is that such effects cannot be put down simply to the overall dynamics of the encounter with each participant making an equal contribution, as it were, to the general outcome. It is true that in many cases the unevenness of contribution caused by personality differences will be cancelled out during the give and take of the proceedings and thus the direct effect of the psychological characteristics of particular individuals will be minimal. However, there are other instances in which specific personalities have a profound impact on the emergent characteristics (tone, atmosphere and substance) of encounters.

Another relevant issue here turns on the concept of subjectivity and what we mean by it. I want to suggest that subjectivity cannot be understood entirely in discursive terms. Although there is an important discursive component that underpins subjectivity, there is also a great deal of interpretive work going on in any encounter that derives partly from the uniqueness of individuals themselves and partly as a result of the exigencies of the situation. Poststructuralist analyses inspired by Foucault typically claim far too much for the influence of discourse on subjectivity, suggesting for example that "discourses are more than ways of thinking and producing meaning. They constitute the 'nature' of the body, unconscious and conscious mind and emotional life of the subjects that they seek to govern" (Weedon 1987: 108). There is some grain of truth in this assertion but as an adequate account of subjectivity as it applies to everyday social activity, it is vastly inflated inasmuch as it overlooks the predispositional nature of self-identities and the emergent nature of situated conduct.

A good example of this is found in Roy's (1973) study of factory machine operatives performing intrinsically unsatisfying unskilled work. One way in which the workers psychologically survived the boredom of the job was to devise forms of diversion and horseplay that also served the serious purpose of structuring the passage of time. Each day was patterned around an ordered series of "times" (peach time, coke time, banana time) that roughly occurred hourly and involved a flurry of horseplay, fooling around and banter centring on the consumption of a "snack" provided by one of the workers. These were interspersed and woven-in with verbal exchanges patterned around "themes" (ritualized "kidding" themes) that broke up the monotony of the work routine and provided rest breaks.

Clearly, such worker "games" are common to many work situations where monotony is a problem. However, the exact form that such diversionary activity takes will depend on a host of factors including the specific circumstances that obtain in the situation (such as the degree of contact with supervisors and management). But also equally important will be the types of relations between the individuals concerned (for example, buddies, mentors, antagonists) and the degree of harmony or internal friction of the work group as a whole. This general tenor or atmosphere of the group's activities, however, will be significantly influenced by the self-identities and psychobiographies of the group members. For example, in Roy's study one of the regular themes that interleaved with the food break times was "the professor" theme – a "serious" as opposed to a "kidding" theme. This revolved around the fact that one of the workers had a daughter who had married the son of a local college professor, and this, in the eyes of his two other workmates, endowed him with superior status. Roy describes them as listening "in awe" to him whenever the subject came up.

More generally, the identities of the three men were reflected in the roles they adopted during the various "times". For example, different individuals would take responsibility for providing the object that defined particular "times" (peach, coke, banana, and so forth). Also particular individuals would invariably adopt the same roles in the ritualized activity that occurred during the small breaks that the "times" provided. For example, Sammy always brought in a banana for lunchtime, but Ike always stole it from his lunch box and ate it himself and this ritual was inevitably accompanied by protestations from George and Sammy. Thus the personalities and self-identities of the three men significantly impinged upon the continuous flow of conduct in their everyday work situations. Motivational issues concerned with the extent to which individuals will continue to maintain ongoing interaction or renew or reproduce it at later points in time are of obvious importance here as J. Turner (1988) has pointed out. The degree to which individuals are motivated to do this is related to the extent to which the needs for group inclusion, ontological security, trust and self-affirmation or confirmation are being met in the situation (J. Turner 1988 : 68).

These sorts of issues cannot be entirely understood in terms of the analysis of discourse, although as I have said it is undoubtedly true that an appreciation is required of the way in which discourses are drawn upon as resources that both allow and limit a person's behaviour. An analysis to the effect that subjectivity is the "site of consensual regulation of individuals" and that this occurs "through the identification by the individual with particular subject positions within discourses" (Weedon 1987: 112) does not come anywhere near to grappling with the intra-psychic and identity issues implicated in the production and maintenance of social encounters. The idea that the "acquisition of modes of subjectivity involves the accumulation of the memory, conscious or unconscious, of subject positions and the psychic and emotional structures implicit in them" (Weedon 1987: 112) does not adequately register the manner in which emotional, motivational and identity issues are continually worked at, negotiated and forever unresolved in encounters – they are not simply "given" or assigned by discourses via the memory of subject positions.

Such an analysis would look no further than the subject position of "unskilled worker" in order to comprehend the activities of the men in Roy's study. It is surely true that the subject positions of these men are not unimportant and certainly the discourses upon which male workers can trade in such situations gives us clues about how they might behave in each other's company. But this could only ever be a starting point for an investigation of how discourses are fractured, spliced, co-opted and otherwise reshaped through the mediation of the minds and selves of the participants and the ever-developing nature of the situation.

Finally, in relation to this example, let me return to an earlier point about Habermas's distinction between "interaction", based on genuine understanding forged out of consensual agreement, and "labour" based upon strategic and instrumental attitudes geared towards the acquisition of money in exchange for their labour power. In so far as Habermas sees the area of work as one that is solely the province of intrumental motives and strategic activity resulting from the encroachment of system impera-tives (the steering mechanisms of money and power) in the context of the labour market, then we must reject this as an over-general claim. It is clear in many empirical studies of worker behaviour (see discussion of Ackroyd & Crowdy 1990 below) that such a clean distinction does not suffice. Motivational processes as discussed by Turner concerning trust, security, inclusion and self-affirmation are constant accompaniments of all social encounters and activities no matter in what setting, field or context they occur. Similarly, all activity calls into play the furbishments of self-identity and personality predispositions that must be mobilized in order for encounters to be initiated, maintained or renewed. The personal and sometimes private worlds of individual subjectivity (in this more rounded sense, than implied in poststructuralism) are an intrinsic feature of face-to-face conduct irrespective of whether the business at hand is significantly influenced by instrumental purposes and strategic motives.

The influence of cultural and collective resources

Ackroyd & Crowdy's (1990) study of a team of workers in a slaughterhouse in the UK both complements and adds to some of the points made in rela-tion to Roy's study. One of the questions the authors wanted to address was the extent to which the culture of the workplace is something that can be created or controlled by management. They argue in the case of the slaughtermen that theirs was a distinctive "occupational" rather than an "organizational" culture that could not be explained by – and in fact was often resistant to – management action. Further, the authors argue that their case study reveals the extent to which there is a complex relationship between the attitudes and behaviour of the workers as they are developed in the work situation itself and the wider community in which the workers live. In this sense the occupational culture incorporates elements from other contexts including the dominant values of society. Thus their argu-ment suggests that worker behaviour and the basic conceptions they have of themselves are "shaped by factors external to the workplace as deeply as by those internal to it" (Ackroyd & Crowdy 1990: 5).

In terms of my more general arguments this study complements the previous discussion of the influence of psychobiography and the emergent nature of situated activity by emphasizing the extent to which behaviour in a particular work setting is influenced by wider cultural resources (of a community and a more general kind). One of the main features of the work of the slaughtermen is the social stigma attaching to the work because of its "dirty" nature. There are two aspects to this. First, the workers cannot avoid contamination by blood, other bodily fluids and animal excreta. Secondly, the job is associated with the killing and dismembering of animals and, although often viewed as necessary by society more generally, it is also regarded as repugnant. Thus the job of the slaughtermen is morally ambiguous in that although they are producing a valued product they do so by causing death. One way in which they dealt with this ambiguity was through the adoption of core occupational values of "realism" (towards the act of killing animals) and "aggressive masculinity".

Adherence to these values involved two kinds of responses to the cultural resources available in the workers' local communities and society at large. First, the general societal value that finds killing repugnant and dirty was inverted in order that the workers could maintain a positive self image and a level of pride in and commitment to their work. Thus, they felt themselves to be special people who can take and do what others cannot by being physically tough and emotionally strong. Highest status in the work groups, for instance, was reserved for those who "stick" or kill the animals since they "most intensely symbolize the dangerous animality of what is being done by these workers" (1990: 11). Also the slaughtermen were unapologetic and aggressive in their attitudes towards their work and celebrated its specialness and "dirtiness" – by wearing dirty clothes, refusing to wash regularly and even splashing blood on their chests before leaving work as a visible sign of their occupation.

This celebration of work that is more widely regarded as distasteful was intertwined with the identification with the aggressive masculine qualities of toughness and realism towards the killing of animals. This realism counters what the workers felt was the hypocrisy of the general public who need and desire meat but who also regard animals with sentimental endearment. Associated with this general and exaggerated masculinity they possessed extremely prejudiced attitudes towards women and homosexuals. The adherence to the values of toughness, fortitude and lack of emotional vulnerability or sensitivity was reflected in their attitude towards the harassments and degradations to which they would be routinely subjected by other workers either to put pressure on others to increase the pace of work or out of a mixture of boredom and generalized aggression. This "ritualized" enactment of a tough self-identity and particular acts of "symbolic subordination" involved such things as throwing entrails at particular workers, filling-up workers' boots with fresh blood, or even spraying liquid excreta out of an intestine in a broad arc across the workshop. Such continual harassments or demonstrations contain elements of symbolic domination and were aimed at younger men in particular. Of course, the whole point about a tough self-image meant that none of the workers ever complained about these incidents.

These attitudes, self-images and values were reinforced in the slaughtermen's relations with their community and their leisure pursuits. They tended towards communal leisure, mixing with other slaughtermen and avoiding contacts with others. Most evenings would be spent in the company of other slaughtermen in a particular pub. Also they rarely went away on holiday since this would necessitate mixing with strangers with whom discussions about the kind of work they do would inevitably arise, and they wanted to avoid the usual reactions of either distaste or "ghoulish interest". Instead of "normal" holidays they typically took five-day breaks from work and often popped back into the plant in between visits to the pub. Many of the men had home-centred hobbies and pursuits related to livestock or hunting such as pigeon-fancying, keeping ferrets and dog-breeding. Clearly, this mode of spending leisure time protected their values and pride in their work from a wider community that was viewed either as hostile or lacking in sympathy or understanding. In a situation where the dominant attitudes and values of the wider society have to be "inverted", this kind of buffering and segregation is essential.

I think that this description of the research makes several points about the nature of social activity in general that are worth spelling out in the more formal terms I have used throughout this chapter. Primarily it highlights the operation and importance of group and cultural resources that individuals may tap into when formulating their conduct in specific situations. In this case wider discourses associated with a stereotyped masculinity played a crucial role in realigning more general social attitudes towards death (and the killing of animals in particular) and recycling them in different forms for their own purposes (for example as pride in the job and "specialness" of their personal qualities). Thus images of "legitimate" masculinity were co-opted in order to imbue their work with elements of "respectability" in their own eyes. Also local communal resources (based primarily on class and gender characteristics) such as subcultural attitudes, tastes, habits, hobbies and so on, buttressed their involvement in an entrenched occupational culture that was insulated from influences or pressures that might undermine it.

Ackroyd & Crowdy's main argument is that to a very large extent this occupational culture results from the combined influences of cultural factors external to the workplace and that it has an independence from – and indeed is resistant to – management attempts to change or manipulate it. (This is in opposition to the main thrust of the literature on "excellent" companies and Human Resource Management ideas.) Now this is an important point since among other things it demonstrates that the settings of activity cannot be thought of as separate enclaves removed from wider social and cultural influences. A similar point can be made about the relation of settings to the individuals and the situated activities that operate within their domains. That is, settings such as work organizations must not be thought of as containing a self-sufficient culture independent of the emergent contributions of situated activity and specific individuals.

From the point of view of the theory of social domains there is always a composite "overlayering" or imbrication of the effects of all the domains. In this respect Ackroyd & Crowdy's case study reveals an instance where contextual resources have an *accentuated* influence in the overall texture of effects. It would be untrue to say that the influence of the setting itself was completely nullified (as I shall go on to show). It would be more accurate to say that its effects were somewhat muted by comparison. The same goes for the relatively autonomous effects of self-identity and situated activity, although Ackroyd & Crowdy's study does not furnish us with enough evidence to be clear about the overall contribution of these domains. This is mainly because the researchers did not focus explicity on situated strips or episodes of interaction as they emerged from the work arena. Rather they focused on "examples" of workers behaviour (demonstrations, harassments, aggression and so on) to make more general points about the extent to which the occupational culture is related to external values and discourses.

This is not an issue unique to this study. Unless there is an explicit empirical or theoretical attempt to focus on problems of trust and anxiety, for example, and the manner in which they are handled by specific individuals in particular settings and situations, or detail is furnished on how specific episodes of interaction are related to the internal dynamics of groups or work teams, there is no way of assessing the impact of these domains on the overall orchestration of effects. Nor is there any means of judging the balance of the influence of self and situated activity with those of settings and contextual resources. Finally, while we have not touched on the question of authority and power especially as it is manifested in social settings, it is clear that without a corresponding analytic emphasis on the lifeworld elements of identity and face-to-face conduct, there is no sense in which one can properly understand their mutual implication in system elements such as power and markets. In this respect, the "methodological bracketing" (Giddens 1984) of lifeworld elements means that it is impossible to trace the subtle web of interdependencies threaded through each of the domains and drawing them together in a complex dialectic of control (Giddens 1984).

Physical and social aspects of settings, fields and contexts
Having "flagged" the issue of power and control let me now consider some of the variable features of system elements as they impinge upon the overall flow of conduct. I must reiterate that although it is necessary for analytic purposes to refer to settings, fields and contexts *as if* they were set within a "frozen" moment in time, the domains must be understood as social processes stretched through time and space. In this respect the domains simultaneously shape, and are shaped by, the activities that give life to them in the present and which reproduce them over variable spans of time. This is most easily grasped from the point of view of the individual as a patterning of involvements as the person moves through the daily cycle (and, of course, subsequently over longer periods of time). For instance an individual will typically shuttle back and forth between a number of different settings and locations of activity – home, work, leisure (pubs, clubs, cinema, sports) – during the course of the day. Other more periodic involvements may punctuate certain days, such as going to visit the doctor or hospital, dealing with mortgages or collecting benefits and so on, depending on the intersection of class, gender and racialized factors that determine an individual's lifestyle, life-chances and standard of living.

This variable set of involvements also implies movement though different spatial or geographical locations as well as a multiplicity of social environments more or less defined and visible in nature. As this movement occurs, there is a parallel movement between the influence of different social domains. Thus for example in the "home" setting, domestic, family or partnership issues may predominate in situated encounters and may be more or less totally absorbed by them, whereas movement into a work setting will be more likely to prompt the activation of other issues and resources. This movement through the repetitive cycles of social involvements and activities follows individual's trajectories that move in and out of the orbit of different settings and social circumstances and their spheres of influence. Thus these social trajectories also map constant shifts in the weighting and accentuation ("presencing") of the influence of different social domains.

As this movement occurs the individual is also subjected to the influence of the social relations that agglomerate at different points (in time and space) as the dialectic between reproduced and free-form aspects of social interaction is variably affected by the transitions and transferences between settings and contexts. Thus the variety of social settings and the movements of individuals (and groups) within and between their spheres of influence are crucial switch points in social systems. In so far as settings are holding points for aggregations of reproduced relations they have a significant impact on the immediate distribution of contextual resources. It is important therefore to appreciate the diversity involved in the form that settings may take and the kinds of social positions and practices that they underscore. Settings are often tightly defined territorial units with a highly structured and visible pattern of position-practices associated with them.

This is typically the case with work organizations like factories or companies, although sometimes territorial clustering does not indicate the singularity of the settings, a "unit" being perhaps one of many such units within a much wider spread. Such settings in themselves display an enormous diversity of internal patterning. For example, work organizations vary considerably in terms of the formalization, definition and codification of the rights, duties and obligations associated with their position-practices as does the degree to which they emphasize hierarchy as against a "flat" internal structure. Other kinds of settings exhibit a much greater permeability of boundaries and a looser definition of spheres of influence and "permissible" practices. Also there are often overlappings of settings and this complicates the spatial spread and reach of influence associated with them. As part of the private sphere (as against the public sphere of work and service organizations) the settings of family, home, and domestic partnerships may produce a bewildering variety of possible permutations depending upon the number of home residents (single occupancy, stable partnership, transient relationships and forms of multiple sharing and so on). Also the often overlapping influence of the family varies to a considerable extent depending on the number of relatives, the regularity of contact between them, their geographical distribution and so on – not to mention the typicality and incidence of such factors as they are influenced by class, gender and cultural or "racialized" backgound.

Other kinds of settings have a less central role to play in society at large, some, in fact, having a less than "legitimate" place in the social fabric as with the example of subcultural and criminal organizations. Although such settings are typically much more amorphous in structure, they none the less display a degree of boundary definition in terms of which a system of rules operates to draw in and bind participants to its moral imperatives. Some settings bridge both the legitimate and non-legitimate worlds as well as the public and private spheres. For instance Wieder's (1974) study of a rehabilitation unit for paroled prisoners identified a "code" that was established and maintained by the inmates (as opposed to the staff) and that was clearly verbalized but not written down or formalized in any way. The code consisted of rules such as "do not snitch on (inform on) other inmates to staff" and "do not steal from other inmates" and so on. The code was used as an interpretive resource with which inmates controlled their own and others' behaviour in terms of a moral order that applied only to other members of the same subcultural group. So although settings such as these seem to be much looser, more amorphous and diverse than many of the "core" institutional forms, they none the less have a definable *bona fide* membership and exhibit a governance of those participants.

Returning to the question of power and control for the moment, we can see in both Roy's and Ackroyd & Crowdy's studies examples of the way in which the physical organization of the work settings influenced the substance of the activities that took place in them. Roy's study in the USA centred on the "clicking room" in which the machine operatives worked and which was physically separated from the rest of the factory. This was of enormous significance for the development of the interactional games, rituals, themes and "times" that structured their working day. The physical separation of the "clicking room" meant that the impingement of authority figures such as foremen or managers on their work area was minimized. The relative isolation of the machine room meant that usual sources of in-group solidarity, such as ill-will towards management, or rivalry and competition with other groups of workers were absent. The workers were thrown back on their own resources to structure their working environment and the passage of time. Thus by having a significant impact on the mediation of authority and external controls, a physical aspect of the setting led to an accentuation of the influence of the internal effects of situated activity.

Settings and the socio-economic environment

Ackroyd & Crowdy's study provides a variation on the theme of the influence of the workplace on attitudes and behaviour within the setting by drawing into the equation the socio-economic context in which it occurs. The gangs of workers were to a great extent autonomous from managerial control but nevertheless they worked hard and largely disciplined themselves. This was because beyond a basic level they were paid by a piecework bonus system according to the number of animals slaughtered and dressed in the week. The workers were motivated by the desire to maximize the piecework bonus and because this guaranteed high levels of effort, the need for close supervision was removed. Many of the harassments and degradations that individuals were subjected to were directly related to the need to do the work as fast as possible, thus men who slowed the teams down overall were consistent targets for attack.

While this is a case of the organizational and market setting of the work exerting an effect on situated activity, my own study of actors' careers in the UK illustrates how in craft-like occupations such as acting, the market is organized on an occupation-wide basis rather than exclusively in terms of particular employing organizations (such as a theatre or a TV or film company). The fixed-term contract basis of much of the work in acting (for the run of the show or for the duration of a film or programme) means that as long as they are relatively successful and in demand, male and female actors alike will move between different employers during their careers. This exigency enforced by the market organization of acting means that contacts and relationships between actors are often disrupted and discontinuous. This is because in this kind of "internal labour market" being "in demand" entails regular movements between different work situations. As a result successful actors are continually placed in work situations in which they have to establish and develop rapport with work colleagues on each occasion from "square-one" since they do not have the benefit of a history of shared experience on which to base them.

The nature of situated activity is therefore rather different from that associated with the work teams discussed above in so far as it is less dependent on previous negotiations, routinized rituals and gaming relations. In particular the establishment of trust between the particular individuals concerned in a dramatic project (a play, a film and so on) and the general provision of a working environment in which trust can be minimally assured becomes a central feature of situated behaviour (Layder 1981, 1984, 1993). This is especially the case in a market environment in which sensitive egos have to be protected against damage produced by the vagaries of market demand, fee-determination and critical censure, as well as the tricky problems deriving from the nature of the work task itself (such as emotional involvement and identification with dramatic roles – the attempt to get to the truth of a performance and so on). Even if actors (and directors) have worked with each other on some previous project the gap between engagements means that working relations need to be carefully and delicately renegotiated and trust re-established.

These examples vividly highlight the manner in which settings and the variations in their social organization critically affect the intersection between lifeworld and system elements. It is not, as Habermas seems to imply, that lifeworld and system elements are somehow "naturally" separated from each other and that system (or market) elements of power and money "drive out" or displace the lifeworld elements. As these examples show the two "meta-domains" are integrally intermeshed with each other. Rather it is the manner in which they are interfused that varies according to the nature of the settings themselves and their relations both with wider (contextual) resources as well as with the situated activities and identities that are a continual or routine feature of them. The occupation of acting is an interesting case in that lifeworld and system elements are equally accentuated in specific work settings as I have indicated and that this has resulted in specific "buffering mechanisms" adopted by those involved in order to manage the tensions that are produced by such a close coupling.

The social fabric: some preliminary conclusions

In this chapter my intention has been to establish the contours of the social fabric – in the form of the social domains as I have described them – from the point of view of the fabric itself. Thus to some extent I have bracketed issues of identity and subjective experience discussed in Chapter 2. However, I have introduced a series of concepts and a framework of analysis that interlocks with the discussion in Chapter 2. Since I have been concerned with creating a general overview I have glossed over some important issues in order to get at the "big picture" before focusing in with a more detailed examination of the constituent parts. Although in this respect I have attempted to give some account of the modes in which social relations (particularly the reproduced features) operate to tie the domains together, I have not as yet described in any detail the various forms of power that exist and the multiplicity of complex connections that thread through social relations, domains, discourses and practices. It is to this task that Chapter 4 turns.

4

Power and control in modernity

The basic theme of this chapter is that power is ever-present and every-where in society. People are constantly subjected to the effects of power, but to varying degrees they themselves also have powers that they deploy to greater or lesser effect. In this sense power spans both the objective and subjective aspects of social life and it is this spread and diffuseness of power at all levels of society that I want to explore in this chapter. First, I must immediately enter the proviso that I do not intend or pretend to offer an exhaustive discussion of the topic of power (which would require at least a book-length treatment in itself). My discussion is strictly tailored to the main theme of this book, which is the understanding of social activity and thus I shall omit a great many issues and aspects associated with the topic of power in the sociological literature (see Clegg 1989 for an extensive overview). Secondly, my treatment of power is in accordance with the theory of social domains and, as I have indicated at various places, one of the main themes in this regard is that the nature and form of power varies in respect of the domains and their influence on each other.

In endeavouring to grapple with this issue, I shall refer to and draw into the discussion a more general body of work, including that of Foucault, Giddens and Habermas, for I believe that each has something important to say about the nature of power in modernity. However, while I borrow much from the work of these authors, it will become apparent as the discussion unfolds that I find it necessary to depart from many of their for-mulations in order to clarify my own position. The main reason that I focus on these authors is they all throw some light on my main theme of the relation between the subjective and objective aspects of power quite

147

irrespectively of whether their overall position is consonant with the one I am here advocating. I shall begin the discussion by examining some of Foucault's ideas on the nature of power in modernity since they usefully set out some of the parameters of the topic that I wish to address.

Foucault and the nature of modern power

In Chapter 3 I pointed out the close links that Foucault posits between discourse (knowledge), power and practice. Let me here concentrate on the implications that flow from these connections for an understanding of power. Much of Foucault's (1977, 1980) work on power is centred on a critique of two "traditional" conceptions of its nature and functions. The first views power as a "commodity" that a person (such as a sovereign) possesses and exercises over a group of subjects who authorize this power. This is a repressive form of power that prohibits, limits and instructs those over whom it holds sway in order to allow power-holders to enact their objectives and requirements. Such a form of power is based on the model of monarchical rule that developed in the Middle Ages against a background of chronic struggle and competition between feudal lords. Another influential model of power very similar to this is that developed within Marxism, whereby it is thought that a group such as a social class exercises power through possession of the state apparatus and control over the means of production.

Both these views of power are based on the idea of "possession" (of the commodity of power) and the idea that it is repressive in nature. In this sense power is inherently limiting and prohibitive. In both cases there is a central "source" that produces all the effects of power and distributes them in a hierarchical fashion to a subjugated population. In Marxism (particularly structural Marxism) this centrality of the source of power is very pronounced and is connected to an all-embracing "grand theory" or "meta-narrative" that attempts to explain the whole sweep of history and social evolution. Thus in Marxism class domination of the economic base of society with its associated control and ownership of the means of production is thought to determine all the other aspects of society and social life.

Foucault insists that these notions based on "single cause" and repressive views of power are out of date and more appropriate to pre-modern societies. In his historical studies Foucault traced the emergence of newer forms of power during the seventeenth and eighteenth centuries that were based on fundamentally different principles. In particular he charts the development of "disciplinary power" in which control over subject populations operates through a regime of continuous surveillance and internalized "self-discipline" rather than the external infliction of punishments – often in the form of public spectacles (as was the case with monarchical rule). For example, Foucault suggests that punishment by torture was replaced by an impersonal system of surveillance which ensured that the focus of this new disciplinary power shifted to the individual's psychology and capacity for self-control. In prisons in particular (Foucault uses Jeremy Bentham's ideas about the Panopticon to illustrate this) but also in other organizational forms such as army barracks, asylums and monasteries, individuals perceive themselves to be constantly under surveillance and begin to oversee themselves – to regulate their own behaviour in the light of its assumed accessibility and visibility to those in control.

This system of disciplinary power extends into many other areas of life such as hospitals, schools and factories and involves three typical forms of control of conduct. First, there is a constant and minute surveillance of the routine activities that take place within the organization. This is also reflected in the architectural design of such places as schools, army barracks and workshops or factories, which allows the spatial distribution of human bodies according to function or rank into isolated locations and spaces. The second form of control hinges around the practice of the "normalizing" judgement that aims to bring into line any violations of the duties and regulations having to do with bodily discipline and conduct in general, by the administering of admonitions and punishments. Thirdly, conduct is controlled through the method of the "examination" that combines the idea of a hierarchical form of observation with the practice of normalizing judgements. The examination puts people under scrutiny (a normalizing "gaze") and makes it possible to individualize them, and therefore to classify, qualify and/or punish them.

This system of disciplinary control is effected in conjunction with various techniques of bodily training in order to encourage individuals to function on an automatic basis as "docile bodies". I have already mentioned the idea of the spatial distribution of bodies according to rank and function aided by architectural design and this allows individuals to internalize and reaffirm their place within the organization. Also bodily gestures and movements concerned for example, with the use of tools or weapons are strictly defined and regulated in time and space. Forms of training (in the use of weapons, tools, manufacturing procedures or simply in the acquisition of certain kinds of knowledge) are operated in a sequential and cumulative manner in order that they can be planned and organized. Finally, from the point of view of disciplinary control it is necessary to make sure that the activities of trained bodies are tighly co-ordinated and synchronized with those of all the other individuals involved.

The normalization of behaviour and identities achieved by disciplinary techniques relies heavily on individuals' capacity and willingness to monitor their own behaviour. This is dovetailed with the organizational use of "examination-like" procedures including the use of dossiers, marking, classification and appraisal systems in schools, prisons, factories, hospitals and other organizations that give individuals some sense of their position within, or progress (or lack of it) through an administered hierarchy. As Poster (1984: 103) remarks, this provides a "technology of power" (or means of control) that can be deployed at many different locations in capitalist society. Poster goes on to point out that Foucault fails to note that in the late twentieth century, bureaucracy and the computer have expanded the nature of disciplinary control. Bureaucracy and computers have meant that mechanisms of information processing have extended the boundaries of behaviour-monitoring beyond the limited confines of organizational spaces. Traces of behaviour such as credit card activity, telephone bills, welfare files, income transactions, loan applications and so on can be tracked by computer to give "a surprisingly full picture of an individual's life". Thus the "normalized individual" not only exists in massed groups in the workplace, school, the military and so forth as Foucault observes, but also extends to the "isolated" individual at home or in the mundane activities of everyday life (Poster 1984: 130).

Foucault identifies another form of power – "bio-power" – that he views as critical to the emergence of modernity. As we have seen, disciplinary power involves some aspects of bodily training and therefore overlaps to some extent with bio-power. However, the distinctive feature of bio-power lies in its specific targeting of the body and its concern with the behaviours and subjective identities of whole populations instead simply of individuals or groupings of them within organizations. In *The history of sexuality* Foucault (1979, 1986, 1988) charts from the eighteenth century onwards, a growth in governments' attempts to control birth and death rates, life expectancies, fertility, health and frequency of illness and so on in relation to whole populations. From this point onwards the area of sexuality became the focus of intense discursive scrutiny in an effort to adminster, regulate and define the "normal" (permissible) forms of sexuality, and as a result, to begin to give shape and name to various "deviations" and "perversions".

In such an effort to control large masses of people there is also an attempt to impose forms of subjectivity – to define permissible or normal feelings, ideas and behaviour as an effect of discourses or bodies of knowledge that legislate "the truth" (particularly scientific truth) about areas of everyday life such as sexuality, health and illness, "normal" versus antisocial behaviour. In this manner, power is linked with discourse (knowledge) and practice. First, the power to define proper or "normal" behaviour and practice on the basis of various claims to valid knowledge (such as its "truth" or its scientific nature) is a discursive power dependent upon access to, and proficiency in, specialist areas of knowledge. Secondly, discourses construct forms of identity and subjectivity (feelings, thoughts and attitudes) which in turn feed into "normalized" forms of activity for individuals operating within certain social milieux. Thus the close connections between power, discourse and practice are secured in Foucault's framework of ideas.

Implications of Foucault's view of power

Apart from the intrinsic links between discourse, subjectivities and practices, Foucault's depiction of the newer forms of power is predicated on several related assumptions about the manner in which they operate. Let me examine these and then try to show how certain elements of Foucault's overall view of power in modernity may be used in conjunction with the theory of social domains. At the same time of course, I shall pinpoint what I take to be the more inadequate aspects of Foucault's analysis – especially with regard to his attempt (though not necessarily "intentional") to go beyond the subjective–objective and agency–structure dualisms.

Power: productive or prohibitive?
First, Foucault's vision of power reverses the idea implicit in more traditional (particularly the sovereign) conceptions – that power is necessarily repressive and prohibitive. Instead, Foucault insists that power should be understood as inherently productive and creative. That is, both disciplinary power and bio-power are based fundamentally on the construction of capacities and skills within people such that they can be held within the

scope of the regime, or technology of power and encouraged to operate "normally" therein. In the sense that people identify and act in accord with the regime then their subjectivities are constructed within the parameters "allowed by" the discourses and the practices of the regime. Similarly practices are created out of these capacities and subjectivities and the bodies of knowledge that are associated with and give shape to them. This applies equally to superordinates as to those below them – they are both subject to the powers and discourses that construct the parameters of their identities as well as their positions and functions within the organizational forms they inhabit.

Clearly the idea that power is productive and creative rather than a repressive and prohibitive "device" is an important dimension of power of a certain sort. That is, from the point of view of domain theory, power may assume a number of different guises and possess varying properties and dimensions – in this sense productive and creative types may exist alongside others which tend to emphasize more repressive and prohibitive characteristics. This raises a general difficulty with Foucault. He often speaks as if the newer forms of power have completely displaced the older ones and thus more traditional conceptions of power are now without foundation. This assumption seems to be unwarranted since there seems to be little empirical support for the view that traditional repressive (and "top-down" or "sovereign") modes of power have completely disappeared. Nor does such an assumption seem logically or theoretically necessary. There is plenty of room for a multiplicity of forms and conceptions of power so why should it be necessary to view power only in the terms that Foucault proposes in respect of disciplinary and bio-power?

Power as possession and the influence of agency

This leads us to the consideration of a second characteristic of power as Foucault sees it. For him power inheres in a constantly shifting network of alliances rather than existing as a commodity or property possessed and exercised by a person or a group. This suggests that power is an intrinsically relational phenomenon and therefore it cannot be viewed as a substance or capacity that people exercise and deploy according to their objectives and intentions. (Among other attributes this distinguishes Foucault's "relational" view of power from that offered from a symbolic interactionist perspective – see Luckenbill 1979.) Of course, this position has to do with the poststructuralist abandonment or "decentring" of the subject that it inherits unquestioningly from structuralism. I say "unquestioningly" since although poststructuralists of all shades have been heavily critical of almost the whole legacy of structuralist thought, the question of the position of the subject and agency in poststructuralist theory has been the glaring exception to this rule.

Since the poststructuralist movement was developed, among other things, to rid critical social analysis of the severe limitations imposed by various versions of structuralism (including structural Marxism) it is indeed very surprising that the abandonment of the subject (which includes humanism and a general concern with intentional human agency) was retained as a viable premise of the new body of poststructuralist theory. I say this since one of the most obvious weaknesses of poststructuralist thought is its inability to deal with the subject and agency, especially as they are portrayed in humanist schools of thought such as symbolic interactionism and phenomenology. While some writers have grudgingly acknowledged the limitations of poststructuralism in this respect (see Barret 1991) there is very little in the way of progress on this issue. It may be that the poststructuralist enterprise is inherently limited in the sense that it is incapable of making a conceptual and epistemological leap in this regard. Certainly this would follow from its commitment to a form of social analysis that abandons the dualism entailed in the agency–structure or macro–micro distinctions. All this is directly applicable to Foucault's work in so far as his notion of a synthetic unity of power-discourse (knowledge)–practice is pitched at a level somewhere between structuralism and systems theory on the one hand, and humanist theories of the subject on the other.

However, I would argue that the only way forward, as Habermas has shown with his attachment to a systems perspective, is to attempt some *rapprochement* with genuinely humanist strands of social thought exemplified in the work of G. H. Mead and other symbolic interactionists including Blumer and Goffman – although I would argue that Goffman's work cannot be so easily pigeon-holed. With respect to the question of power therefore, Foucault's approach is inadequate in so far as it rejects the idea of a subject partly independent of social construction in discourse and the associated idea that intentions and agency have decisive consequences for social processes. From the point of view of the framework that I am elaborating, I see no real reason why the Foucauldian conception of power as a network of shifting alliances, strategies and tactics should not exist alongside conceptions that emphasize the exercise of power by human agents and the notion that there are subjective aspects of power that they possess.

This is possible within the terms of domain theory since, like Habermas's work, it is not hampered by a dogmatic exclusion of the possibilities that dualism holds for social analysis. Indeed as I mentioned in Chapter 3, the theory of domains actually holds to an even more complex and manifold ontology (in the form of the domains) than is implied in simple dualism.

In particular there has to be room in a comprehensive understanding of power for the idea that the domain of self-identity and psychobiography is one in which various dimensions of power are located. Clearly certain people are "powerful" in a variety of ways, for example, in the sense of having physical power or possessing persuasive or dominant personalities or as some aspect of their personal style. Also charismatic qualities are based on the unique personality and physical attributes of a person and may lead to the acquisition of authority and leadership over others. Weber (1964) has described the characteristics of charismatic authority as the foundation for forms of social domination and in this respect we can clearly discern the overlap between personally possessed powers and their connection with social settings and contexts. Thus the importance of personal powers for an understanding of power in the social arena should not be underestimated in the way that is implied by Foucauldian or poststructuralist analyses in general.

Apart from its inscription in self-identities and personalities, power is exercised and individualized in a slightly different manner – as a result of its implication in social agency in a more general sense. As Giddens (1984) has noted, to be a social agent requires not only that a person has objectives and intentions that lock him or her into a social world of reciprocal ties and obligations, but also that the person is capable of "making a difference" in that world. That is, to be a social agent is to be someone who possesses a "transformative" capacity. In Giddens's terms, this ability to transform the social environment or to make a difference is absolutely central to his larger vision of social analysis that is avowedly against objectivist approaches in all guises (structuralism, poststructuralism, functionalism). For Giddens, any approach that draws upon the basic assumptions of objectivism is also committed to the false doctrine of determinism – the idea that human behaviour is simply the result of the influence of social structures or systems that operate independently of the intentions and activities of people. For Giddens this also involves an illicit reification since it assumes that social phenomena have a life of their own beyond the grasp of the transformative and productive activities of human beings.

For these reasons Giddens's general conception of social analysis involves a radical humanist element in which all social phenomena must be understood as inherently and indissolubly tied to human reasons and motivations. Unfortunately Giddens's approach requires an absolute break with any form of objectivism and any sense of the independent properties of system or structural phenomena. To a certain extent it is possible to go along with Giddens's conception of agency as transformative capacity as an implied critique of Foucault (as well as structuralist and other poststructuralist positions). However, Giddens's overall vision of social analysis eliminates an equally important dimension that is present in Foucault's work – that is the interlinking between discourse, power and practice at an objective level beyond people's intentionalities, reasons and motivations. It is also untenable to accept Giddens's rejection of any form of systems theory (as it appears, for example, in Habermas's work) since this is based on the mistaken assumption that objectivism is a necessarily extreme doctrine without any redeeming features, whereas domain theory establishes links with a moderate objectivism and does not lead to the errors associated with the extreme version.

Therefore I want to retain the notion of human agency as involving transformative capacity without adopting the rest of the assumptions of structuration theory (or any other humanist approach that rejects dualism and objectivism out-of-hand, such as symbolic interactionism and phenomenology – see Layder 1994). This is absolutely central to understanding the manner in which power operates in the realm of situated activity. It is also relevant to an understanding of how more structural or systemic forms of power (as an aspect of contextual resources) connect with social activity. In short, the notion of power as a feature of human social agency is essential to an appreciation of the reciprocal links between activity and its institutional, systemic or macro-structural contexts as they are reflected in the processes of social production and reproduction (see Ch. 5). However, in this respect we must be careful not to repeat Giddens's tendency to treat transformative capacity as a sort of generic aspect of human agency. This is because such capacities vary in terms of two important dimensions.

First, an individual's ability to "make a difference" varies according to personality and identity attributes. For example, if someone is too shy to intervene in a situation, that person can hardly be said to be exhibiting a strong transformative impulse or capability. Conversely, if someone exudes a surplus amount of confidence, that person may make more of a difference as a result. Secondly, transformative capacity is conditioned by system (or social-structural) factors that constrain the power resources that individuals have at their disposal. Thus for example, oppressed or sub-ordinate groups are by definition excluded from positions of power and denied access to resources (including psychological skills) and this clearly impinges on their ability to "make a difference" in the first place – both in terms of sheer intensity of response and in terms of the locations in which such capacities are allowed expression. It has been argued, for example, that the extent of women's ability to "make a difference" is significantly influenced by the subordinating effects of patriarchal power in society in general (Smith 1988, Wolf 1993). Similar arguments can be marshalled in order to understand the position and experiences of other subordinated groups such as those of a class or "racialized" nature. Giddens's rather open-ended assertion that the ability to make a difference is a defining fea-ture of social agency does not properly incorporate these "prior" condi-tioning features.

Power: continuous or discontinuous?

One of the assertions that Foucault makes about the operation of power in modernity is that it is continuous in nature. By this Foucault is drawing attention to the fact that monarchical or sovereign forms of power operate on an intermittent basis, for example, where a feudal lord extracts the products of labour of those working on his land or where a public torture is undertaken to demonstrate and affirm the powers of the monarch. By contrast Foucault points out that disciplinary and bio-power are continu-ous in their operation and effects. Individuals who are subjected to them can never step outside the net of power and its influence. In this sense power is everywhere (as is resistance to it) so that people's identities and subjectivities are necessarily constructed in its image and within the parameters of the discourses (knowledges) that underpin it.

The operation of bio-power most clearly and obviously conforms to this model of functioning in so far as it refers to, and influences, whole masses and populations of people. There are no visible or obvious boundaries to its scope of influence or its spheres of operation. On the other hand, in so far as disciplinary power is understood to be a feature of particular organi-zational locations such as hospitals, factories, barracks and so on, then it does not "automatically" conform to the idea of continuous operation except *within* the boundaries of the organizational location. However, if considered in the wider context of Foucault's view of the development of disciplinary power at the societal level, then it is clear, as Honneth (1993) has pointed out, that he is dealing with the general augmentation of bourgeois power and that "systematic" links between locations and sites and positions of power have to be taken into account. Honneth even goes on to argue that Foucault reverts to a systems view of power from a previously "strategic" conception in which there are shifting networks, in an effort to explain stable forms of domination. For present purposes, whether or not this is a fair interpretation of the movement of Foucault's work is neither here nor there. Honneth's observation is interesting in that it highlights some of the problems faced by a purely discursive conception of power that attempts to eschew any residue of structural analysis. Principally such a conception runs into manifest difficulties when faced with the problem of explaining durable forms of domination.

It would seem that the presupposition of the continuous nature of the operation of power and its effects needs to be approached with a certain amount of caution. There are a number of senses that can be distinguished when we speak of continuity in relation to power. First, there is a very general sense – that I would want to uphold – in which power operates "continuously". This has to do with the ubiquitousness or the "everywhereness" of power that Foucault expresses as the inability of individuals to step outside the net-like grip of power. However, a crucial difference in my own rendering of this principle lies in the idea that although power spreads itself everywhere in society, the form and nature of this power is not necessarily the same. Thus power as an aspect of subjectivity is substantially different from (although related to, and overlapping with) power as transformative capacity or power as a system property (such as a resource allocation or distribution) or even power as an aspect of the everchanging balance of power in face-to-face conduct. In this sense although there is a continuous spread of the operation of power, there are also levels of discontinuity in terms of the processes and effects of power in relation to different social domains.

There is another sense of continuity implied in Foucault's view with which I would be less inclined to agree on any interpretation, and that is the idea that the different organizational locations of disciplinary power are somehow connected with each other in such a way as to allow for a concerted (and thus continuous) flow of power effects. This idea presupposes far too much interrelatedness of the locations and sites of power than can be supported by empirical evidence. Thus we cannot assume some kind of concertedness or unifying of the influences exerted through the different locations of disciplinary power. This is so even between the organizations that Foucault cites as examples – schools, the military, monasteries, factories and so on. There is far more interruption and division between such organizations in terms of the social functions they serve and their relation to other centres and positions of power than there is "continuity" – even if we concede that there is a similarity in the disciplinary nature of the powers that they contain within them. In fact, the idea that there is a level of continuity of the operation of power as a result of the "systematicity" of the relations between sites of disciplinary power is rather at odds with the poststructuralist enterprise in its avowed attempt to move away from essentialist or reductionist ideas about social structures or social totalities and their organizing principles. As I have pointed out, bio-power does not raise this problem since although it focuses on whole populations, its specific target is the individual body, and thus no further sense or level of social organization is brought into the picture. Although disciplinary power also targets the body it does so under the auspices of a structured organizational context and this then begs the question of how, and to what extent, it is related to other aspects of societal organization. This issue relates to other aspects of Foucault's move away from Marxism and structuralism, which I deal with below.

I have said that even if we refer to the organizational examples that Foucault uses we cannot assume some kind of concertedness or interrelation between them, but this is even more true of examples of settings to which Foucault pays scant or no attention. This particularly relates to areas of "everyday life" in modernity such as shopping, walking on city streets, going to restaurants, participating in sporting events and so on. Other settings and areas of "private" or personal relationships, such as the family or romantic love, receive little attention from Foucault (even in his three-volume work on the history of sexuality), despite the indisputable fact that these areas and settings of activity play such a monumental role in modern life. If we consider the linkages between such areas from the point of view of the spatially and temporally patterned involvements of individuals, we can assume nothing like a sense of continuity or evenness of the effects and influence of power. Of course, from a poststructuralist point of view such a "humanist" perspective would accede too much in the way of deferral to the subject and the powers of individual human agency. Obvious grave injuries to theoretical adequacy are the price to be paid for such (unnecessary) inflexibility.

There is yet another sense in which Foucault's concern with continuity can be identified in his reference to the operation of power (Foucault 1980:78–108), and I would again want to uphold this meaning as long as we are clear about its specific implications. This has to do with general processes of social reproduction. In so far as power is implicated in social reproduction and if social reproduction is, necessarily, a continuous process – in that it is an integral aspect of all social activity – then sure enough there is an element of continuity in the operation of power. However, Foucault's whole analysis is couched exclusively in terms of social reproduction (mainly because he ignores the autonomy of human agency) and thus has little or nothing to say about social production and the creativity of face-to-face conduct. However, although social reproduction is an essential feature of social practices it is quite false to assume, as Foucault does, that this represents the whole picture as far as social practices are concerned, or that social reproduction itself is an even and uniform process. I shall deal with social production and reproduction in some detail in Chapter 5, although here it needs to be noted that both processes have to be understood as perpetually partial, incomplete and "in question". In this sense although the process of social reproduction is a continuous aspect of activity, *in itself*, it is not something that is necessarily smooth, even and complete, and in certain circumstances it may even be subject to interruption, disjuncture and punctuation. All in all then, the idea of power as a continuous process has to be treated with caution. In some respects it tells us something important about the nature of social power but in others it is quite misleading – especially since Foucault does not distinguish between the different senses of continuity that I have identified.

Power as dispersed and plural

Part of Foucault's attempt to move beyond both Marxism and structuralism involves the insistence that power has to be understood as a dispersed, fragmented and plural phenomenon rather than as emanating from a central source or location. Among other things this is clearly a critical response to structural-Marxism whereby social relations are understood as totalities or wholes that are governed by some overriding and determining principle. As such the social whole is thought to be internally consistent with the determining principle and subjects everyone within it, to its influence and effects. The idea that power is dispersed within society rather than existing in the form of a monolithic block or central source allows Foucault to distance himself from both this particular structuralist position as well as that of Marxism in general. A common thread here is the idea of a totalizing theory that tries to explain everything in terms of a unified and comprehensive set of concepts.

Marxism envisages domination as emanating from the capitalist mode of production viewed as an all-embracing unity that provides the basis for explaining all conflicts and power struggles. However, since the 1960s Marxists themselves had become aware of the limitations of Marxism in understanding domination outside the factory and workplace environment as it was experienced by groups such as women, children and students (Poster 1984). Foucault gave expression to this inadequacy in Marxism by suggesting that technologies of power are not located in some central or "core" agency such as the state or government, but on the contrary, exist at multiple points throughout the social body. In this manner the forms of power and domination experienced by such groups as gays, women, prisoners, mental patients or ethnic minorities cannot be explained by or "reduced to" single-cause factors such as the mode of production.

In this respect Foucault is concerned with an "ascending" analysis of power rather than a descending one in that he is interested in the form of its dispersal in time and space. For Foucault analysis should "be concerned with power at its extremities, in its ultimate destinations, with those points where it becomes capillary, that is in its more regional and local forms" (Foucault 1980: 96). This localization also implies an interest in groups that had hitherto been considered peripheral or marginal in importance in modern society (such as gays or prisoners). This reverses the traditional Marxist "descending" analysis of power that views it as flowing downwards from the state or centrally from the economy and ownership of the means of production. As Foucault says, he is interested in the capillary form of power and its circulation at all levels of society right down into the micro-practices of everyday life (see Fraser 1989).

Now I think this claim is somewhat overstated because although, in principle, Foucault clearly wants to incorporate the analysis of "everyday practices", he evinces considerable difficulty in couching his analysis in terms of every day life especially as it is expressed in the lived experiences of real individuals. As I pointed out in relation to the analysis of the settings of disciplinary power and bio-power, Foucault misses out the more mundane leisure-time activities like going to pubs, clubs and theatres and various other forms of socializing such as inviting others round to dinner, romantic attachments, friendships, popular culture and so on – a myriad of factors that are strangely missing from his analytic "vision" of everyday life. In this respect it could be said that his analysis of everyday practices starts out from a point fairly high up on his ascending analysis. Expressed otherwise, his analysis is stuck at a somewhat elevated level of understanding of "everyday practices" rather than linked with a more down-to-earth conception of everyday life. In fact Foucault's theoretical and epistemological commitments lead him to suppose that everyday practices are about the reproduced features of social life and hence prevent him from grasping that they are in good measure about the emergent and interpersonal dynamics of situated conduct. In Foucault's scheme of things there is no recognition or discernment of what Goffman refers to as the "interaction order" and which I believe has such a pivotal role to play in any account of everyday life and social practices.

However, not withstanding this rather crucial problem let us return for the moment to Foucault's insistence on the dispersion of power and its congregation at multiple centres or sites. As we have already noted there is a tension between the idea of power as something that circulates in a chain-like manner (and is mobilized in a strategic sense), and that in modernity the number of linkages and contacts between centres of power are increased. This is because this latter idea seems to endorse a "systemic" conception rather than one of a shifting network of mobile force-fields. None the less I think there is every reason to go along with Foucault's dispersed and multi-centred view of power. In this respect a poststructuralist vision of social relations certainly has an interesting point to make. However, Foucault refrains from taking the question of linkages any further in the theoretical and empirical sense of suggesting why or how any potential linkages between centres of power might occur.

From the point of view of domain theory I would agree that we should steer clear of single-cause or unifying principles (economic reductionism and so on) in any absolute or fixed manner. To a limited extent the social world must be understood as aggregations of organizations, institutions and various practices that obey no internal logic of form or consistency. However, to adopt the opposite extreme and suggest that all the elements are entirely contingent (Hirst 1983, Laclau & Mouffe 1985, Barrett 1991) seems to court all sorts of empiricist dangers. It would seem theoretically wiser and empirically more sound to leave open the possibility for elements of both – a degree of systematicity in conjunction with a certain amount of contingency. This applies to the position that I have hitherto been outlining, particularly in Chapter 4. In this respect I argued that to some extent the manner in which settings and locations of activity stand in relation to each other can be understood to be "unprincipled", additive and empirically contingent. This is most easily appreciated from the point of view of an individual moving between settings in a daily (or some other temporal) cycle.

However, if we switch perspective and consider the distinctions between settings in terms of the social functions they fulfil or the nature of the social positions and social relations that they aggregate, we can see that in terms of the routines of capitalist society (the circulation of capital, the operation of markets, forms of bureaucracy, for instance) certain centres and areas of activity clearly are more closely related to each other. Habermas's distinction between lifeworld and system is useful here in that he distinguishes system elements in terms of their implication in the generation and reproduction of money and power. Now although I would disagree with the idea that power is exclusively tied to system elements (see comments below) I do think there is some point in the assumption that particular settings and spheres of social life are more *directly* implicated in the generation and reproduction of markets and power. Let me be absolutely clear, this is not to suggest that the effects of system factors are completely blocked or filtered out of the interaction order (lifeworld elements), but rather that they are in Goffman's terms "loosely coupled". I am also not completely happy with Habermas's rather unrefined identification of system elements as markets and bureaucracy and this is why I prefer to speak of a distinction betweeen different kinds of settings, types of contextual resources and various fields of activity. Habermas's construal of system elements is too homogeneous and uniform in this sense; it does not allow for the variations that I identify in form, function and degree of connectedness between them. Nevertheless Habermas does highlight the point that any overall conception of economic and social relations in modernity (including institutions and organizations) cannot be understood entirely in terms of contingency.

Power and ideology

I dealt fleetingly with the question of Foucault's attitude to the concept of ideology in Chapter 3 along with a discussion of the role of discourse, however, the explicit link with power needs to be made here from the point of view the theory of social domains. Foucault is very suspicious of the classical Marxist position on the question of ideology because it presupposes a unified "truth" that lies buried beneath the distortions produced by the ideology of the ruling class. Apart from moving away from an exclusive and restrictive concern with class domination in order to incorporate an interest in the diversity of power networks and centres, Foucault was influenced by Nietzsche's perspectival view of truth. That is, following Nietzsche, Foucault believes that all truths are partial and reflect the particular perspective from which they derive. Thus there can be no all-embracing truth that is disfigured by the distortions of a ruling ideology. For Foucault there are many "truths" associated with particular fields of knowledge and the perspectives that different discourses lend to them. In this respect Foucault is not interested in truth claims in themselves and whether they stand up to scrutiny, but rather in the power effects of various truth claims. For Foucault the concept of ideology seems wedded to the discovery, or unearthing of the truth behind the "false" rationalizations of ideology.

Since power for Foucault is a multiple phenomenon and associated so closely with discourses and the various truth claims they enshrine, he has no real need to uphold the Marxist idea of an ideological superstructure that rests upon the economic base of society. For Foucault discourses are not tied to the mode of production in order to achieve their effects, thus there is no need for a base-superstructure model as there is in Marxism. Now granted that there is definite merit in breaking away from some of the more restrictive and defective features of Marxism, I do not think it necessary to jettison completely the notion of ideology. The danger of Foucault's "relativizing" of truth claims is that it prevents us from asking questions about the specific functions of certain bodies of ideas (discourses) in relation to their power effects. Questions such as "in what way does a specific discourse achieve its effects?" and "is it different from other discourses in this respect?" While there is also some advantage in viewing discourses in a plural sense as part of a diverse cultural array, there is a danger that we homogenize their influence as a generic "power effect" of truth claims.

Both these dangers can be averted and the original core concerns of ideology may be restored by retaining the concept of ideology itself, although stripped of the crude Marxian baggage that Foucault identifies. Ideology must refer to the manner in which power relations are facilitated and stabilized through forms of rationalization and mystification. In this respect the concept of ideology should be reserved for a special form of discourse that is explicitly concerned with the rationalization of domination and control and not simply with producing power effects as Foucault defines them (normalizing conduct, disciplining bodies, creating subjectivities and so on). In this manner one can still retain Foucault's emphasis on the perspectival nature of truth claims as they are inscribed in discourses without abandoning the specific notion of ideological discourse as centrally concerned with the rationalization of power and control. Further, one has to understand ideologies as ranged along a continuum of greater and lesser degrees of sophistication and varying degrees of intended scope. In this respect the cruder but more far-reaching political versions rely on substantial "economies of truth" such as facist and racist ideologies, while the more sophisticated variants (such as those associated with professional and occupational groups) involve narrower areas of application and more "benign" attempts to disguise the nature of their control over client groups.

Giddens on power

Let me now shift focus and consider some of Giddens's views on power. As I have already indicated one of the most significant differences from Foucault resides in Giddens's view of the inherent tie between power and human agency that is summarized in his notion of "transformative capacity". I have also said that it is of paramount importance that some sense of the powers of individual agents must be retained in order to understand the multiform nature of power as it relates to different domains. This means rejecting Foucauldian and poststructuralist views on the abandonment of the subject (although at the same time retaining some sense of the discursive construction of subjectivity). However, in endorsing Giddens's appreciation of the importance of the "active subject" in social analysis, we must be careful not to import some of the more unnecessary and debilitating features of Giddens's theory of structuration. In this respect, I believe that Giddens overstresses the importance of action and agency in the understanding of power and power relations and consequently underemphasizes the nature and role of systemic (or structural) power and its influence on activity – particularly the role of "constraints". Conversely, Giddens's view of power as transformative capacity tends to leave out of the account some of the subjective dimensions that play a significant part in social activity. Moreover Giddens's refusal to acknowledge the partly independent nature of what Goffman terms the "interaction order" means that he does not properly address the issue of power in this area. As a result, Giddens's approach compresses and ultimately dissolves various dimensions and characteristics of situated power into the notion of transformative capacity and thus they are lost to analysis.

164

The crux of the issue lies in Giddens's outright dismissal of objectivism and dualism in social analysis. The fact that he sees no redeeming features whatsoever in these means that Giddens is unable to co-opt whatever useful features they possess and thus he becomes committed to a mode of analysis that is unnecessarily constricted (both epistemologically and ontologically). I would argue, however, that there is sufficient elasticity and flexibility built into the terms of structuration theory for these inadequacies to be glossed over (Layder 1994). Part of the problem here is how we define objectivism and dualism and thus what we take them to imply in social analysis in general. In essence Giddens understands dualism in a traditional philosophical sense as implying separation and opposition between two entities or sets of ideas. In terms of social analysis on this definition, dualism involves a separation or gulf (a standing apart) between social orders (or domains) that is untenable. For example in this respect agency and structure would not interrelate in a way that they obviously do, and must. Now if this were the only meaning that could be given to dualism then sure enough such a position would be inadequate for a thoroughgoing understanding of the relation between different social domains.

However, dualism does not necessarily mean separation and opposition especially with regard to understanding the connections between different social orders. It simply means that activity and social context are distinct but interlocking domains and that their partly independent characteristics must be understood as having an important influence on their mutual implication and modes of operation. Giddens's approach does not allow for this possibility and thus he prefers to talk about the *duality of structure* in which two orders are reduced to one, and which is then said to have a dual nature. But by following a theoretical strategy that attempts to combine and fuse what are, in fact, two distinct domains in their own right, one loses analytic grip on the independent characteristics that each possesses. In a very positive sense dualism allows us to distinguish between distinct orders, domains or levels of society (or social reality) and to assess their interrelations and mutual impact (Archer 1995). As is consistent with the theory of social domains my own position goes beyond a simple dualism in the sense that it distinguishes between *several* interrelated orders. The notion of power therefore has to be understood as both multi-form and as a series of variably overlapping effects and influences.

The main problem for Giddens in recognizing a partly independent "system" (or macro-structural) realm of power is associated with his rejection of objectivism. Thus he assumes that all forms of objectivism presuppose that actors' reasons and motivations are of no account (or are at least minimized) in understanding social activity. Now while certain versions of functionalism and structuralism are guilty of this error there is no reason to think that all approaches that draw upon objectivist elements are destined to follow the same path. The theory of social domains by contrast underscores the idea that there is a social system realm (otherwise and variously termed "macro", "structural", "institutional") that is partly, but only partly, independent of actors' reasons and motivations. However, it also suggests that people's reasons and motivations are closely bound-up and implicated in these structural or institutional forms. In this sense there is an "external" dimension to social power (as a distributive aspect of resources or as institutionally "contained") as well as an "internal" subjective or psychological dimension (see Lukes 1977, Crespi 1992).

Since Giddens rejects the idea of an external world via his rejection of objectivism, he is unable fully to incorporate theoretically these aspects of social life. On the one hand his insistence that power is logically and intrinsically tied to agency (Giddens 1979: 92, 1985: 9) means that he cannot fully conceptualize power as a partly independent system property. On the other hand, his view that power is defined in terms of a socially conditioned transformative capacity neglects the more subjective and situated aspects of power. There is a sense in which Giddens's analysis of power as transformative activity reduces the diversity of moments and elements of social reality into a single unifying principle – and the effect of this is quite opposite to that which Giddens intends. Instead of freeing social analysis from the (assumed) limitations of dualism and objectivism, structuration theory rather limits the possibilities for social analysis by positing a one-dimensional view of social reality. This is not to say, of course, that structuration theory has nothing to offer, as I have already pointed out with regard to the important role that human agency plays in social analysis. Similarly Giddens's discussion of what he terms the "dialectic of control" is a useful counterpoint to views of power that view it simply as a top-down phenomenon emanating from a single source.

The dialectic of control

This principle follows on from Giddens's idea that to be a human agent involves the ability to make a difference in the world by altering one's social circumstances – that is, to have power. Giddens adopts a relational view of power and suggests that power relations are never "zero-sum" affairs where one party is thought to have all the power while the person or group who is subjected to it has none at all. Subordinates always have some level of power available to them. As Giddens notes:

> . . . actors in subordinate positions are never wholly dependent, and are often very adept at converting whatever resources they possess into some degree of control over the conditions of reproduction of the system. In all social systems there is a dialectic of control, such that there are normally continually shifting balances of resources, altering the overall distribution of power. (Giddens 1984: 32)

Giddens gives the example of prisoners using "dirty protests" or hunger strikes in order to put pressure on the authorities. Clearly Giddens is right to suggest that no matter how meagre a subordinate's resources may be, there will always be some that allow them to carve out small areas of autonomy and thus to alter the balance of power in particular relationships. This applies not only to relationships between individuals but also to the relative position of social groups from a historical perspective – Giddens (1982) offers the example of the development of worker rights through forms of protest, collective action and the evolution of citizenship rights.

This is a useful idea and allows us to chart the continual shifting in balances of power within relationships as both parties manipulate resources. However, it is not just a matter of appreciating the fact that the dialectic of control operates at different levels. Something that Giddens does not emphasize is the degree to which alterations in the balance of power between parties to a power relationship may be largely determined in advance by more enveloping dialectics of control. In particular here I am referring to the notion of power as a social system (or macro-structural) resource and the fact that the relations of control that stem from it, exert a partly independent effect on the dialectic of control of actors in face-to-face conduct. Giddens certainly envisages what are conventionally referred to as forms of domination and what he calls the "institutional mediation" of power. He also recognizes that the analysis of power has to to do with investigating "relations of autonomy and dependence between actors or collectivities of actors" (1979, 1985). However, since Giddens is very keen to distance himself from "objectivist" schools of thought he does not view these relations of autonomy and dependence as aspects of a system partly independent of, but exerting some influence on, social activity and people's capacities – in this case the exercise of power. In this sense structuration theory does not ask questions about whether or to what extent relations of autonomy and dependence between actors or collectivities are pre-structured via the historically emergent conditions that set the institutional parameters (including current configurations of power) of societies as social systems.

The "dialectic of control" seems to presuppose a rather fluid give and take between actors or groups in terms of what immediate resources they have to manipulate, and therefore alter, the balance of power between them. Such a position does not seem to entertain the possibility that the terms of the dialectic may be formed in advance by the historically emergent conditions under which it operates. That is, although *some* resources may be available to subordinate groups or individuals, many other resources may not be accessible because of the dominant party's prior command over and ability to restrict access to such resources. Thus prisoners may be able to engage in dirty protests or hunger strikes and this may slightly alter the balance of power with the authorities, but in themselves these forms of protest are not enough to *change or transform* the basis of the control or domination. Such matters are dependent upon prior position within the system and command and access to other resources (such as the force of law and the legitimate use of the means of violence).

Similarly, the example of theatrical agents (or "personal managers" as they like to be known) and their actor clients in the acting profession in the UK (Layder 1984, 1993) illustrates the point that the dialectic of control between individuals or groups is always conditioned by a prior distribution of power. For instance relationships between particular actors and particular personal managers are characterized by a dialectic of control in that at different phases of the actor's career a different power balance will obtain between them. Typically at the start of a career an actor will be in a subordinate position to the manager, but if the actor eventually becomes very successful, a "star" even, then the position may be reversed with the personal manager being "eased" into a more lowly position. The exact level of power that actors have *vis-à-vis* their manager will also be dependent on the position of the latter relative to other managers and agents (since there is a strongly defined hierarchy among them). Nevertheless we can see that according to variations in market demand for the actor and the prestige of the manager, the balance of power between them may continually shift accordingly.

However, if we scrutinize the power positions of personal managers (and agents) *as a professional group* in relation to actors' as *a client group* we have to reassess the control relationship between them. In this respect the relationship of control does not conform to the model of a continually shifting balance of power in the same manner as it is worked out at face-to-face level. The level of control that personal managers exert over actors' careers has to be traced over a long period of time and is dependent upon long-term social changes and shifts in the mobilization of resources. Such things as the actors' trade union's attempt to secure a minimum wage, the ability of personal managers to impose a code of ethics on their membership, the open-market craft-like nature of the occupation and the career and so on, have to be taken into consideration. Such long-term changes, struggles, conflicts and the shifting mobilization of resources they entail have very different connotations as compared with face-to-face relations between individuals – and I think the same considerations apply to Giddens's example of the development of worker rights.

In this respect we are dealing with an issue of group access to resources and group possession of resources. This, I believe, takes the problem out of the orbit of an exclusive tie between power and agency and brings into the account the influence of system (or structural factors). In this sense we have to understand power as a property of structures and systems and not, as Giddens insists, as exclusively (and logically) tied to agency, the exercise of power, or the deployment of resources. The two "levels" of control relations are strictly incomparable and thus cannot be subsumed under the same rubric of the "dialectic of control". The same can be argued I believe for the example of the position of women in society. At a system or structural level, patriarchal domination is based on access to positions and resources of power for women as a group compared with men and this influences the face-to-face level, but individual power relations between men and women cannot be understood simply as a mirror image of the systemic aspects of patriarchal domination.

Therefore in relation to the nature and operation of power we have to question Giddens's assertion that "resources do not 'automatically' enter in to the reproduction of social systems, but operate only in so far as they are drawn upon by contextually located actors in the conduct of their day-to-day lives" (1985: 8). Here we can appreciate in full the difference between Giddens's notion of "system" and the one that I am employing here. For Giddens, "social systems only exist in so far as they are continually created and recreated in every encounter, as the active accomplishment of human subjects" (1977 : 118). This makes his conception of system very different from traditional usages (particularly as employed by Parsons and

Habermas) that endeavour to indicate a level of independence from situated activity. My own usage (drawing particularly from Habermas – see Chapter 3) underscores this emphasis but does not do so at the expense of a concern with human agency and its close connection with the reproduction of system features. Part of the definition of system therefore involves the idea that it is not *exclusively* tied to action and agency – people's reasons and motivations. That is, in itself it is not identical with activity (although it is a human product created out of, and susceptible to change through, transformative activity). As I pointed out in Chapter 3, systems represent the historically formed standing conditions of society as an ongoing concern that confront human beings in their daily lives. As such these conditions act as constraints on their activities but at the same time they are a fund of resources that also enable people to make things happen in the social world.

Unlike in Giddens's formulation, the concept of system that I employ allows us to say that while *one way* in which resources may enter into the reproduction of social systems is by being drawn upon by actors in their day-to-day conduct, this is *not the only way* that system reproduction occurs. In this respect domination and general relations of power and control can also operate through forms of possession and "closure" of access to resources. It is important to stress that the resources upon which domination and control are based may be reproduced in a number of ways. First, reproduction of power and domination may occur as a consequence of actors drawing upon resources in the exercise of power, or by being denied the use of certain resources. Secondly, reproduction may occur through forms of possession and closure (or "ring-fencing") of resources. This type of reproduction is important since it does not necessarily involve action – although it definitely has implications for future behaviour in the sense that possession and closure will pre-empt certain courses of action for some groups and individuals or may even encourage inaction.

For example the very possession of information about job opportunities and control of access to contact networks provides the resource basis for the power of personal managers over actors as a group. Since access to such information, contacts and opportunities is restricted, actors themselves cannot readily draw upon them as resources independently of intermediaries such as agents and personal managers. This is what entices actors into their orbit and persuades them to part with a percentage of their fee for a job acquired through the agent or manager. It is the continuing existence of these conditions (possession of, and restricted access to, resources) – rather than any activity or exercise of power as such – that underpins and reproduces the asymmetrical form of their power relations with actors. This principle not only applies to subordinate groups. The dominion of powerful groupings is often buttressed by their reluctance to use certain resources as sanctions to secure the compliance of subordinates. In fact it is the possession of the resources upon which sanctions are based that secures compliance because it is the *threat* of their use, rather than their actual use, which is most effective in securing such an outcome. Thus an employer's threat of "the sack" is a potent means of averting strikes. Also as Weber has pointed out it is the possession of the means of violence that is an important foundation of state power. Too frequent deployment of the means of violence as a way of maintaining the status quo is more likely to result in a questioning of the legitimacy of the power structure and to lead to the destabilization of state power. In a similar way domination is not inherently tied to the use of various resources.

In this respect domination does not necessarily express the *behavioural (or action) dimension* of control over others, it expresses the prior relations that groups or individuals have with each other according to their position in relation to some scarce resource. Domination is not necessarily or simply the implementation of control through the activities of the powerful. Domination expresses the power that one group or individual has over another by virtue of their possession of resources and their ability to defend and stabilize this position (through forms of closure and restrictions of access as well as through ideological means, such as the engineering of consent). Configurations of power that, like this, have been established over time (typically as the result of conflict and struggle), *define* levels of autonomy and dependence between groupings and individuals in the present. Thus they define in advance much of the scope, range and intensity of possible behaviour for subordinates and superiors alike. In this respect power exists in a structural or systemic form as well as in activities, human agency or the exercise of power. In opposition to Giddens then, we must conclude that power is inherently and logically tied to system elements as much as it is to the transformative capacities of human agents. The relation between the two different forms of power is complex involving variable levels of mutual influence and intertwining.

Habermas and systemic power

Having argued for the absolute necessity of distinguishing power as a system element or property from power as an effect of agency and activity, let me elaborate a little further in the context of a discussion of Habermas's view of power. Although I would endorse Habermas's notion of system-steering media in the guise of money and power (particularly as they are reflected in markets and bureaucracy), I do not want to follow his arguments completely. As I pointed out in Chapter 3 Habermas's distinction between system and lifeworld has some unfortunate implications. The most important of these is the idea that the two spheres are cleanly separated from each other. I have made it clear that while it is possible to speak of the different properties of systems and lifeworlds, the two spheres also intermingle, coalesce and co-exist in various states of tension or harmony. Always, however, they mutually influence each other. In this respect we must reject Habermas's tendency to see the lifeworld of social interaction as a power-free zone, while conversely the system elements cannot be conceptualized as entirely lacking in moral regulation and forms of agreement born out of communicative action.

None the less some of Habermas's views on the way in which system elements have reclaimed and "colonized" parts of the lifeworld are extremely important. Habermas argues that over many years of societal evolution, system elements are gradually differentiated out of, and uncoupled from, the everyday lifeworld and have become independent specialized sub-areas of society (such as the economy, markets, government and bureaucracy, and so on). Power and money come to play such a dominant role in modern societies because they reduce the need for mechanisms of social integration based on shared agreements, consensus and moral imperatives. Money and power provide means of co-ordinating behaviour behind people's backs through the operation of markets and bureaucracies that short-cut the need for agreements based on linguistic (face-to-face) communication. This means that motivations of self-interest tend to hold sway in these areas rather than those based on judgements about sincerity, rightness or appropriateness in the circumstances. Thus also these areas become neutralized in terms of moral or normative standards. Instrumental motives and strategies take the place of attempts at understanding each other and reaching agreements in terms of notions of rightness, justice or fairness. Habermas argues that having uncoupled themselves from the lifeworld, the system elements re-enter and colonize it in the same manner as colonial overlords, displacing and intruding into areas of the lifeworld that were formerly "free" of them (at least in relative terms) or that were once "better defended" from the incursions of money and power (such as the private domain of personal relationships and mental health – see comments below).

In one sense Habermas is here arguing that modernity is characterized by the intrusion of system elements into the lifeworld and thus power takes root in the lifeworld via the re-colonization by system elements. On this argument power begins to play an important role within everyday life and is not simply corralled within the system domain. However, there are two senses in which Habermas's view of power does not allow him to view it as a "natural" part of everyday life. First, he understands power entirely in systemic terms (as an aspect of markets and bureaucracy). Power is not viewed as an intrinsic feature of individuals and their psychological make-up, nor is it an emergent from the give and take of social encounters. For Habermas, power exists in one form – as a system steering property. Secondly, Habermas conceives of the existence of power in the lifeworld in entirely "pathological" terms as part of the domination of the capitalist system and its encroachment on ever more areas of everyday life. In this sense it is viewed as an "impurity" of the lifeworld that must be expunged. In fact this is the focus of the "new political movements" of the late twentieth century, the existence of which requires us to rethink Marx's notion of a labour-driven politics of dissent centring on class conflict and struggles over the distribution of goods and services. The new political movements – ecological groups, the peace and women's movements, gay rights, and so on – are concerned with reclaiming the "quality of life" that has been severely compromised by the process of colonization.

Of course, to say that Habermas finds no room for the existence of "natural" forms of power in the lifeworld is not to say that there is no substance in his view of the pathological consequences of the colonization of the lifeworld in late modernity. Rather it is simply to point out that there is space for both views if one expands one's understanding of modern forms of power. In fact, from the point of view of a critical theory of society, the notion of the pathological consequences of the spread of system elements explains a good deal about the nature of modernity and the psychological costs of the infiltration of system elements into the heartland of the lifeworld. In this sense, if we reject Habermas's tendency to view the lifeworld as naturally "pristine" and unaffected by system elements or power of any sort, there is still a substantial core of his analysis which

173

throws light on the nature of capitalism in late modernity.

This core lies in the observation that late modernity has witnessed an "overloading" of the lifeworld by system elements and has had the effect of disfiguring and distorting the nature of social relationships. This in turn has had a knock-on effect in terms of the nature of the psychological demands made on people in their daily work and personal lives. Smail's (1993: 56–159) brilliant analysis of the effects of the business enterprise culture of the 1980s in the UK on the mental health of those most caught up in the psychological demands made by this market-lead culture is a telling example of the empirical implications of Habermas's colonization thesis. From the point of view of the theory of social domains such an analysis provides an essential insight into the processes by which system elements become inscribed in the principal domains of everyday life – social settings, situated activity and individual psychobiographies.

Power as multi-form and interlocking

The theory of social domains insists that power is a basic, ever-present feature of social reality and that it is ubiquitous. Power, therefore, is just as much a part of face-to-face conduct and individual identity (and personality) as it is a feature of the operation of markets and bureaucracies. In this sense, the theory of social domains tends to accord more with Foucault's view of the omnipresence of power – that it is found everywhere right "down" into the finest capillaries of society – with the important proviso that power has to be understood as a multi-form phenomenon rather than the ontological unity that Foucault presupposes. Similarly, while Giddens's notion of power as transformative capacity has an advantage over Habermas's in that it fully appreciates its groundedness in everyday social interaction, it tends to reduce the variegated nature of power to a single unifying principle – in this case transformative capacity. On the other hand, Habermas, as I have said, tends to see power as exclusively tied to the steering capacity of societies (the political and economic principles of capitalism and the markets and bureaucracies that serve them). In this respect he views power as associated with the overall relations of domination in society (the system level) rather than as part of the give and take of everyday encounters and the capacities of individuals.

None of these authors views power as a multi-form phenomenon, they all see it (in vastly different ways of course) as associated with particular levels of application in society and as having an intrinsic, unified nature. Part of the problem here is that the theoretical commitments of the authors often preclude various possibilities in this respect. For example Giddens's humanism (and anti-objectivism) prevents him from understanding power as possessing properties independent of actors' reasons and motivations. Conversely, Foucault's strong aversion to humanism prevents him from embracing a notion of power as an aspect of face-to-face conduct. Habermas's commitments are the most "open" and therefore the most promising in this regard, in so far as his theory of communicative action is an attempt to combine elements of humanism and objectivism (action and systems theories). However, even though the preconditions for a more embracing conception of power exist in Habermas's work they do not seem to have "worked through" into his actual theory or analytic framework. The theory of social domains shares the open commitments implied in Habermas's aim of synthesizing aspects of action theory and systems or institutional theory (Habermas 1987: 151) but tries to develop a more embracing notion of power. Thus conceptions of power that understand it as operating according to some single principle or sphere of influence do not do justice to the diversity of types and modes of power in society. Power has to be understood as a multi-form phenomenon that varies in terms of the different social domains in which it is implicated. It is very important to emphasize that this does not mean that the different forms and modes of power are sharply or cleanly separated from each other. On the contrary they meld into each other to varying degrees in different empirical circumstances. Similarly, the perception of different mixes and combinations of influence will to some extent vary according to the particular vantage point and interests of analysts and observers.

As I have suggested in passing, a preliminary requirement for a multi-form view of power is to posit the notion of "subjective power". This is quite distinct from the notion of a discursively constituted subjectivity as found in the work of Foucault and the poststructuralists, and from the idea of the active subject as portrayed by Giddens (as well as interactionists and phenomenologists). Both of these conceptions – in their markedly different ways – posit an overly social conception of the human being. I am certainly not rejecting the substantive core of truth contained in these models but I am suggesting that they do not adequately deal with the psychological dimension of human behaviour, particularly its emotional aspects and its relation to the analysis of activity and power. Perhaps in the case of Foucault this is more readily apparent since Foucault rejects the importance of the human subject and the validity of approaches that concentrate on subjective experience and face-to-face conduct. Thus the poststructuralist vision is one in which the human being is entirely socially contructed within the available discourses. On its own this leads to a crude behaviourism whereby psychic processes are understood as the result of constant conditioning (see Honneth 1993: 189). In this sense the individual behaves simply in accord with the parameters determined by the interplay of discourse.

On the surface it would seem that Giddens's notion of the active subject embraces individual subjectivity in a more rounded sense. However, as Craib (1992) has noted, Giddens's view of the person lacks emotional depth and suggests a model of personality that seems overly enmeshed in social routines as a means of staving-off (ontological) insecurity. Although Giddens does envisage a role for the unconscious in human behaviour, it is considerably muted in terms of emotional expression in social interaction. Also his notion of transformative capacity is presented as a generalized social attribute acquired through experience and engagement with the social environment, rather than as something that is significantly conditioned by subjective factors that vary from individual to individual – such as strength of motivation, level of ambition, charisma, leadership skills and so on. All in all, the notion of the active subject in Giddens's work stresses the socially constructed dimensions of human agency to a point where one asks the question "is this an 'oversocialized' view of human beings?", rather in the way that Dennis Wrong originally asked this question of Parsons's work (Wrong 1967). In short, the question of power must be directly connected to the notion of the individual as a unique being with specific motives, personal qualities and changeable mood states.

In this sense, the notion of subjective power refers to variable capacities of specific individuals – their abilities, inclinations and ambitions, as well as their psychological abilities to express whatever powers they possess and to take on power roles. In this sense although power or "transformative capacity" may be conditioned by a person's group membership and wider social position, specific individuals will be either comfortable or uneasy about the exercise of power. For example, as Smith (1988: 66) has argued, women's lives are "organized and determined external to them" and that they have little opportunity for the exercise of mastery and control in the ordinary situations of their lives. However, it is also clear that specific women vary in terms of their psychological predisposition towards the exercise of power – regardless of the extent of power or "mastery" available to them (see Naomi Wolf (1993) for comments on women's attitudes towards power). This indeed is also the case with men, some of whom shrink from opportunities to exercise of power both in terms of a public career or in the domestic or private arena.

Although Lengermann & Niebrugge-Brantley (1992) argue primarily about the position of women and their exclusion from certain areas of social interaction, they also make a general point about social analysis with which I find myself in broad agreement. They suggest that inter-actionist sociology tends to subsume the notion of subjectivity under the micro-analysis of face-to-face interaction. In this respect they argue that the individual's interpretations should be taken into account and subjec-tivity should be treated as a distinct level in its own right. Lengerman and Niebrugge-Brantley argue that this is especially important from women's point of view since people who are treated as subordinates (as women often are), typically experience the world in very different ways from those who dominate and in terms quite different from the prevailing culturally established definitions. This is true but the point applies to *all subordinates*, not just women (and this includes men in subordinate positions). So although from a feminist point of view the issue of subjectivity may be important I think that it is crucial for the study of human beings *per se*.

The reasons for this require us to generalize and elaborate on the points made by Lengermann & Niebrugge-Brantley. First, their characterization of interactionist sociology is largely accurate. Symbolic interactionists and phenomenologists concentrate on inter-subjectivity rather than individual subjectivity. That is, they are interested exclusively in the social aspects of individual behaviour and often this is combined with a rejection of indi-vidual psychology (Mead 1967, Blumer 1969). This is an unfortunate ten-dency and some version of it can even be observed in Goffman's (1967) work as I mentioned in Chapter 2. This does mean that subjectivity as a general aspect of individuals is rather sidelined and displaced by the sup-posedly more important "social" aspects of their behaviour. The symbolic interactionist view of power underscores this deficiency by defining power exclusively in terms of the interactional processes involved in asymmetri-cal social relationships. That is, it focuses solely on the adjustive and flex-ible responses of targets and sources of power (Luckenbill 1979). The emotional or psychological demeanour of those involved is of little or no account.

Secondly, the point about women as subordinates viewing the world in ways different from dominant groups is important, but as I hinted earlier this must be understood in a much wider sense than just women. There are many subordinate groups in society that include men (such as those based on class, and underclass or "racialized" characteristics) but there are also many *individuals* who are in positions and relations of subordination sometimes quite independently of their wider group membership or structural location. To understand the basis of this individualized subordination we can utilize the notion of social setting, as I have previously defined it in conjunction with Foucault's notion of disciplinary power and Weber's (1964) view of legal-rational authority. These all indicate the way in which the reproduced social relations that define the internal structure of various organizational settings hinge around the principle of hierarchy as a mechanism of control. This applies to members at all levels of the organizational hierarchy. Thus middle-ranking members (such as managers and administrators) are differentiated from each other in authority and status terms (as in a promotional or "career" hierarchy) as much as they are from lower ranking members (shopfloor workers, manual workers, cleaners, functionaries). Edwards's (1979) research on industrial organizations in the USA suggests that the principle of bureaucratic hierarchy and control also plays an important role in distinguishing between workers themselves (in terms of pay-scales and other inducements and "career" rewards). Edwards argues that "bureaucratic control" also has the effect of disciplining the workforce and thereby producing compliant and "enthusiastic" workers.

In such hierarchically organized settings, the basis for individualized forms of subordination is increased in an exponential manner and thus it is extremely important to include them within the purview of other group (systemic or macro-structural) forms of subordination. This is not only because such individualized forms of subordination exist in tandem with the group forms, but also because the combined effects sometimes cut across each other – as in the case of white middle-class males in lowly organizational positions such as routine white-collar jobs (or conversely, black women who achieve high organizational rank against the odds). The way in which subordination is individualized within social groups such as the working class or the middle class is an important pointer to understanding the way in which this kind of power and control operates to fragment potential forms of in-group solidarity and opposition to the dominant regime (the divide and rule principle). In these cases it is important to investigate subjectivity in order to understand the way in which subordination is managed, resisted and psychologically dealt with by those subject to it. Also, however, to fully understand domination and control there is no point in restricting the investigation of subjectivity to subordinate groups. Thus the subjectivities of those who hold power over others is absolutely pivotal to an appreciation how power and control "works" via the psychological predispositions of those who wield it, even if the power they wield is socially based and generated.

The conception of "subjective power" that I am outlining here is in some respects similar to that described by Crespi (1992), although there are significant differences. I agree with Crespi that social activity is always influenced by subjective factors such as the desire for honour, prestige and loyalty and other feelings and motivations such as insecurity, bewilderment, identity, care and responsibility and so on, and moreover, that these factors push against the influences and pressures of social norms and expectations in an effort to preserve some measure of autonomy for the individual. In this sense the individual is able both to identify with social structures and systems as well as to generate distance from them. Thus the individual's attitude towards social structures is fundamentally ambivalent (Crespi 1992: 132). For Crespi power is what allows the "specific contradictions of the relation between determinacy and indeterminacy to be dealt with" (1992: 99). Thus subjective power has both "inner" and "outer" aspects. The "inner" aspect is concerned with the tensions that arise between the subjective world of the individual (self-identity and so on) and the concrete situations that individuals find themselves in, and which may threaten or compromise these subjective factors. The outer subjective aspect has to do with the individual's ability to deal with the contradictions arising in the social context.

However, Crespi goes on to be very specific about the type of power that is entailed in inner power. He says it is concerned with wisdom, love, responsibility and so on. Crespi notes that "inner power as such is not connected with a will to dominate others: on the contrary, the more inner power an individual has, the less he needs to look for reassurance by possessing or controlling others" (1992: 104). Thus the person who has inner power has no need to seek reassurance in the "false" certainties provided by the social world in the form of social roles, ideologies and the dogmatic assertion of "the truth", nor have they a desire to exercise power over others. If such a person has to exercise power it will be out of duty rather than choice. There is no doubt that this type of inner power involving a sense of self-knowledge and wellbeing exists to varying degrees in particular people and that this plays a part in a person's attitude towards power and the manner in which it is exercised. However, as an inclusive definition of subjective power it is surely far from complete.

It may be the case that the extent to which individuals can balance the contradictions (probably more accurately described as "tensions") between affirming their relative autonomy from others but at the same time recognizing some dependence on them, will be helped by a person's "inner power" in the sense of self-confidence, feelings of security, self-awareness and "being in touch with our inner lives" (Jampolsky 1994: 104). However, this definition seems unnecessarily restricted – it neglects the manner in which power is a diffuse and intrinsic feature of social life. It does not square with the fact that people are always enmeshed in power relations and that their subjectivities are already to a great extent formed in and around various powers in the shape of capacities as Foucault describes them. (In this sense we do not have to accept the Foucauldian exclusion of the "inner life" in order to accept the kernel of truth in his argument about the diffuseness and ubiquitousness of power.) Also the idea that to be a human agent involves transformative capacity is not registered in Crespi's conception of "inner subjective" power.

In this respect Crespi juxtaposes inner power with the desire to dominate, manipulate or control others and, furthermore, sets up an opposition between duty and choice as the stark alternatives in relation to the exercise of power. These sets of alternatives do not adequately represent the possibilities and tend to impose a view of power that reaffirms both the sovereign and zero-sum conceptions. By drawing an extreme contrast between inner power and the desire to control others, Crespi puts all the focus on the person who dominates a relationship as the one who possesses power – as if the subordinate had no power, or did not use whatever resources are available to affect the balance of power. This, of course, is entailed in Giddens's conception of the dialectic of control and it surely implies that all human action involves the capacity to "make a difference" no matter how reduced or limited it may be. Resistance to the attempt by others to control our behaviour is a form of power even if this is passive resistance (such as the option of silence in an argument or interrogation). Since we can never step outside the net of power as Foucault observes, then we are always involved in some sense with resistance as well as attempts to control the behaviour of others (irrespective of whether they are trying to control our behaviour). As social beings we are necessarily involved in many ties of dependence with others (of varying qualities, types and strengths) – including family and friends – and thus we cannot avoid being drawn into the orbit of power both as a source and a target at different times and places.

Apart from this, the idea that inner power can be contrasted with its assumed opposite – the desire to control and manipulate others – casts the latter in an unremittingly negative light. It can never be a power that is benignly exercised (even if it is ineptly executed) – it is an inherently malign force with nefarious objectives. This view of inner power leaves out of account the fact that people do choose to manipulate and control others in every facet of everyday life. These interventions range from the attempt to control the subject matter of conversations and their outcomes (to win an argument, to secure agreement, to explore areas of disagreement), the attempt to control the feeling states of self and others (to make people angry, to placate them, to defer to them, to insult them). Even inviting someone round to dinner has elements of power and control attached to it. For example, one might want to impress the invited person – a boss, potential partner, or friend – or one might simply want to make the other person feel good or socially acceptable and desirable. These are exercises and assumptions of the mantle of power that are not the result simply of a social duty (although some may indeed be influenced by feelings of "duty" and responsibility). More often than not these attempts to manipulate and control others are the results of deliberate choices that conspicuously lack malicious or malign intent. They are undertaken not simply to control others for the sake of it, but in order to achieve desirable outcomes from the point of view of the person initiating things.

Even if power and control are linked to more formal settings such as a work organization, there is no reason to suppose that instances in which control over others is exerted are the result of black and white alternatives such as duty versus choice. Just as choice need not be associated with less-than–respectable motives, so "duty" may be a banner beneath which very unsound intentions may be concealed. There is nothing intrinsic to "duty" that makes it morally superior to choice in the exercise of power, and both choice and duty may be related to positive and negative intent as far as the exercise of power is concerned. Thus a power-related action taken by a superior in a hierarchy is not necessarily motivated by duty (the obligations and rights associated with the organizational position) nor is it necessarily motivated by a desire to suppress the careers or thwart the ambitions of subordinates. There are a great many stations in between these two alternatives that can supply "appropriate" motivations, intentions and objectives. The superior's actual intention may have been to "sweeten" the atmosphere surrounding the relationships between subordinates of a particular rank. Of course power-plays in formal organizations, as everywhere else in society, may in fact be intimately tied to motives of the most venal or Machiavellian kind. The point is that the will to power, in itself, is neither one thing or the other. What the will to power turns out to be as an intervention in the social world by a particular human agent is an empirical question and this is the whole point about the investigation of the subjective dimension of power.

Whereas his vision of inner subjective power tends to constrict its terms in a rather idiosyncratic manner, in a more general sense Crespi does decidedly underwrite the notion of subjective power in an important and valuable way. This contrasts somewhat with the view offered by Smail (1993) in his analysis of the origins of unhappiness and personal distress. Generally Smail's analysis is very challenging, insightful and innovative. In many respects it is an important corrective to approaches that tend to apportion the blame for unhappiness on individuals themselves – on something "inside" them that is inherently defective. In this I think he is undoubtedly correct. Many psychotherapeutic and psychoanalytic approaches tend to "pathologize" the individual in the sense that they imply that the origins of unhappiness and distress lie inside the person. Importantly, Smail turns the spotlight on to the external world and the operations of power (coercive, economic and ideological) and the person's location in a field of power. A person's feelings of wellbeing or unhappiness will depend upon the experience of and capacity to exercise control within this field of power. The details of Smail's specific analysis of unhappiness do not concern us here, what is interesting is his conception of power from a subjective point of view.

I would certainly want to agree with Smail that it is often a mistake to "pathologize" the individual, as many forms of psychology and psychotherapy tend to do, by neglecting the role of the social context in producing mental distress. However, I think that Smail goes too far down the road of assuming that there are no such things as "inner worlds" or that there are no unique, private motivations that individuals "possess". While taking the point about the necessity of viewing individuals as intrinsically related to the social environment in the form of ties and social bonds of interdependence with each other, the idea that we are nothing other than vehicles for the flow of socially located powers seems to be an overreaction of some magnitude. In fact Smail's account adopts the Foucauldian view of individuals as constructed through discourse and power. Thus Smail says "our experience of being permeated by social power necessarily imparts the illusion that we *originate* action, but, in fact, we would more accurately be characterised as *loci* in social space *through which* power flows" (emphasis in original, 1993: 228). He goes on to say that "there are no such things as 'inner worlds', but personal powers acquired (embodied) over time" (1993: 230).

The abolition of the notion of the "uniqueness" of the "inner world" of the human subject is not required in order to reinstate the idea that people are enmeshed in social networks of interdependence. The idea of the human individual as predominantly constructed through discourses and the powers they confer is a rather impoverished view of human beings and their social behaviour. It is unnecessary in that it is perfectly possible to reject the atomistic view of the individual that often emerges from overly psychologistic approaches without abandoning the claim that human beings *do* originate action in a certain sense, that they *do have inner worlds* and unique characteristics that make them different from other people, and that these things play a significant role in human behaviour. People are caught up in the dialectic of separateness and relatedness (as I stressed in Chapter 2) and this in no small way has to do with the unique psychological characteristics of individuals as they intersect with the demands and obligations of their social interdependencies. The notion of subjective power both as an indication of an individual's felt sense of efficacy and potency with regard to "making a difference" in the world and of their preferred personal style of deployment of such powers is absolutely essential to an understanding of social behaviour and is intimately related to the manner in which the dialectic of separateness and relatedness is resolved.

To say that we are simply "loci in social space through which power flows" reduces human beings to the status of ciphers for the expression of social powers and as conduits through which power circulates around the social body. It denies autonomy and personal efficacy to the human agent and ignores the social influences that push in the direction of the creation of unique individuals. To say that the human agent has a level of personal autonomy and is capable of originating action is not to deny in the least the influence of any of the social forces that constrain and mould the individual (I take up the question of constraint in Chapter 5). To say that the individual is in a specific sense a point of origin of action is to understand the precondition for the establishment of self-identity in a social context. For it is in the area between social constraint and psychobiography that individual selves are forged. Although the human self has a large social component it is never simply a social product; there is always something unsocial or anti-social about it and it is the dialectic between these two aspects of the self that constitutes individuals in their difference (uniqueness) from each other. To deny a significant level of autonomy to individuals both in terms of the origin of action and in terms of the existence of inner worlds is to overestimate the constructive capacities of general social forces as well as wrongly to assume or impute the perfectibility and integrity of these forces.

The idea of the social construction of the individual to the point where individual difference is obscured, ignored or viewed generally as a false premise of social analysis is to impute powers and influences to the social order far in excess of those that it actually possesses. In particular this kind of social constructivism assumes that processes of socialization, training, and social control are perfected and complete in terms of the formative influences they have on people. It also rests on the prior assumption that the underlying processes of social reproduction that ensure the continuity of socialization, control and training are themselves perfectible, "finished" and irrevocable. This, of course, is hardly the case. All social processes are subject to the resistance, pummelling and subversion by all manner of means via the transformative energies of people (individuals and groups) "bucking against" the social order (Wrong 1967). In this sense forms of socialization, training and social control are always "in question" and thus their grip upon human desire, emotions, intentions and cognitions is inherently partial and incomplete. I agree with Crespi (1993: 81–94) that there is always an "unsocial" side to the human being that has to do with an attempt to stave-off, or at least keep at bay, the insistent claims of social forces (obligations, expectations, sanctions and so on) in an effort to preserve and maintain a continuous sense of self-identity. This involves the anchoring of a firm sense of personhood to a complementary feeling of ontological security. In this sense ontological security is not so much an effect of the attachment to and enactment of routines as such (although this does play some role), but to the apprehension of a sense of personal efficacy and self-worth that is reflected in the assertion and demonstration of a distinct self-identity – the uniqueness and individuality of the person.

Power and social encounters

Much of the preceding discussion on the multi-form and interlocking nature of power has concentrated on establishing the credentials, so to speak, of the idea of subjective power. This is because this dimension has so often been neglected or ignored in sociological discussions of power. My intention has been to establish that subjective power exists in its own right but at the same time empirically interlocks with other forms of power. Thus subjective power is not "open-ended" and unfettered by social-structural or system factors as I made clear in my earlier discussion. The scope and depth of subjective power is largely conditioned by the parameters set by the contextual resources that are available at a macro-level to various groups and collectivities. I want now to examine briefly those social areas in which both subjective and objective forms of power enter into the constitution of everyday social activity itself. For this purpose, I shall focus on the domains of situated activity and social settings with a view to understanding the link with power.

The first observation to make is that it is in the intersection of settings and the social activities that guarantee their continuity in time and space, that the intermixing and mutual conditioning of the different forms of power is highlighted. In this sense it is absolutely crucial to view power both as an irreducible social force (in true Foucauldian manner) *as well as* an irreducible property of human agents and their activities (the inter-actionist preference). In the arena of social activity there is a melding of personal, interactional and system-based forms of power. Thus people deploy a blend of these powers to varying effects in face-to-face conduct in their everyday lives. Situated activities, therefore, provide environments in which the metamorphosis of powers that derive from objective and subjective sources takes place. A sort of shape-shifting occurs whereby personal (subjective) powers are transmuted, enhanced and decreased in the volatility of face-to-face encounters. At the very same time, discursive and other system-based powers are shaped and redefined (in terms of scope, relevance, efficacy and so on) as they become entwined in the settings and activities of everyday social life.

This shape-shifting is an important feature of my overall argument. On this view power is not a uni-modal phenomenon – it is never a once-and-for-all "thing" – it has to be understood as constantly reformulating itself as we trace through its effects at different points in time and locations in social and physical space. The imagery that Foucault uses in his analysis of power is a useful point of comparison here. Foucault is very keen to say that power is something that "circulates" and "functions in the form of a chain" (1980: 88), and this draws us away from the false idea (according to Foucault) that is possessed by some and not others. Moreover, Foucault insists that power "is never localised here or there, never in anybody's hands, never appropriated as a commodity or a piece of wealth" (1980: 88). I have drawn attention to the limitations of this all-or-nothing attitude to the conception of power. In this respect it seems that either we accept Foucault's "new" account of power or we are trapped in a false and inadequate "traditional" view. Foucault's rigid and constricted commitments to a particular kind of analysis prevent him from embracing the notion of the co-existence of types of power or of the related idea that there may be "hybrid" types. Of course, my own position rests on the assumption that a recognition and acknowledgement of these latter possibilities is exactly what is required in order to capture something of the variegated nature of power.

However, if we consider for the moment the overall imagery that Foucault employs in relation to his discussion of power we may detect elements in common between his and my own views. Like Foucault I want to say that power circulates and that it has a net-like organization. But my construal of the actuality and practical implications of this power imagery is very different from Foucault's. In my view it is necessary to say that although power is a circulatory medium, it shifts shape as it circulates and thus it is not exclusively tied to discourses and their effects. Similarly, I would want to agree that power is never localized in the specific sense of being isolated from other sources and centres of power and limited only to localized areas of application. However, I strongly disagree with Foucault's implication that power has no localized manifestations and spheres of influence that are relatively autonomous force-fields which are, in themselves, important aspects of the operation of power. Furthermore, at times it is necessary to conceive of power as "being in people's hands" – as a property of their personal powers, their social position or some combination of the two.

The implications of these differences are nowhere more keenly pertinent and sharply observed than in the area of situated activities and the localized settings that are their ever-present environments. Foucault's account of the general nature of power rides roughshod over these complex and subtle aspects of the "capillary" nature of power because he omits reference to, and analysis of, social life at the level of symbolic communication between people on a face-to-face basis. Foucault is unable to broach issues concerned with what Goffman calls the "interaction order" and thus his analysis of power is blunted at the point where it should be as finely honed as possible. Now although Goffman may be remiss in terms of underemphasizing this aspect of the analysis of the interaction order, none the less the whole area is replete with power and control issues. As identified by Rawls (1987) the main concerns covered by the umbrella concept of the interaction order are the care and maintenance of selves, the underpinning "morality" characterizing face-to-face conduct, the production of meaning in interaction, and the obdurate nature of the interaction order itself in the face of external threats to its existence. Although I do not agree with Rawls's overall account of the interaction order, I think the latter is a fair summary of the general concerns indicated by the term except in one important respect – the issue of power.

Goffman never explicity addresses the theoretical issues of power and control in interaction although there is much in what he has written that either incidentally or implicitly bears upon them. Certainly, Goffman provides many examples of the effects of what he refers to as asymmetrical relations in describing various interactional scenes or episodes. The question of power and control is brought into play in respect of considerations germane to the care and maintenance of selves during social encounters – and in particular in relation to what Goffman refers to as the "sacred" nature of selves. In an essay on the nature of deference and demeanour in social life, Goffman says "it is therefore important to see that the self is a ceremonial thing, a sacred object that must be treated with proper ritual care and in turn must be presented in a proper light to others" (Goffman 1967:91). Playing this "sacred game" – which is what we must do in the course of our daily lives – involves a great deal to do with the control of others and control of ourselves. To effect good demeanour and composure requires that selves are truly "presented" to others in ways that achieve the desired effects. Conversely in order to acknowledge the sacred character of selves we must treat others with the respect and deference they deserve and this almost always involves subtle forms of control (as when at a party someone is prevented – by the quick-wittedness of another from making a gaffe). Goffman's underlying thesis of the dramaturgical nature of the self – that it is in some sense a "performance" that is scripted and edited for presentation to a specific audience – is highly pertinent to the theme of power and control as a means of achieving various interactional outcomes (1959). The manipulative aspects of this view of self-presentation are undeniable with each person attempting to fashion a "line" and image of themselves fit for the situation at hand. However, this has to be tempered by recognition of Goffman's equally undeniable emphasis on the moral issues that surround the interaction order which are implied in his concern with issues of trust, respect and deference.

Goffman is much less concerned with how power and control issues link up with other "social orders" as he calls them. Thus he does not discuss how institutional power (or power related to the social system) infiltrates into the arena of face-to-face conduct. Here it is important to try to link Habermas's thesis of the colonization of the lifeworld by system elements with Goffman's ideas about the production of meaning, the sacred character of selves and so on in encounters. In this sense it is crucial not to see the lifeworld of everyday encounters as somehow sealed off from wider influences as some commentators have implied. However, it is also necessary to dispense with Habermas's one-sided view of power implicit in the colonization thesis in order to appreciate the way in which social activities resist some colonizing influences and in the process transform and press them into the service of the interaction order. My own view is that situated activities and their settings must be understood as mediators of both wider system elements and of subjective dimensions of power. It is in the intersecting and overlapping of these areas that the shape-shifting or processes of transmutation occur in the nature of power and control.

The relative autonomy of situated activity is a crucial feature of the theory of social domains and one, among others, that sharply distinguishes it from Giddens's structuration theory. From the point of view of domain theory, the ability of people to make a difference in the world is conditioned by the interaction order itself. Thus transformative capacity has to be understood in relation to the emergent dynamics of situated activity such that the latter may significantly affect the former. For example, a particularly dominant personality (male or female) may find that the mix of personalities or characters that they confront in say a formal meeting, or even an informal encounter, is such that they cannot command the centre of attention as is their usual habit. Conversely, the fact that a person holds a position of high rank in a government or business organization does not necessarily guarantee their power to control events or situations in other settings in which they are involved – for example, a meeting of Alcoholics Anonymous or a therapeutic encounter.

Significant transformative potential is exhibited by the domain of situated activity in so far as it is a "centrepoint" in a nexus of power types and influences. Thus the idea that human agents are defined in and through their transformative capacities does not adequately reflect the subtlety and flexibility associated with this aspect of human agency as it is both shaped by, and shapes, situated activity. I also noted at an earlier point that

Giddens's notion of transformative activity does not distinguish between the effects of the power of system elements nor of "subjective power" in the manner here defined. Therefore the notion of a uniform "dialectic" of control needs to be treated with caution, while the idea of differing dialectics of control (some being enfolded within others) seems to be more promising. Both the notion of transformative capacity and the dialectic of control are not sufficiently elaborate enough to deal with the complexity of the social forces involved in the intermeshing of objective and subjective aspects of power.

Conclusion: power and everyday encounters

I have argued that everyday encounters cannot be understood without reference to the different forms of power that exist in society at large. Social domains are the sites of different forms of power that interlock and meld into each other while encounters themselves are always at the centre of a maelstrom of complex social processes (including shape-shifting). In this respect, power is multi-form and transmutable in ways that many current conceptions of power find difficult to conceptualize. Thus I have argued that Foucault's, Habermas's and Giddens's very different, but equally overgeneralized, notions of power must be viewed rather as different aspects of the multi-form nature of power. In this manner the insights of these authors can be utilized to develop a more embracing conception of power and its relation to everyday encounters.

5

Creativity and constraint in social life

In this chapter I focus on the manner in which people engaged in social encounters contribute to the ongoing nature of society and how society in turn influences the daily activities of individuals. This raises questions about the extent to which people are free and creative in their social lives and the degree to which they are hedged in by social constraints and the obligations of social arrangements and circumstances. In more formal terms I shall be dealing with various aspects of the problem of social production and reproduction. My argument will be that it is necessary to examine these terms in some detail and to unpack the issues associated with them in order to develop a multidimensional view of these social processes.

Particularly important in this respect is the idea that from the individual's point of view, we can distinguish between psychological reality and social reality although the two are intrinsically interrelated. Furthermore, our understanding of this social reality requires us to distinguish between internal and external aspects of social constraint and enablement. It is necessary to rescue this feature of social analysis from those approaches that would abandon the idea of an external social reality (and the notion of external constraint), by collapsing it into the notion of an intersubjective world. The view that all reality is a social construction effectively denies the distinct characteristics of psychological phenomena and situated activity, both of which have their own partly independent features.

Next I move to a discussion of the nature of social interaction and discourses. In this respect the notion of discourse connects with the analysis of social reproduction and production in ways not envisaged in Foucault's own work (and subsequent poststructuralist analyses in general). I also examine some of Habermas's ideas on the nature of communicative action and suggest that there is a connection between his work on validity claims and the push towards shared understanding, with the analysis of discourse and subjectivity. Having made these connections I develop some of Goffman's ideas on the "interaction order". Goffman is a key figure in sociological analysis but the linkage between his work and that of the classical sociologists (particularly Durkheim) have been overlooked. In this respect he has closer affinities with various forms of objectivism than others have assumed. For my purposes Goffman's notion of an interaction order that is loosely coupled in various ways with other social orders is an essential ingredient of the theory of social domains.

This discussion feeds directly into an examination of the processes of social production and reproduction as they manifest themselves in face-to-face conduct. Lifeworld and system have to be treated as parallel social domains in which different aspects of creativity and constraint are worked out in the context of very different social conditions and circumstances. Many theorists have neglected this distinction and tended to treat production and reproduction as rather uniform and mechanical processes that operate within a similarly uniform social landscape. Despite the vast differences in their starting points and the implications of their approaches, writers as divergent as Foucault, Giddens, Blumer and Garfinkel are at one on this. For very different reasons these writers overlook the mediating influence of situated activity (as it is shaped by the partly independent effects of the interaction order) and as it articulates with social system elements. Also, as I have argued in Chapters 1 and 2, day-to-day conduct is an inherently emotional enterprise in which elements of unique psychobiographies are impressed upon, and become constitutive of, the emergent nature of encounters. The role of psychological and emotional factors in the processes of production and reproduction must therefore be registered in our theories.

The nature of social constraints

Constraints have to do with the manner in which social behaviour is both facilitated and limited by social circumstances and arrangements. In this respect they may be treated in a similar fashion to the analysis of resources since indeed they can be understood as types of resources (such as cultural, discursive phenomena) that shape activity. My fundamental argument is that social constraints exist in three dimensions – they possess an internal (subjective or psychological) existence, an external one as an aspect of social systems (including both the domains of settings and contextual resources) and an intermediate one as the lived experience of situated activity. Certain dominant trends in social theory seek to abandon the idea of external constraints explicitly (as in the case of Giddens and various ethnomethodologists and symbolic interactionists) and adopt a position in which social forces are understood as entirely internal to an ongoing intersubjective process. These approaches fail to appreciate that interaction is but one social domain among others that are equally important in the analysis of creativity, constraint and the reproduction of social life. Other forms of social constructivism that reject a phenomenological starting point (as found in Foucault or Elias) and opt for some synthetic unifying principle (such as discourse/power or "figurations" or "process analysis") conversely fail to recognize the importance of both the inter-action order and the realm of psychobiography in the constitution of social life.

Unless the three different but related aspects of constraint are acknowledged then social analyses will deploy a faulty and very limited notion of constraint. Although it is easier for sociologists to acknowledge that the social world is a source of constraint that is, in principle, external to individuals it is harder for certain of them to acknowledge that social constraints may be distinguished in terms of their existential status in the social world. Thus constraints as they are experienced and enacted in face-to-face encounters have a status that corresponds with the thereness of the participants, the motives and reasons they have for their behaviour, and the situated or bounded character of the interaction. The virtuality of these constraints is to do with the fact that they exist in time and space only in so far as they are in the process of being employed by people in their behaviour and activities. They appear to exist only for the practical purposes of the activities of participants since when the encounter terminates they seem to "disappear" as the activity and the people themselves disperse. In the sense that specific constraints are mobilized and involved in the scene of activity then they can be said to be evanescent.

For example individuals may feel constrained to display "involvement" in some talk about which they have little enthusiasm (so as not to let colleagues or family members down). Once the encounter is over then this particular constraint ceases to have any hold over the proceedings and for all intents and purposes "ceases to exist" for those taking part in the encounter. However, although it ceases to exist as a factor in this situation, the general nature of "involvement obligations" continues to exist as a wider cultural constraint in the sense of being something that people need to attend to in all encounters. In this sense it has an existence external to particular situations and represents the preconditions under which particular instances or displays of involvement are enacted. The two are different but related. The general constraint of involvement demands that people exhibit attention to what others are saying and doing in any face-to-face encounter. In specific encounters, however, the extent to which that demand is pressing and how it manifests itself in the unfolding situation varies according to the circumstances of the encounter such as the type of relationship that the participants have with each other (family, friends, strangers), the state of the relationship (good, bad, "so-so"), the emotional tone of the proceedings (whether they getting on well with each other, whether they have had a recent argument), and so on.

So although we can understand the operation of specific constraints as internal to situated activity – a function of the emergent and ongoing nature of the encounter – how should we understand the more general cultural constraints from which they derive? In this respect we have to borrow from several traditions of thought that underline the objective character of certain social phenomena. In particular, Popper's notion of a "third world" of objective knowledge – or knowledge without a knowing subject – is again pivotal here in understanding the "externality" of these constraints (as it was in the discussion in Chapter 3 on the nature and analysis of discourse). Such a conception of cultural knowledge and ideas as they are exemplified in art, science, language and so forth, is absolutely central to understanding the distinction between situated activity and the broader settings and contextual resources that feed into such activity.

Although these aspects of lifeworld and system are intrinsically related to each other as I have tried to make clear throughout, it is of paramount importance to view them as quite different orders of social reality with some similar – but also, crucially, with some very different – characteristics. Popper's idea of third world phenomena is a useful way of conceptualizing these features as relatively autonomous from the situated activities that make up the day-to-day substance of social life. At the same time such phenomena are not divorced from human agency or social life in any way. In fact they enter into the constitution of daily life in four principal ways. First, they are themselves human products (institutions, cultural resources) that represent established ongoing social processes and conditions that influence people and help shape their activities. Secondly, they enter directly into social life as resources that people draw upon to help in the formulation and construction of their behaviour. Thirdly, as a by-product of this process these phenomena are an important ingredient of, and provide a focus for, processes of social production and reproduction. Fourthly, as Popper argues, the very fact that they have an objective existence allows them to be examined, criticized, extended, revised or completely changed. That is, their very external form makes them amenable to transformation through human activity.

This particular aspect of Popper's work is in line with a tradition of social thought that emphasizes the importance of a dualism between an internal world of subjective experience and an external world of social structures, institutions and culture ("system elements" as a generic term). This is reflected not only in the work of Habermas with his lifeworld–system distinction but also in the work of Durkheim, Marx and Parsons. However, unlike this tradition of thought the theory of social domains accords due weight of influence to the situated character of social activity and to individual psychobiography, both of which are either muted or missing in the work of the above authors. As long as these latter amendments are brought into the equation then I feel it is possible to tap into, and borrow from, this tradition since it provides us with means by which the objective features of social life are acknowledged and given adequate weight in social analysis. Several strands of modern social theory have tended to erode, obscure or simply reject the distinction between social practices and system elements. This includes a diversity of authors and approaches who have very different reasons for denying or obscuring the distinction. Whatever the reason, I believe that it is a mistake to take this step and that it is important to retain a notion of constraint that underscores the multidimensional nature of social reality.

What is at stake is an understanding of the independent, though related, effects of different domains on the form and functioning of social constraints and thus on social activity itself. There are a number of positions in social theory that fail to recognize the multiplicity of effects or appreciate their importance for various reasons. The work of Foucault (and poststructuralists who take their lead from him) analytically suppresses the notion of an interaction order and the importance of individual psychobiography by couching everything at a general impersonal level of discourses and practices. Now certainly this position can be brought into the service of a more embracing notion of constraint by underlining some of its important objective features. However, on its own such a one-dimensional view of social life lacks subtlety and leads to a rather mechanical view of subjectivity. Others such as symbolic interactionists and ethnomethodologists simply reject the idea of objective constraints because they believe that there is nothing "external" to, or partly independent from, social activity itself.

Although expressed in a sophisticated and subtle manner, Giddens takes a very similar line on the question of what he terms structural constraint and thus his remarks provide a useful focal point for mounting a challenge to this view. The fear expressed in Giddens' work (as it is in symbolic interactionism and ethnomethodology) is that the idea of a social world which contains external properties is the product of a falsely scientific and objective line of thought in social theory as exemplified in functionalism and structuralism. On this view it is thought that sociologists have adopted a version of scientific inquiry from the natural sciences that is wholly inappropriate to the analysis of the social world. For example, in criticizing Durkheim for adopting the idea of externality in his famous discussion of "social facts", Giddens says that "he wanted to find support for the idea that there are discernible aspects of social life governed by forces akin to those operative in the material world". He goes on to say that "of course 'society' is manifestly not external to individual actors in exactly the same sense as the surrounding environment is external to them" (1984: 172).

Taking their cue from Durkheim subsequent authors have adopted this false line of thinking and "have tended to see in structural constraint a source of causation more or less equivalent to the operation of impersonal causal forces in nature" (1984: 174). Importantly Giddens suggests a corrective to this view:

> Structural constraints do not operate independently of the motives and reasons that agents have for what they do. They cannot be compared with the effect of, say, an earthquake which destroys a town and its inhabitants without their in any way being able to do anything about it. The only moving objects in human social relations are individual agents who employ resources to make things happen, intentionally or otherwise. The structural properties of social systems do not act, or "act on", anyone like forces of nature to compel him or her to behave in any particular way. (Giddens 1984: 181)

I would want to agree with Giddens that it is quite inappropriate to sug-gest that society is like the natural world and that it is a serious mistake to understand constraints as operating as if they were natural forces that are independent of social life in general. However, this is not my view when I suggest that social constraints possess an external dimension. Here, I am suggesting that social constraints are multi-dimensional and that they exist in different but related forms. Thus as I have already intimated, as an ingredient of situated activity constraints are linked *directly* to people's rea-sons and motivations in two ways. First, constraints are tied in with the emergent and variable activities and behaviours of the specific people involved in particular encounters. In this sense constraints have to do with the way in which people creatively deal with the demands produced by specific situations. Questions of how to deal with other people in situations that are always unique in some respects requires imagination, skill and knowledgeability. Thus these constraints are directly implicated in the means through which social life is accomplished by individuals and has to do with their being able to successfully manage, sustain or terminate encounters. Constraints in this sense are what interactants have to take into account about the behaviour and reputations of others included within the membrane that defines the boundaries of the encounter.

Secondly, constraints are also directly linked to people's reasons and motivations in the sense that they form part of their behavioural predispo-sitions that are the resultants of psychobiographical influences. Again, however, although there is a direct link with the motives and reasons of individuals, this should not lead us to assume that these subjective controls on behaviour are of the same type as those concerned with the interaction order. Further, although it is true that a merging and melding of these two sources and types of constraints takes place in the arena of face-to-face conduct we cannot assume that this somehow "neutralizes" the effects of their different characteristics. Both of these assumptions are implicit in the view that constraints can be identified with agents" reasons and motives (in Giddens's scenario) or in the ethnomethodological assumption that the investigation of local practices defines the limits of social analysis (see Hilbert 1990).

To leave the analysis of constraints at the level of interpersonal processes would indeed be to reduce and limit our understanding of social phe-nomena to the realm of intersubjective processes – a point with which Durkheim and Marx (as well as subsequent functionalists, neo-functional-ists, systems theorists as well as structuralists and poststructuralists) all concur. While we do not have to adopt *in toto* the ideas and implications of any of these authors or schools of thought, we certainly have to take seriously the point that social analysis is predicated on a collectivist assumption (Alexander 1985) and that to account for social order we must begin with the premise that there is a collective or institutional level of social life in parallel with (and not reducible to) an interpersonal domain. Expressed in rather different terms we have to conceive of macro or system elements as a parallel reality that provides the society-wide context in which situated activities take place in order to conceive of society as an ordered whole in the first place. To start with interpersonal relations and to deny a macro reality leads to an image of society and social processes as random and formless (Alexander 1985).

In order to understand the importance and necessity of conceiving of social constraints in an external sense as an aspect of a wider macro reality we simply have to pose the question "how do cultural and institutional elements of social life influence people's behaviour?" Functionalist, structuralist and poststructuralist approaches attempt to answer this question while many other positions in social theory cannot even pose it since they do not recognize the reality of an external macro-order. Now while functional and structural schools of thought are deficient in their analysis of human agency and subjectivity, those who wish to restrict the notion of social constraints to actor's motives and reasons as a purely internal feature of interpersonal processes are likewise inadequate in two ways. First, they have a partial account of subjectivity because their internal account of constraint severs its connection with reproduced system elements and thus fails to acknowledge the extent to which subjectivity is dependent on collective (system) elements. Secondly, they have a partial view of social reality in so far as they deny the existence of social processes that exist beyond situated activities and are, therefore, external to them in some way. Thus those who offer an exclusively "internal" account of constraints underwrite a version of social analysis that is based on a subjectivist premise.

In order to go beyond the limitations of this subjectivism and properly to come to grips with the process of social reproduction we have to entertain some of the ideas of functionalist and structuralist schools of thought in relation to the notion of external constraint. In addition to this we have to borrow from an objectivist epistemology such as that proposed by Popper (1972) to undergird the assumptions of this line of thought. In this regard I shall try to adapt some of Foucault's ideas on discourse to the understanding of objective social constraint and social reproduction in the next section. However, before this let me spell out some of the characteristics of the notion of external constraint and give some practical illustrations. The most important characteristic that I want to emphasize is the fact that externally based or system constraints are linked *only indirectly* to individual's motives and reasons. That is, they do not operate independently of reasons and motives to determine or cause the behaviour of people (without their being able to do anything about them), but they do exist in an objective, autonomous sense as reproduced cultural products. Such constraints are associated with power and resources that may be drawn on by individuals to facilitate their behaviour or, conversely, mobilized against them (and thus act as barriers to behaviour). In this sense they enter into the context of situated activity *but they are not identical with motives and reasons.*

In fact social activity is possible only by virtue of the existence of system resources like language, ideas, cultural norms and so on, that people draw upon to inform their behaviour and literally to "make it happen". System constraints are therefore resources that can enable forms of behaviour as well as exert limits on what is possible within certain kinds of settings and contexts. As such, people are compelled to take them into account once they come up against them. This can happen in a variety of ways. First, an individual may be required to take such constraints into account by moving within the orbit of certain networks of constraints as entailed, for example in entering a particular setting, institution or mileu in which rights, obligations or expectations attach to social positions, roles and relationships within them. The extent to which a person will have to take into account the constraints of a setting or milieu will depend upon three things: the degree of "coerciveness" of the institution or setting, the negotiated definitions and agreements that emerge during situated encounters, and the decision-making capacities of individuals as they are conditioned by the first two factors.

The idea of differing degrees of "coerciveness" has to be understood in rather broad terms. In one sense we can understand institutions, settings and milieux as ranging along a continuum from extremely coercive organizational forms (such as prisons, detention centres and secure units of all kinds), through moderately authoritarian ones like military institutions and the armed forces, to less formally controlled and prescribed settings such as the family, friendship and personal relationships. Clearly the degree to which conformity to rules, regulations, obligations and expectations occurs will vary according to the nature of the organization or settings and the configurations of power that underpin them. However, we must remember that power and influence can operate in ways other than direct coercion. Forms of inducement and reward as well as the internalization of moral standards about appropriate behaviour and the psychological mechanisms of guilt and shame all play a role in "encouraging" levels of conformity. Similarly the degree of sedimentation of roles and institutions in time and space and the "moral aura" that surrounds them (as reflected in respect for standards, traditions, values and authority) are very persuasive factors in producing assent to social demands. For example, the roles of father and mother in most cultures are so deeply embedded and entrenched in the cultural mores that deviations from expected patterns of behaviour associated with them may produce extreme reactions both by legal institutions and society at large – as witnessed, for example, in the public outrage provoked in instances of child abuse.

As can be appreciated, my use of "coerciveness" as a general characterization of the effects of a range of organizational forms shades into factors associated with moral persuasion and influence that include factors to do with individual responsibility and moral choice. This simply means that in the less coercive settings and milieux, there is less external imposition of demands for conformity and more latitude for individual discretion and choice about the details of behaviour that are required to fulfil social requirements. This point connects directly back to the discussion in Chapter 3 on settings and the duality of social relations. I do not want to repeat in detail what I said there but it is important to note the link with social reproduction. The more that settings and milieux are sedimented in time and space, the more the reproduced aspects of social relations will have a hold on the behaviour of those within them and the less will participants be able to innovate and extemporize.

However, this is complicated by the fact that some settings and milieux, such as friendships and personal relationships, are not "policed" by an intermediate organization that interposes itself between an individual's private life and the wider cultural and social milieu (as in work organizations or carceral institutions characterized by disciplinary power). In the context of the latter kinds of organizations, there is a conjuncture of power and the capacity to regulate the time, bodies and mental lives of large sections of the population that is largely missing from areas of social life concerned with leisure, intimacy and personal relations – the "private" sphere. As I have said, however, this does not mean that these settings and contexts are any less constraining and compelling in a moral and social sense. In this respect they are "policed" by the social community at large rather than any definite intermediate level of formal control and surveillance. They do, however, allow for a greater range of behaviour associated with their reproduction and also are more tolerant of behavioural variety and diversity.

Let me recap. The level of compulsion entailed by the external character of constraints is largely mediated though the reproduced social relations that constitute particular settings and milieux. As such, the compulsion is intimately bound up with power, control and the modes of policing and surveillance of such settings, as well as with moral identification with them. Prisoners will be "compelled" to the same degree – in the sense of experiencing the same intensity of pressure to conform – by the curtailment of their freedom as much as parents will be compelled by the moral injunction not to hurt or abuse their children. This is not to say that either prisoners or parents could not (and do not) do otherwise – as evidenced in prisoners' riots, dirty or hunger protests, child abuse (both physical and psychological) – but rather that there is external pressure to conform and that this will vary in intensity. It is possible that these external considerations, as I said before, will be conditioned by the situated circumstances involved in actual instances of face-to-face interaction. Thus, if settings and circumstances allow, people may arrive at "informal" agreements about the extent to which external considerations will come into play in the immediate circumstances. Parents may say to their children that they cannot do this or that, even though other parents allow such behaviour; this may be enforced in a number of ways ranging from simple coercion – Bernstein (1973) calls this "positional control" – through the powers of persuasion (personal control) to the negotiation of trade-offs such as allowing other indulgences or freedoms.

Bittner's (1967) study of the police on skid-row in a city in the USA is a classic example of the way in which occupational practitioners make *ad hoc* decisions about whether to arrest or to refrain from arresting drunks for petty offences depending on their assessment of the likely consequences for "keeping the peace" in a particular section of skid-row. The point is that the police make such decisions on the basis of intimate knowledge of the situations and circumstances and "personal" knowledge of the down-and-outs concerned, in order to "keep the peace" – rather than uphold the letter of the law. The patrol officers used the law simply as a resource to deal with the practical problems that they confront in their jobs as law enforcement officers. Sometimes this means overlooking infractions of the law for the wider purpose of avoiding further trouble in the long run. At other times it means trumping-up charges for "non-existent" or minor offences in order to keep particular men out of trouble with others on skid-row. Although the law exists as an external constraint that can be called upon as a resource to help keep the peace, it is used selectively by the patrol officers on a situation-by-situation basis. Thus the formal constraint of the law as a means of punishing infractions is employed as a resource that is given shape and expression on the basis of situational understandings and agreements about what is best in the circumstances. In this sense occupational practitioners work out practical solutions to problems encountered in the work situation.

Finally, social constraints are conditioned by an individual's internalized moral standards and psychological dispositions as they have been fashioned through the person's psychobiography. Thus, for example, parents might be "strict" with their children, or very lax, or something in between, according to their preferences, behavioural style and personality and upbringing. Individuals will have their own interpretations of the roles, positions and relationships in which they are involved and these will vary within certain defined limits. The extent of this permitted variation, as I have pointed out, will depend very much on the kind of setting, relationship or role in question but in the final analysis as Sartre (1966) has pointed out, individuals are free to decide what kind of person they will be regardless of the degree of constraint involved. Thus slaves are patently unfree in one sense but in another they are "free" to be a particular kind of slave – acquiescent, resistant, cunning, manipulative and so on. Such "freedom" is a direct consequence of a process of psychological development in which internal constraints entrench themselves in the individual's psyche to predispose that person to be a certain kind of individual and to adopt a distinctive behavioural repertoire.

Let me deal with one example briefly to show how all instances of constraint contain within them traces of the three dimensions that I have described. This is important especially in cases where, on the surface, there may appear to be no external compulsion involved. There is no coercive arm of the state that compels certain people to be university lecturers. People decide to become academics – presumably on the basis of their psychological predispositions as individuals, their upbringing and early experiences, as well as later educational opportunities and so on. However, once they have decided to become an academic there are certain external constraints that come into play that stand in the way of achieving such an ambition. A person has to undergo a form of professional training in which examinations have to be passed, interviews have to be completed successfully, expertise in a particular specialism has to be demonstrated, evidence of aptitude for teaching and publication in professional journals has to be presented and so on. These are constraints whose existence lies outside the personal motives and desires of individuals and beyond their power to transform. Clearly, once an objective or goal (such as to become an academic) has been adopted by an individual it becomes an internal constraint bound up with personal desires and ambitions. However, the end itself is socially constructed as are the social channels, requirements and means of achieving it. As such, they are external constraints that pre-exist and place limits around such personal motives.

This example highlights the point that in many settings and contexts no-one is "compelled" to adopt certain aims, goals, values, strategies and ambitions. However, once individuals have engaged with them – brought them within the realm of internal constraint – they are compelled to negotiate a series of external hurdles in order to realize their goals. They become enmeshed in external constraints that define appropriate behaviour in relation to the achievement of certain outcomes and as such limit the range of options available. Such objective constraints do not determine the behaviour of people (like natural forces) but they do enforce attendance to them in that they compel individuals to deal with them in the pursuit of their ends. Thus although motives and reasons become part of the means of dealing with external constraint they do not define or delimit the constraints themselves that are predefined and mandatory, as long as the end itself is desired or sought after. The whole notion of social constraints is dependent upon the idea that they exist in a general sense as reproduced cultural forms that have an existence that is external to *particular* people and groups (including their motives and reasons) and specific situated encounters. Obviously, they are not external to *all* situated encounters or people, and in that sense they are firmly locked into the continuity of social life – but they enter into the interpersonal realm in a transformed and indirect manner.

Discourse and social reproduction

In this section I want to pursue the question of the impersonal nature of social products and their constraining qualities in a different guise by examining the role of discourse in the reproduction of social life. In Chapter 3 I insisted on the irreducibility of social phenomena to subjective or intersubjective processes, and claimed that subjectivity is in part shaped by social discourses (and other contextual resources). Of course the "in part" caveat distinguishes my own position from that of Foucault and other poststructuralists (as well as structuralists) who view subjectivity as constructed exclusively in discourse(s). I want to argue that there is a core of truth in the image of the individual as "constructed in discourse" and I want to defend the idea that individuals are in a certain sense *nodal points* at the intersection of available discourses. This aspect of human subjectivity is central to the process of social reproduction. In particular it accounts for what I would call the push towards *idiomatic stylization* in face-to-face communication and linguistic usage and which, in turn, is linked to the problem of the continuity of social reproduction.

However, it is possible to defend this view only by insisting that it is a deliberately partial image of subjectivity that serves the purely heuristic purpose of highlighting an aspect of social interaction that may otherwise be obscured. Thus my argument also asserts that the individual is far more than a nodal point in the intersection of discourses. In this respect human beings are active and transformative agents as Giddens notes (bearing in mind the qualifications I have previously spelled out, especially in Chapter 4). Thus the human being is not a simple plaything of social forces operating in the social stratosphere, beyond the reach of human agency. Further, to understand the process of social reproduction properly we have to consider the interactive and communicative context of social behaviour. I think Habermas is right to concentrate on developing what he calls a theory of "communicative action" since basic features of social life are embedded in this domain and cannot be ignored (as they are by poststructuralists). Among others (including Wittgenstein, Austin and Gadamer), Habermas draws on Mead's work on symbolic communication to inform the theory of communicative action and again I find this a very fruitful line of attack, especially considering Habermas's objective of bringing these strands of "action theory" together with a version of systems theory.

Habermas concentrates mainly on the question of how people reach shared understandings by making "validity claims" and negotiating with

others in respect of these claims. While there is much in his notion of differing validity claims for the understanding of communication in a generalized sense, I think that it provides only a partial account of the way in
which shared understanding is achieved. I want to focus on two aspects of
communication that I believe Habermas underplays in his attempt to deal
with this issue. First, he does not consider the general issue of communicative style as an essential precondition for the achievement of understanding (and shared definitions of the situation) in human communication.
Although it is not necessarily precluded from Habermas's schema, he
tends to view it as a sideline to the main issues of understanding as an
adjudication of validity claims. In this sense the cognitive aspects of communication are unwittingly elevated above others. I say unwittingly
because Habermas is at pains to include some reference to emotional
or expressive factors by suggesting that claims to sincerity and self-presentation (as in Goffman's work) are important in arriving at shared understanding (Habermas 1984: 75–101). However, this element is regarded as
just one of several kinds of validity claims that are sorted through and contribute to some overall agreement about how to proceed. Habermas tends
to see this process in linguistic terms as a formal process of reasoning in
which people "yield to the better argument". He does not envisage the
process of communication as driven by less rational forces in which the
expression of feelings and emotions become an overriding issue for those
concerned.

Secondly, Habermas fails to note the connection between the general
process of communication and its situated character and hence underplays those emergent elements of face-to-face encounters and the psychobiographical features of individuals that automatically intrude into the
flow of communication. In particular Habermas's view of communication
in interaction stresses the centrality of reason in the sorting through of
validity claims and thus characterizes it as a primarily cognitive, rational
and reasoning process. As a consequence he does not acknowledge the
importance of the expression of affect in shaping communication and generating *shared* understanding. Sharedness of understanding is never simply
a cognitive phenomenon and in fact may be of minimal importance in
particular instances of communication. In this respect face-to-face communication is just as much about empathy, identification, fellow-feeling,
gelling, compatibility, force of personality, and a whole host of variable and
unpredictable factors. In terms of communication such elements are often
signalled through the employment of idiom and style. It is at this crucial

juncture that the link between social reproduction and situated activity is effected and this is missed in Habermas's focus on the overrriding importance of validity claims.

In so far as idiom and subcultural style exist as choices for speakers then they can be understood as externally based resources that are drawn into specific situations by specific people. In so far as personal styles or idiolects are expressions of unique personalities then these too are imported into situations by participants. Both these communicative resources meet up in actual situations of use in which elements of each are selected on the basis of their appropriateness and effectiveness in the specific situation. It is the importance of the emergent character of situated activity and psycho-biography and the manner in which they condition the choice of idiomatic forms that distinguishes this present formulation from Bourdieu's notion of "habitus". Clearly "habitus" as a person's dispositions resulting from their group affiliations is important, but it does not represent the whole story by any means (see comments in Chapter 3, and later in this chapter). The employment of idiom and style to "make things happen" and to produce certain communicative effects has the consequence of reproducing the social forms – the discourses – in which they are expressed. In this manner reproduced discourses are resources that feed into situated encounters and directly contribute to their emergent and fragile nature. In this respect idiomatic stylization is the background reproductive "noise", which is a constant accompaniment of face-to-face communication.

For example, ways of expressing agreement or disagreement (or of any of the shades in between) say, are just as important as its formal statement. What we do not say but is tacitly acknowledged and understood (Tannen 1992), as well as the tone of voice and facial expression (Austin 1971), is crucial to the felt *sense* of agreeing with or understanding someone. Furthermore sharedness of understanding can also be signalled by a specific choice of words, or selection of phrases and styles of expression. Appropriate usage is important since the employment of similar style and the consequent overlapping of cultural references is itself a demonstration of union, a tangible sign of sharedness of meaning. This also has to do with what J. Turner (1988) – referring to the work of Garfinkel – describes as the sense of sharing a similar factual world. However, it also has to do with a more embracing sense of sharing a similar emotional-affective world. This more than anything creates a generalized sense of "feeling right" in encounters in terms of sensing a "rhythm, flow and predictability" (J. Turner 1988: 206) and leads to reduced anxiety in participants. The continuity and unfolding of activity is never completely dependent on the play of validity claims since communication is not simply about the rational adjudication of reasoned claims – it is in equal measure about empathy, acceptance and a willingness to agree or not agree. Also as J. Turner (1988) and Collins (1983) have pointed out, among other things social interaction is driven by the need for confirmation of self, the need to be closely bonded (feelings of solidarity) with others, and the need to feel included, "in touch with" and "part of" events. All these factors are underpinned by changeable feeling states and emotional responses that are signalled not necessarily through explicit (reasoned) argument or formal agreement but through the adoption of specific forms of communicative response.

This interactive and communicative context – which includes varying levels of emotional intensity – provides the background against which the process of social reproduction can be viewed more generally. Let me now return to the proposition with which I began this section – the idea that human beings are, in a special sense, nodal points at the intersection of discourses. Having outlined the qualifications concerning the nature of face-to-face communication and the self as a force-field of feeling, in terms of which this proposition has to be understood, we can now approach the issue of the relation between social reproduction and discourses more realistically. My thesis in the foregoing has been that a crucial aspect of shared understanding (and the emergent negotiations and definitions of the situation that flow from it) is the push towards idiomatic usage. I have argued that since the situated circumstances of activity and the psychological inputs of individuals always condition the impact of idiomatic forms, they are never simply, mechanically or deterministically related to activity. None the less the choice and incorporation of idiomatic forms speaks to the fact that discourses (and thus reproduced resources and practices) play a central role in shaping face-to-face encounters and activities. The regular employment of reproduced forms is a continuous feature of routine social interaction because it is a source of solutions to the general communication problems thrown up by interpersonal encounters.

These problems hinge around three criteria having to do with the issue of communicative flows which are related to the ability to "carry on" in encounters and make an essential contribution to what Turner refers to as the rhythm, flow and predictability of events. Communicative flow – the ongoing and cumulative character of interpersonal exchanges – is dependent upon the satisfaction of three criteria associated with the quality of the communications concerned and the specific circumstances in which they are embedded. They are acceptability, effectiveness and appropriateness. These represent the tangible link between external resources (particularly in the form of discourses) and the internal dynamics generated by the interpersonal and intra-psychic domains. In this particular sense they represent the "transformation rules" that selectively allow a series of interchanges between the personal and impersonal (system or macro-structural) aspects of social life. These rules then allow for a crucial possibility. This concerns the fact that although acceptability, effectiveness and appropriateness all have their counterparts and indicators in situated activity – that is, behavioural solutions geared to and shaped by the local circumstances of the encounter – reproduced idiomatic forms may also provide ready-made solutions that serve as temporary or transitional "holding points".

In this sense the use of idiomatic forms acts rather like a parallel set of meta-communications which produces the background "noise" that forms a constant accompaniment to face-to-face communication. It establishes a framework of communicative rapport (feeling right, emotional intensity, identification and so on) in terms of which the foreground of interpersonal negotiations may take place. In so far as interpersonal negotiations take time then the use of idiomatic forms can establish instantaneous rapport by the symbolization and auditory indication of agreement and understanding and thus act as a "holding scaffold" for the participants. That is, it can function as a preliminary working agreement on understanding, a promissary note or template that can be revised, amended, torn-up or remodelled in the light of the unfolding nature of the interpersonal situation. In this sense idiomatic stylization short-cuts the need for communicative negotiation and the sorting through of validity claims in order to arrive at a preliminary shared understanding, even though these processes may be going on in parallel and will eventually feed into the preliminary agreements either to supplement and buttress them or to undermine or revise them in some way.

In this respect, interpersonal encounters proceed via participants' deployment of a split-level communication system that involves a melding of different timeframes. One frame involves the "real" time of the encounter and the other involves the condensed historical time of reproduced social forms (discourse, idiom and style). Habermas's version of the achievement of shared understanding tends to presuppose a one-channel mode of communication that progresses in a linear fashion through competing validity claims to arrive at some "reasoned" conclusion. The use of idiomatic forms (which incidentally include ritualized actions such as the entry, avoidance and leaving rituals mentioned by Goffman (1967) as well as ritualized linguistic exchanges such as "polite" conversation, chit-chat, passing the time) allows for the fact that definite conclusions may not be reached and that shared understanding (apart from the possibility of non-agreement) may indeed include the eventuality that things will be "left in the air" in an inconclusive manner. Therefore while the use of idiomatic forms conveys some messages unambiguously (such as general assent or rapport), it has the added advantage that in other respects it may also imply other communications that are fuzzy and vague in nature. In this sense idiomatic stylization provides both interim "cover" for the simultaneous and continuous development of more detailed understandings as well as providing for a degree of latitude in interpretation no matter what turns out to be the case. The degree of freedom of interpretation accorded to the receiver allows for the possibility that messages may be misinterpreted or misunderstood as they often are in social life. (In some cases the leeway for interpretation entails deliberate ambiguity on behalf of the sender.)

In that in a very real sense people always employ idiomatic forms, they are drawing on reproduced social discourses and practices because they provide ready-made solutions to "problems" of interaction and communication that are a continuous feature of face-to-face conduct. Thus at a general level they satisfy the demands for acceptability, effectiveness and appropriateness that are an ever-present aspect of communication. At every step of the way, however, adjustments, trade-offs and interchanges are taking place between ready-made solutions and those that are being continually worked at and negotiated in the situation itself. An appropriate signalling of assent or agreement at the general idiomatic level (politeness, rapport-talk) may have to be adjusted in order to accommodate an emergent disagreement in a conversation, thus the appropriate situational solution – in these circumstances with this person – may be to make definite signals of annoyance or disapproval. Thus while people and their communicational subtleties are never fully "determined" by discourses and practices (including all the idiomatic modes and styles) they are always in part the willing conduits of reproduced social forms since they provide the necessary cover (refuge, time-out) from the imminent and very pressing demands of face-to-face encounters.

As willing conduits people are also actually the unintended captives of reproduced discourses in the sense that they live their lives partly within and through them. As such people cannot do without idiomatic forms since they enable interaction to proceed apace and in tandem with emergent understandings, negotiations and definitions. It is in this sense that people stand at nodal points in the intersection of the numerous discourses (and the practices they represent) that are available to them at their particular point in the social system (principally their class, "racialized" and gender positions). People live within the parameters of available discourses by "carrying them around" in their heads. In more formal terms these idiomatic forms are deeply internalized resources, and as such are significant identity props. Thus by drawing upon them as resources people both reproduce and reaffirm the social forms themselves as well as significant chunks of their own identities. Social reproduction is thereby linked to psychological reproduction (although it should be noted that both the social and the psychological worlds are only partly served by these replications since they both have areas of autonomy and both are conditioned by the influence of situated activity – also see later comments).

The reproduction of identities (and psychobiographies) that occurs as an unintended outcome of the use of idiomatic forms also points to the emotional inner core of human beings in so far as levels of emotional connectedness are conveyed through their deployment, as I have pointed out. However, it is not only expressed affective relations with others that are thereby signalled, but attitudes and feelings towards self are also implicated. Therefore the process of reproduction holds within its social moment a point at which the relation between the public and private spheres of the self becomes an issue. So although psychological reproduction is partly served by its social counterpart it is never completely so since the individual memory (the unique psychobiography) is always something more than those things that discursively reflect aspects of self-identity.

In saying that individuals are in a certain sense nodal points at the intersection of available discourses I am pointing to the residual grain of truth in the structuralist and poststructuralist idea that subjectivities are "constructed in and through discourse". I am also indicating how I think that the analysis of discourse fits in with an understanding of face-to-face conduct. However, this position can be supported only via considerable modification of the assumptions and premises of poststructuralist thought to a point where they cease to be recognizably poststructuralist. Apart from the fact that psychobiography and self-identity are inherently refractory to monopolization by discursive influences, individuals are never simply nodal points at the intersection of discourses because they never stand completely outside the interactive heart of social life. Communicative acceptability, effectiveness and appropriateness are forever situationally transforming and transformed by the reproductive demands of other social domains.

Goffman and the interaction order

I have made reference to Goffman's ideas on the interaction order in passing at several junctures in this book but here I want to consider its importance more fully, especially its connection with the processes of social production and reproduction. In the previous section (as throughout) I have pointed to the conditioning influence of what I have termed the domain of situated activity. I ended the previous section by stressing that the need for acceptability, appropriateness and effectiveness are communicative problems that require behavioural solutions to be realized in the immediate circumstances of encounters. This idea links strongly with Goffman's views on the interaction order, which he regards as a domain of study in its own right and which is distinct from the more usual areas of sociological inquiry (such as the study of institutions). I want to say immediately that what I have termed situated activity is related to Goffman's notion of the interaction order but is not identical with it. As I pointed out at the begining of Chapter 3, I see the "interaction order" as a broader area that includes situated activity. I think much of what Goffman wrote about and dealt with implies the existence of situated activity in my terms, but he never explicitly dealt with it as a specific manifestation of the interaction order.

In order to illustrate what I mean by this let me first outline what Goffman means by the interaction order and its relation to social life as a whole. Goffman (1983) addresses this issue by suggesting that the interaction order represents a domain of issues and problems that can be studied sociologically but which is distinct from other social orders such as the institutional order, and other aspects of social life that are usually studied and defined in society-wide (macro) terms. In this respect the interaction order is explicitly about face-to-face conduct in which there is a focus of attention on the encounter by the participants and which is enclosed by a permeable membrane that provides a temporary boundary between it and adjacent social activities. As such the focus of analytic attention is trained on the manner in which the behaviour of those involved is influenced by the responses of the others present. Much of Goffman's work centres around the social organization of such encounters and he claimed that this is a valid and important area of inquiry even though mainstream sociologists tend to be more concerned with larger-scale matters of seemingly greater importance. In this respect Goffman was responding to the fact that some sociologists (for example Gouldner 1971) had suggested that this preoccupation with face-to-face encounters reflected an unwarranted concern with the trivial and fleeting minutiae of social life and that sociologists should be concerned with more "worthwhile" matters.

The charge of triviality in relation to the subject matter of encounters is completely misplaced since Goffman himself recognized that these microprocesses were related to wider issues of social order and social structure even though his own work does not always explicitly concentrate on such links. Subsequent commentators (Giddens 1987, Rawls 1987) have recognized the importance of Goffman's work for an overall account of society and social processes and I agree with them that Goffman's work cannot be dismissed as dealing with lightweight issues or that it reflects a wrongheaded and irredeemably "subjective" view of social life. While I also think that they are right to stress the importance of Goffman's work for our understanding of social organization in general, I feel that his work itself has suffered from some misinterpretation in the process. In so doing the continuity between Goffman's work and classical sociology has been minimized and its relevance to an understanding of the processes of production and reproduction has been neglected.

To understand these points let me elaborate further on Goffman's vision of the interaction order. In Chapter 4 I briefly mentioned Rawls' (1987) discussion of the four main concerns covered by the term the "interaction order" and since I feel that these aptly summarize much of Goffman's intentions let me recap. The first area of concern has to do with the care and maintenance of the self (and selves in general) in social interaction. In this respect Goffman's work is very much in line with Mead's social psychology in so far as it recognizes that the self is dependent on the responses of others both to provide support and to provide a reflected image (or "face") with which to meet and deal with other people. The manner in which people attempt to deal with others in pursuance of their own needs and intentions by projecting certain kinds of self-images and employing various (sometimes manipulative) strategies creates inherent problems for other people. In this sense the interaction order provides a framework of ground rules and moral constraints that protect the sacred character of selves.

This emphasizes a second intrinsic feature of the interaction order – its moral nature. The obligations and constraints that pervade the interaction order are "moral" in so far as people implicitly agree not to deliberately violate or destroy the working consensus that builds up in encounters and the self-images that people are projecting, for fear of destroying the whole fabric of the interaction itself. Thus people typically employ face-saving tactics on behalf of others to avoid embarrassing themselves and others and thereby allowing for the possibility that the embarrassment will "infect" the whole of the assembled company. There is an element of self-interest involved in so far as it is assumed that other people will do the same if we ourselves are in difficulties. None the less there is a fair amount of trust, tact and altruism at work also since the order and continuity of encounters depends upon the protection and support of the selves that people are projecting in particular situations. All in all this aspect of the interaction order has to do with the commitments that people make to a morality of fair dealings in face-to-face conduct based in large part on trust and tact and in which the sacred character of selves and the honour that is due to them is a central issue.

The third characteristic of the interaction order, which again has striking overlaps with the work of Garfinkel (1967), Mead (1967) and Blumer (1969), is its capacity to produce meaning. Thus the give and take of encounters involves interpretive work on behalf of the participants who fashion understandings and agreements about the meanings of objects and events around which the encounter revolves. These meanings are properly explicable only in terms of the inner workings of encounters; they are not externally "imposed" by institutional objectives or role expectations or "given" in dictionary definitions of words. As Blumer insists, the meaning of an object or event resides in the responses of those who are a party to the interaction and the emergent definitions and understandings that arise. Finally, the interaction order is characterized by its resilience and durability in the face of external threats to its existence. This means that the central concerns of the interaction order cannot be driven out or entirely extinguished, even though they may be forced underground by the imposition of external authority. The example of the flourishing "underlife" of mental hospitals wherein the selves of inmates find refuge and sustenance and that support various "unofficial" kinds of activities is something Goffman (1961b) himself has studied.

These are the characteristics of the interaction order as Rawls describes them and although they do throw some light on Goffman's general views, they are also in need of some important additions, qualifications and amendments. In Chapter 2 I stressed that a full understanding of the interaction order must take into account the problems and issues of involvement, civil inattention, situational propriety as well as the framing devices that people use to order their social experiences and which constitute important aspects of Goffman's overall approach. In one sense, these issues can be considered to be supplementary aspects of the care and maintenance of selves, the production of meaning and the morality of the interaction order. However, it is also important not to lose sight of them as elements in their own right. Furthermore, as I have already mentioned in Chapter 4, Rawls's list needs to be supplemented by issues surrounding power, control (and hierarchy), which I argued were a feature of Goffman's writings on face-to-face interaction – even though he often dealt with them only in an implicit and partial manner. Leaving this aside for the moment let me comment on the other characteristics described by Rawls. I shall take the last mentioned characteristic first since it summarizes the problems associated with them all.

Although the idea that the interaction order is typically durable and resilient is valid up to a point, it needs to be specified more exactly in order to be commensurate with Goffman's own views and for it to be a serviceable instrument in social analysis more generally. There is in this rather bald construal of durability and resilience the implication that the interaction order, apart from being a domain in its own right, is somehow autonomous from other social orders (principally the institutional order) and that this is how it manages to maintain its continuity in the face of external threats to its existence. Moreover Rawls's depiction of the interaction order accords it an inflated importance in social life generally and this is confirmed in other aspects of Rawls's account. For example, she claims that according to Goffman "the needs of interaction and the self are a source of consistent social constraint which does not originate in social structure" and that "individual and structure . . . are the joint products of an interaction order sui generis" (Rawls 1987: 138). Further on, she argues that Goffman supports a view of "involvement obligations" as constraints but insists that these "do not arise from the social structure, class relations, the division of labour, or cultural ideas, but rather from the requirements of self and sociality" (Rawls 1987: 140). As a final illustration she suggests that "Goffman's notion of trust is directed toward the interaction order sui generis, for its own sake, and not directed toward the reproduction of social structure at all" (Rawls 1987: 145). All these statements attest to a view of the interaction order as quite independent of other orders. At several points Rawls also seems to imply that the interaction order actually generates other orders – as where she says that "individual and structure" are "joint products" of the interaction order.

One of the reasons behind Rawls's arguments is her objection to Giddens's suggestion that Goffman's work is important because it provides a link between the encounters of everyday social life and the reproduction of social structures and institutions. Giddens argues that this link is forged both by the routinization and joining together of social encounters as well as through the "duality of structure", which has the effect of reaffirming and re-creating existing institutions. On this view people creatively construct their behaviour in social encounters and simultaneously reproduce the wider social orders (structures, systems, institutions, cultural ideas and so on) in which they are involved. In this sense there is a direct link between the micro-activities of everyday life and the wider institutional structure. As a consequence, according to Giddens the routines of everyday life are directly implicated in the fixed appearance of social institutions (Giddens 1984: 69). Rawls objects to this line of reasoning because it ignores the importance of the interaction order in its own right. According to Rawls, Goffman's concern with trust and tact and so on have to do with the protection of the self via rituals of interaction; they are not concerned with the protection and continuity of the encounters themselves nor with the wider institutional reproduction that allegedly stems from it (according to Giddens).

Rawls believes that all reproductive effects of encounters are geared to "preserving presentation of self and the interaction order which sustains it" (Rawls 1987: 144) and have nothing to do with social reproduction in general. While there is some truth in the idea that there is a different type and level of social reproduction operating in face-to-face activity, it is misleading to suggest that there is no underlying link with more general aspects of social reproduction. People employ elements of language, idiom and style as well as myriads of social rules, cultural conventions, and skills in order to be able to interact with others on a meaningful basis and thus the continuity of social reproduction is perpetuated in each encounter. Encounters never are, and never can be *entirely* separate from the reproduced order of institutions (or other social orders) as Rawls (1987: 144) seems to think. In any case Rawls's views do not square with Goffman's own ideas on the nature of the "loose-coupling" between social orders that accommodates the idea that there is a link between encounters and general social reproduction. It also underscores the fact that the interaction order has its own distinctive reproductive problems, processes and constraints that are not reducible to, or identical with, these wider processes.

That Goffman's position allows for this crucial possibility brings us to the issue of Giddens's (1987) interpretation of Goffman. In presenting the case for Goffman as a far more important social theorist than he has hitherto been credited, Giddens inadvertently constricts the versatility of Goffman's own theoretical position. Giddens insists that the closeness of the links between encounters, routines and general social reproduction (which stem from the "duality of structure") makes it unnecessary to conceptualize a distinct interaction order. This has to be understood against the backdrop of Giddens's general critique of dualism in social analysis, whereby distinctions such as agency–structure, individual–society, macro–micro, and so on, are thought to be the product of, and to encourage a line of thinking that implies a false separation and opposition of, the entities denoted by the terms. One of the central aims of Giddens's structuration theory is to break down such "false oppositions" and produce a conceptual framework that unites them in various ways. For Giddens to acknowledge the importance of a distinctive domain called the interaction order would be to uphold a form of dualism in social analysis (the dualism of agency and structure) to which he is strongly opposed.

However, the inflexible belief that all dualism is wrong falsely assumes that it always implies separation, opposition and unrelatedness – in this case between encounters and institutions. But this is not implied in the theory of social domains and nor is it in Goffman's work. Goffman does not argue that the interaction order is separate (and therefore opposed or unconnected) from other orders, he merely says that it is a domain in its own rights which is "loosely coupled" with others. Therefore, this view of the interaction order suggests that it is *different from* (that is, possesses its own problems, needs and constraints), but is in various ways *connected with* other social orders. I think that part of Giddens's critique is correct in so far as he points out that in the main, Goffman does not elaborate on the links between the interaction order and the institutional order to any great extent and thus, perhaps, the emphasis on social reproduction as an important connection between them is somewhat subdued. However, there are scattered comments throughout Goffman's work and most definitely in his Presidential Address to the American Sociological Association in 1983, which make his wider position clear.

Goffman and the "loose-coupling" of social orders

Although Goffman understands the interaction order as having its own distinct characteristics he also envisages it as loosely coupled with others, particularly the institutional order. This loose-coupling allows for a variety of forms of relationship between the interaction order and other social domains as well as an array of mechanisms that service the connections between them. However, as I pointed out in Chapter 2, one of the drawbacks of Goffman's construal of the interaction order is reflected in his commitment to a psychology "stripped and cramped to suit the sociological study of conversation, track meets, banquets, jury trials, and street loitering. Not, then, men and their moments. Rather moments and their men" (1967: 3). This version of psychology is fine in so far as it relates to an "internal" understanding of the interaction order (and more generally to a sociological orientation), but it does not do adequate justice to the psychodynamics of individuals and their psychobiographies. There is no reason to suppose that a richer, more textured version of individual psychology could not be loosely coupled with the interaction order and the other social domains as I have outlined them. I am suggesting that Goffman's vision of the loose coupling idea is consistent with the main thrust of domain theory – particularly its general conception of the relations between domains.

One of the radical implications of the notion of a distinctive interaction order is that it challenges us to rethink the received wisdom on several areas of sociological analysis. I have already tried to show how several issues, questions and problems of social analysis may be tackled by taking into account the partly independent character of the interaction order. In this respect it is clear that the issues of creativity and constraint are involved but it is also clear that these are also related to questions of social change and the transformative power of human agents, as well as the processes of production and reproduction of social structures and systems. By embracing a theoretical position such as domain theory or Goffman's notion of the loose coupling of social orders, we are necessarily led to abandon the idea that any one order or domain is preeminent or that it is the principal locus of these processes and mechanisms. Similarly, we are required to relinquish "synthesizing" or "unifying" principles that reduce the complexity and multifaceted nature of these processes to a single dimension of analysis (such as the "duality of structure", "figurations" or "discourse-practices"). Such strategies do not adequately register the

216

multiplex couplings and connections that result from the closely inter-related nature of the different layers and domains of social reality – and that manifest themselves empirically in diverse ways.

Let me first unpack a little of what Goffman has to say about the loose-coupling principle and then concentrate on the implications for the above issues. Goffman is clear that the interaction order never stands alone with regard to other orders and that no matter how strong its effects are, they never succeed in entirely blocking the influence of other orders. In this respect the loose-coupling idea is likened to the action of a membrane that defines the boundary or "skin" between social orders and that selectively allows certain influences through while blocking or filtering others. Another image that Goffman offers here is the notion of a set of "trans-formation rules . . . selecting how various externally relevant social dis-tinctions will be managed within the interaction" (Goffman 1983: 11). Thus the influence of status, authority, seniority, gender, class, ethnic back-ground and so on are selectively filtered in and out of the behavioural dis-plays and the substance of the encounter. The amount and direction of this filtering and the social consequences that flow from it will vary accord-ing to different empirical circumstances, but the influence will always be mutual and diffuse.

This applies to what Goffman describes as the "purest" instance of the workings of the interaction order, the phenomenon of queuing to complete a service transaction. On the face of it, waiting in line for a train or bus or at an airport check-in or a supermarket check-out seems to be an almost pure example of the interaction order at work since the influence of external social characteristics and distinctions such as class and status, "which are of massive significance outside the situation" (Goffman 1983: 14), would appear to be completely blocked out. Queuing proceeds on the basis of an understanding that those in line will be treated equally without favour or prejudice and that they will be dealt with on a first-come first-served basis. Those in the queue make a commitment based on this understanding and immediate considerations concerning its orderliness and maintenance, all of which are independent of the external objectives of those in the line (such as where they are going and why) or their external statuses (occupation, class, gender, seniority, ethnicity). However, Goffman points out that the assumption of equality of treatment is just that – an assumption based on the apparent irrelevance of externally based attributes and goes on to argue that the latter are "given routine, systematic 'recognition'" (1983: 14) dur-ing service transactions and that equal treatment is in no way sustained. In

217

fact, all manner of subtle and not so subtle forms of discrimination and preferential treatment take place (better seats, more courteous handling, quicker or more thorough service) without disturbing the orderliness of the queue or the apparent "fairness" of the system.

In the case of the queue then, a *sense* of the prevalence of equal treatment is generated because the influence of certain external attributes are, at certain points, blocked from the service framework. However, the sense of equal treatment is more apparent than real and Goffman's general point is that even in this, the seemingly purest example of "local determinism", the interaction order is, in fact, impinged upon by other social orders in the shape of external considerations and the forms of discrimination and preferential treatment that prevail as a result. Goffman's argument against any form of local determinism (or "rampant situationalism" as he terms it) is further strengthened by his observation that there are always elements that are external to the domain of face-to-face interaction such as language, speech styles and shared cultural knowledge that people draw upon as resources to make the interaction happen. People clearly create meaning in situations as Blumer, Garfinkel amd others have argued, but Goffman insists that they do so against the backdrop of external resources that people "bring with them" to situations. In this regard Goffman's position is not unlike that of many more structurally minded or system-oriented sociologists who conceive of a dialectical relation between micro and macro social orders (such as Bourdieu, Turner and Alexander & Colomy). Another factor that, for Goffman, underlines the importance of extra-situational influences is the history of prior dealings we have had with others who share our cultural knowledge of the regulations and expectations that apply to particular situations (1983: 6).

Although all these are in principle consistent with the presuppositions of domain theory I would argue that what Goffman's position lacks is an explicit understanding and delineation of situated activity as distinct from the interaction order in general – although I think that the idea of situated activity as I define it is implicit in Goffman's writing. Further, Goffman's position does not in and of itself underwrite the pivotal distinction I make between the situated and reproduced aspects of social relations, practices, discourses and power. I shall return to these questions presently (particularly the question of power), but for the moment let me round out Goffman's outline of the loose-coupling idea. He is against the idea of determinism either of a situational or a structural kind and the loose-coupling idea allows for a mutual but variable influence rather than any prior assumption that one particular order is more important. However, the interaction order is always related to the other orders and is influenced by them. Goffman expresses the relationship thus: "minor social ritual is not an expression *of* structural arrangements in any simple sense; at best it is an expression advanced *in regard* to these arrangements. Social structures don't 'determine' culturally standard displays, merely help select from the available repertoire of them" (1983 :11).

Other aspects of causality are raised by Goffman when he goes on to consider how wider collective social movements may originate from social forms "having merely an interactional life". The organization of West Indians in London as a politically self-conscious group began as an annual Bank Holiday street-band carnival in Notting Hill. In this case the multi-ethnic block party was "more the cause of a social movement and its group formative effects than an expression thereof" (1983: 10). This is a case of a phenomenon that begins with a strictly interactional life as Goffman phrases it, and generates a self-conscious political movement where no such phenomenon had existed previously. Of course this is not an inevitability; very often ceremonial or celebrative occasions, like many others in which face-to-face encounters figure prominently, result in nothing more than "a one-time intersection of variously impinging interests" (Goffman 1983: 10). Likewise the influence of interactional forms that are critical of established institutions and inequalities (or system elements like markets and bureaucracy) may be minimal in terms of changing the structural arrangements that are being questioned. Here Goffman gives the examples of women and blacks who have breached segregated public places with lasting consequences for access arrangements but with little or no change in the place of blacks and women in the social structure. Goffman also cites examples of interactional fads and fashions deriving from wider social movements but which have variable influence in terms of lasting effects on structural arrangements. For instance the increased informality of dress and greetings in the business world that resulted from the hippie movement did not affect the overwhelming influence and importance of status, hierarchy and economic power in the wider society.

These examples highlight the flexibility and range of applicability of the loose-coupling idea. The exact nature and degree of influence of the different orders on each other is not something that we can predict independently of knowledge of the empirical circumstances. What we can say is that there is a mutual filtering upwards and downwards of influences and effects, with each social order or domain conditioning the others. Sometimes the interaction order succeeds in blocking or filtering out most of the effects of structural or systemic arrangements, at other times the effects of these latter predominate (as in instances of coercion or confinement). Similarly, the transformative and creative consequences of forms of interactional life are variable – sometimes producing profound changes and durable social arrangements as a result. At other times they simply represent temporary fads and fashions of interactional style or "cosmetic" changes of a ceremonial or ritual kind without any lasting wider effects. Clearly also Goffman's loose-coupling idea is rather general in that it allows for a wide range of possibilities but does not provide more detail about specific forms of coupling. Nor does Goffman directly spell out the implications of this idea for a more general understanding of creativity and constraint, the transformative potential of human activity and the processes of production and reproduction. Let me now attempt to deal with these issues.

The multi-form nature of social processes

Goffman's work is consistent with domain theory in that it implies that the processes of production and reproduction are multi-levelled instead of uniform and unified. However, Goffman's account does not go far enough in this direction especially with regard to the psychological and emotional dimensions of everyday life. There are also conceptual problems with Goffman's account of the relations between different orders in that he does not adequately define the "boundaries" of the interaction order. In this sense it is hard to say where its influence begins and ends and this is both a strength and a source of confusion. On the one hand it seems to destabilize the idea that the interaction order is a distinct order in its own right – and this lends support to Giddens's claim that it "is most assuredly not the case . . . that situated interaction and more embracing institutions are different orders of phenomena" (Giddens 1987: 135). On the other hand, the very same ambiguity lends support to Rawls's claim that Goffman envisions the interaction order as "a self-ordered and separate domain" (Rawls 1987: 146).

From the point of view of domain theory, a number of crucial distinctions are missing from Goffman's account. First, he does not distinguish the notion of situated activity as a more specific feature of the interaction order – although this is implied in his work. Secondly, Goffman does not recognize or distinguish the reproduced aspects of social relations (and their underpinning powers and discourses) from their more free-form aspects. Thirdly, he does not propose variations in social settings and fields in terms of the mandatory quality of their reproduced features (and the degrees of compulsion and constraint associated with them), although this again is something that is often implicit in his work. Fourthly, as a result he does not therefore appreciate the interlacing of situated activity with the reproduced aspects of the social relations that intersect with them. Recognizing these aspects of social life would have allowed him to give definitive boundaries to the emergent character of situated activity while at the same time it would have allowed him to secure a more definite link with a distinct institutional order through the process of social reproduction. His own version of the interaction order hovers unsatisfactorily between the situated (and emergent) aspects of interaction and their more far-reaching institutionalized features. Thus he speaks of the interaction order sometimes in terms of the latter and sometimes in terms of the former (Rawls 1987: 147).

The point is that Goffman never satisfactorily conceptualizes the distinction between these two aspects of the interaction order, although he undoubtedly recognizes them both as integral elements of a full account of face-to-face conduct. Thus awareness of and attention to both aspects is a constant feature of his work and analyses, as the following examples vividly show. First, Goffman's development of role theory as expressed in his essay "role distance" (1961a) points to his exquisite awareness of the interconnections between the institutional and interaction orders. Role distance expresses the extent to which individuals may "stand apart" from the institutionally defined roles that they are called upon to occupy at various junctures. Goffman argues that the ability to distance oneself from a role is missing from those accounts of role behaviour that see it primarily in terms of the enactment of institutional demands. In this sense roles should not be understood as a kind of straitjacket of institutional expectations to which individuals rigidly conform, but as "resources" with which individuals can preserve a space for themselves and the situational requirements that emerge during the course of routine interaction.

For example, a surgeon in an operating theatre may express distance from the role of "surgeon" when critical incidents occur during operations. The surgeon may talk about home life (invoking the role of parent or spouse) or tell humorous anecdotes or even joke about the situation (the role of comedian) in order to divert attention away from the seriousness surrounding the mishap in the operating theatre. The employment of role-distancing techniques has the effect of draining the tension from the situation and smoothing out the interaction surrounding the patient, enabling the operation to continue in a controlled and efficient manner. The ability to make this creative departure from formal role requirements is to some extent dependent upon a conception of the individual as a skilled and accomplished social agent. However, more importantly the need for the departure in the first place is an emergent outcome of the specific situation itself – as reflected in the accumulated "seriousness" and tension of the interaction in the operating theatre. A primary need centres on the sustenance and maintenance of the professional self-identities of those involved so that the interaction may proceed towards a successful outcome. In a sense constraints of a situational kind require the invocation of role-distancing techniques and thus create the interactional consequences that follow from it.

An elastic and temporary membrane encloses the situation and the activities to set them slightly apart from the formal role expectations and institutional requirements until the drama has fully unfolded. A set of situated behaviours and features are created by the participants that co-mingle with the formal requirements of the institutional backdrop to produce a unique amalgam. At the same time the institutional context itself is being reproduced unintentionally by the participants. In particular the authority and professional competence of the surgeon is reaffirmed – by a subtle form of control and morale-boosting – as is the hierarchical structure of the hospital – in so far as the other nurses and doctors concur with the surgeon's authority by responding to the "invitation" to come to grips with the crisis. Furthermore, the collective "creative departure" from institutional requirements (initiated by role-distancing) to meet the demands of the situation (the unfolding of the crisis) creates the conditions in which the institutional anchoring of the behaviour is re-established. In other words the status quo is quickly restored after the disruption caused by the mishap. This example clearly underlines the dual emphasis on the partly independent character of the interaction order and its simultaneous link with institutional reproduction.

The same is true of Goffman's treatment of trust and tact as reflected in his analysis of civil inattention and face-work as well as of other aspects of social life such as involvement obligations. This is contrary to Giddens's (1987) argument that Goffman limits the implications of his work solely to the interaction order. It is true that Goffman often tends to highlight the importance of the interaction order because it has often been overlooked or downgraded by sociologists in general, but Goffman is always aware (as in the example of role distance) of the intrinsic link with the institutional order. Giddens, on the other hand, in elevating the importance of the link between institutional reproduction and face-to-face conduct, glides over the independent conditioning influence of the interaction order.

For example, Giddens insists that although Goffman speaks of the use of mutual support mechanisms such as tact as a means of establishing trust between co-present individuals, he fails to acknowledge how this makes possible "the existence of contacts and relationships that stretch across contexts of co-presence" and that trust not only "influences and orders what we do in co-present interaction . . . but equally importantly by the very same token it orders our relations with them across a diversity of contexts" (Giddens 1987: 135–6). Of course in a general sense this is true. If trust is to be a feature of co-present encounters it must also exist in a general sense beyond and across such situations in order for it to be a meaningful resource that people can "draw into" their encounters. Goffman recognizes this in his view of the relation of the interaction order to the wider institutional environment and this is exemplified in his view that civil inattention is accorded to all strangers (on the street, in a lift and so on) as a general rule. However, Giddens construes trust primarily in this more general sense – as implicated in institutional reproduction – and thereby misses out the more particular properties and features of trust that are negotiated emergents of particular situations.

To see trust primarily as a generalized resource that cuts across situations, diverts attention away from the variability of form that trust takes in different situations and the diverse ways in which people deploy trust in encounters. In this sense trust in social life is a many-faceted thing; it is not simply and solely a generalized resource. The latter view of trust prevents us from entertaining questions such as why do we not trust everyone we meet? What kinds and levels of trust are there, and how fragile and enduring are they? These sorts of questions are marginalized in Giddens's schema with his overriding insistence that institutional reproduction is primary and that the interaction order produces no independent effects. (This is reaffirmed through the duality of structure principle that short-cuts any engagement with an intermediate domain of interaction.) Goffman's work includes attention to such questions without denying that trust has more general implications for social relations across a diversity of contexts. The situated nature of trust points to its interactional achievement as the negotiated outcome of either one-off situations or linked episodes of face-to-face behaviour. Thus generalized attitudes or predispositions of a trusting nature are simply a backdrop or initial position from which other types and forms of involvement start life. Subsequent encounters may alter or transform this predisposition in a manner that in a significant sense "brackets out" or masks the influence of an initial general attitude of trust.

Trust therefore has to be understood as a multi-form phenomenon. In some cases it can be understood as a generalized resource that is drawn upon by actors to make the encounter "work" or "happen" and in this sense it is incidental to the internal dynamics of co-present encounters. In other cases the formation of trust is directly linked to the exigencies of situated activity (including elements of psychobiography) and its unfolding character over time. These two forms can be seen in the example of the relations of trust among professional actors in their working environment. First, the work situation in the acting profession is an uncertain and insecure environment in which personal vulnerability is heightened and in which the ability to trust others and to make this trust "visible" is highly valued (Layder 1981, 1984). Elsewhere I have argued that general trust relationships in acting are facilitated by the liberal use of camp language by actors (Layder 1993: 55–6, 87–8). The use of expressions such as "dear" and "love" and "darling" regardless of the gender or sexual proclivities of those involved provides an idiomatic form of discourse (see previous section) that communicates, in the words of one actor, "little cuddles without touching" and thus provides a "safe" medium for interaction. The softness and protectiveness of camp banter, as well as effusive behavioural displays such as actual cuddling and touching, demonstrate trust in an environment where it is a valued resource. At the same time this demonstration or realization of trust serves to reproduce its institutionalized form as a general interactional resource within the occupational milieu.

Of course in each instance the use of idiom has to be renewed in the specific circumstances of a face-to-face encounter and involves various kinds of interactional negotiation, but this reliance on the trust conditions of behaviour manifests itself largely as a continuous background accompaniment to the encounter. As I said in the section on discourse and social reproduction, the invocation of such idiomatic forms is done in a quasi-automatic way and acts to short-cut the need constantly to renegotiate the background understandings and basic assumptions of routine encounters.

While this reproductive process provides a steady-state accompaniment to encounters across different work situations it also frees up the interactional foreground for the negotiation and development of other kinds and modes of trust relationships in specific circumstances with particular people. For example, the very close collaboration between a director and a group of actors rehearsing for a specific production (a play or a film) requires the establishment of trust between those involved.

Since the director is in a position of authority over the actors and needs to induce optimum dramatic performances from them, the director also needs to be able to trust that they can and will do so. The actors, in turn, need truly to believe that the director "knows" and understands the characters and the structure of the play in a manner that enables them to "give" themselves fully to the task and to accept the authority and competence of the director. They need to be committed psychologically and emotionally and this requires a highly charged and personalized trust. This may develop more or less immediately, or it may take time (days or weeks) and involve a complex and subtle "testing out" of each other. Alternatively real trust may never fully develop at all. The consequences of the latter may manifest themselves in a below-par production as a whole or less-than-peak performances from particular actors. The director has to assess the psychological make-up or personal chemistry of each of the actors so as to be able to push them dramatically without undermining their confidence. During this process the director also has to allow the actors to explore their illusions about their characters in order to achieve truthful performances in the end. From both the director's and actors' points of view, an atmosphere of mutual trust in the work situation must emerge from the face-to-face encounters between specific individuals in rehearsal.

Such trust is not something that is taken-for-granted or a natural part of the continuity of institutional reproduction; it has to be constantly earned, negotiated and battled for in each situation and interpersonal exchange. It is necessarily a precarious and fragile trust based on highly personalized relations that rely upon the continuous emotion-work of those involved – as well as the complex interweaving of the authority relationship between actors and director. The substantive core of this kind of trust is developed over a short period of time in relation to a specific work task – the unique interpretation of dramatic characters for a particular production. The short-term contract basis of much of the work in acting (Layder 1984) means that trust in similar but separate work situations has to be renegotiated each time to take account of the changing personalities, dramatic objectives and the levels of character and role-identification required. (Even if the director has worked with particular actors before, this will serve only as a "starting position" for the development of trust in different circumstances.)

The two modalities of trust that occur simultaneously in the work context of acting simply highlight a more general point about the nature of everyday life. This centres on the fact that there are different "trust requirements" demanded by the multiplicity of settings and contexts of social life and that these are always mediated, to varying degrees, by the interaction order and situated activity. In this sense the interaction order can never be completely severed from the institutional order (nor from other social domains) and thus Rawls's insistence that there is a morality specific to the interaction order (surrounding the care and maintenance of selves) has no basis since morality (or trust or involvement obligations) has no definite boundaries. Like power, moral elements leak into every sphere of social life – large and small, trivial and important, fleeting and persistent. In this manner all the principal domains of social (and psychological) reality are interlinked and cannot be artifically separated. However, each has its own level of autonomy from the others and thus can resist any complete "determination" by other domains. Similarly the interdependence of each with the others means that no single domain can ever be fully self-determining.

Thus all aspects of the interaction order – the care and maintenance of the self, morality, resistance (as well as all those things that Goffman concerned himself with in the study of face-to-face encounters such as trust, involvement, the framing of situations and so on) cannot in themselves be considered to be exclusive properties of the interaction order. What is crucial is that these elements take on different guises within and between domains and this is what makes the influence of different orders distinguishable. As I have argued, I also think that a distinction between the more general notion of the interaction order and the more specific notion of situated activity is absolutely essential here. Only in this manner can we achieve conceptual purchase on the general properties and needs of face-to-face interaction (which are linked to the institutional sphere) as distinct from the actual manner in which they are dealt with by specific participants in situated encounters – and which are by nature evanescent.

The creation and replication of society and social life

What is distinct about situated activity (as opposed simply to the inter-action order) is that compared with other domains it functions as a "delivery" mechanism rather than a "supply system". In this sense the institutional order *sanctions* and legitimizes various notions of morality and behaviour such as rules of involvement (looking at another while talking to them) or civil inattention (not staring at strangers in public places), but it does not *guarantee* the observance of these in particular circumstances, nor does it provide the contents and substance of the actual behaviour indicated and sanctioned by it. The interaction order translates and trans-forms these into terms that refer to those generalized aspects of face-to-face encounters such as care and maintenance of self and so on. In this sense the interaction order acts as a selection membrane, as Goffman says, allowing in only those influences most pertinent to the encounter, but it is also decisive in setting the generalized shape of encounters as reflected in the ceremonies and rituals of interaction. What Goffman failed to do was to distinguish between the interaction order as furnishing a pattern that reflects "the syntactical relations among the acts of different persons mutually present to one another" (Goffman 1967: 2) and situated activity as the mechanism that delivers unique instances of actual conduct.

It is also clear, as I have already argued, that Goffman was aware of the specific nature of situated activity (actual encounters) as compared with the interaction order and this is clearly hinted at when he says "a normatively stabilized structure is at issue, a 'social gathering', but this is a shifting entity, necessarily evanescent, created by arrivals and killed by departures" (Goffman 1967: 3). Here we get the recognition of the tension between social patterning and actual conduct that obeys a different sense of reality and temporal rhythm. However, Goffman never developed the distinction nor made it part of his overall conceptual apparatus and thus I think this has contributed to the confusion surrounding the nature of the interaction order and its relation with other orders (or domains). Similarly the delivery of conduct through specific participants has to be contrasted with the psychobiographies of individuals that operate in a dual fashion partly through memory traces (as suppliers of predispositions, attitudes and so on) and partly through the bodily enactment of various behaviours. This again is missing from Goffman's version of individual psychol-ogy that he deliberately "stripped and cramped" to suit the analysis of "moments and their men" rather than "men and their moments".

Taking into account the diffuse interrelations between social domains means that we must view the processes of social production and reproduction as complex and multi-levelled. By definition this view demands that we jettison accounts of them that stress, or give the impression that they are compressed and "unitary" processes that are forged by the drawing together of subjective and objective aspects of social life (albeit in a number of different ways). Such accounts are present in the work of many sociologists although they vary in the form they take and their background development. The most sophisticated of these attempt to combine the analysis of activity with that of institutions by insisting that there is a sort of defining moment in every instance of social activity (every encounter) in which society is simultaneously produced and reproduced (created and recreated). This kind of "solution" is present (although in different forms) in the work of a whole range of authors including Berger & Luckmann (1967), Giddens (1976, 1977, 1984), Bourdieu (1977) and Bhaskar (1979). These authors see the solution as a binding together of agency and structure and macro and micro elements. Other sociologists such as Blumer and Becker see the solution exclusively in terms of interaction or intersubjective processes and reject the idea of social systems external to activity. Yet others claim that social processes must be understood in terms of some "unifying" concept such as "discourse" (Foucault) or "figuration" (Elias) – see Layder (1994) for the details of these variations.

What all these solutions have in common is the reduction of complex social processes to a simplified unity – even though what this unity actually is, and how it operates are understood in different terms by different authors. These positions are best summarized in Giddens's and Bourdieu's work in which the processes of social production and reproduction are clearly envisioned as two sides of the same coin that occur simultaneously and lead to effects of equal strength and intensity. For instance Giddens (1976: 123) says: "every act which contributes to the reproduction of a structure is also an act of production a novel enterprise, and as such may initiate change by altering that structure at the same time as it produces it". Production here involves the creative abilities of individuals and this gives rise to what Giddens calls the "double involvement of individuals and institutions" in which "we create society at the same time we are created by it" (Giddens 1981: 14). Further, Giddens states that "social systems only exist in so far as they are created and recreated in every encounter, as the active accomplishment of human subjects" (1977: 118). Strikingly similar statements can be found in the work of Berger & Luckmann (1967), (Paci 1972: 381), Bourdieu (1977: 79) and Bhaskar (1979: 44).

Such statements are predicated on the assumption that society and social life are unitary and one-dimensional and thus the processes of production and reproduction are themselves unitary processes. I believe that such statements are misleading and simplify what in fact are far more complex processes. My argument is that these processes must be conceptualized as multiplex phenomena that take place within and between three principal social domains – psychobiography (self-identity), situated activity and social systems (treating settings, fields and contextual resources under the composite heading of social systems). Thus statements that stress the simultaneous production/reproduction or creation/recreation of social life make overgeneralized and oversimplified claims about the unitary nature of these processes and the nature of social life itself. I shall deal separately with the several related issues that this raises in more detail.

First, let me distinguish three modes in which social activity contributes to social reproduction. This entails specifying three levels at which the reproduction (and production) of social life is accomplished through everyday encounters. The types and levels are implicated in each other in complex, diffuse and overlapping ways. Rather like the domains themselves they are simultaneous processes and are mutually constitutive – although they each possess quite distinctive characteristics. The most encompassing form is what I term "general" or "system reproduction", while the other two, "situated and "psychobiographical" reproduction, are enfolded within the more general type. Since they are mutually constitutive, this "enfolding" simply refers to the differences in the "scope" or reach of influence of the types of reproduction. In this sense system reproduction is the widest reference point for processes of social reproduction.

General or system reproduction

This provides the most enveloping sense that can be attached to social reproduction. It refers to the manner in which the routine use of generalized resources (material, discursive and dominative) by actors in the fields, settings and locations of social life serve to reproduce these very forms. This has to do with the production and reproduction of what Popper calls "world 3" phenomena of a cultural, material or authoritative kind and in this sense such phenomena are subjectless (as in Popper's construal of "knowledge without a knowing subject"). In fact this type of reproduction "works on" already established and embedded social phenomena (cultural, institutional) and represents the manner in which routine social encounters contribute to the structural continuity of societal forms. Although this is essentially about the reproduction of "subjectless" social forms, the latter are realized only through the actual practices and encounters of everyday life.

General or system reproduction is the mode in which the conditions inherited from the past (in the form of tradition, social relations and forms of control and domination) are continually reconstituted in and through the effects of routine everyday activities and encounters. Thus system reproduction is the result of a dual process in which these "standing conditions" enter into the constitution of everyday encounters by influencing their general parameters and forms at the same time as they themselves are recreated or reproduced by these activities. Although this requires the skilful application of rules and resources by the participants, the level of creativity involved is minimal. In this respect the idea that every act of reproduction is also an act of production, a novel enterprise (or that we create society at the same time we are created by it), is quite misleading. We do not create social system features in routine encounters; we merely recreate, replicate or reproduce the social settings, fields, contexts and resources that already exist. Thus those elements of social encounters that contribute to system reproduction are, by definition, primarily concerned with the reaffirmation and revivification of extant social forms. As soon as social activity entails the transformation of system elements, it ceases to be routine and reproductive and must be understood as part of processes of social (system or structural) change. While this latter always remains a *potential* built into all social activity, it becomes actualized only in circumstances that are by definition non-routine or exceptional in so far as they involve the subversion of standardized, reproduced practices.

Since everyday encounters always depend on participants drawing upon system elements to "make them happen" (enablements) and to give them shape (constraints) in the most general sense, as a consequence, they always contribute in some measure to system reproduction. The extent of this reproductive contribution varies according to different settings and circumstances and this undercuts the idea of a unitary and "even" process that is implicit in the established imagery of the process of reproduction. Also while *at times* routine interaction makes a very substantial contribution to system reproduction, it is often the case that this continuity hangs by a thread. This is because of anti-social and unsocial pressures routinely unloosed by the internal dynamics of situated activities and the personalities involved. In this sense situated and biographical reproduction cut into the overall contribution to system reproduction and reduce it to a minimal presence. Thus the density and positive or negative valency of general reproduction may vary within and between encounters.

Situated production and reproduction

Social encounters are not simply concerned with system reproduction since they are situated phenomena with their own emergent needs and problems. In this respect those aspects of the interaction order that I have indicated previously (care and maintenance of self, production of meaning and so on) set up "reproductive" problems for participants connected with the continuity and the "syntactical relations among the acts" of those mutually present. That is, a range of interactive problems that are typically thrown up in daily encounters, such as entering and leaving rituals, involvement, situational propriety, tact and trust, face-saving, establishing a face and line, need to be taken into account or dealt with by participants during the course of the encounter. This makes them problems of social reproduction of the interaction order and this has to do with the continuity of the encounter and its general success or "failure". In Goffman's terms these general imperatives of the interaction order function as the membrane that allows through certain aspects of other orders (such as the institutional order or the influence of contextual resources like language and idiom) while blocking others – and as such there is solid link with general or system reproduction.

Of course meeting the requirements of the interaction order (for example, the need to display situational propriety, or different kinds of involvement) also requires certain (minimum) levels of creativity, knowledgeability and skilfulness on behalf of participants – as indeed is also required in system reproduction. However, the most creative inputs are concerned with situated activity considered as the "delivery system" of behaviour and interactional dynamics in the unique circumstances of the encounter. This pinpoints the way in which the needs and requirements of the interaction order are dealt with or met by particular individuals and in specific situations. In this sense it links with the issue of the continuity of social life in relation to the "smoothness" (or disruptiveness) of the encounter in terms of its contingent features. Smoothness here concerns "how the encounter goes" or "turns out" in terms of whether those involved are gelling with each other (currently as well as in the context of previous involvements), what their purposes are, the emotional tenor of the interaction, the social setting of the encounter, and so on.

The production of localized meanings, interpretations and definitions of events and behaviour is particularly important since it significantly influences the degree of understanding and consensus between participants and the nature of their commitment to and involvement in the encounter – all of which are absolutely pivotal to the outcome. In this sense situated activity is an inherently productive and creative enterprise. However, this production and creativity is predominantly *localized* and works on the raw material of general background resources to construct localized meanings, trust requirements, and so forth. In this sense the transformative implications of face-to-face encounters are limited to the domain of situated activity and its local manifestation. In routine everyday encounters such activity is not transformative or creative of system elements. Rather, since these elements are used as templates for localized creativity, they are simultaneously reproductive of generalized system elements.

This is not to deny that system change and other social transformations may *have their origins in* the routines of everyday life (as with Goffman's example of the Notting Hill Street Carnival) but once initiated – and for the period of transition – the interactional forms have become something other than routine and everyday. They have become part of social movements either explicitly geared to change or some incidental or unintended part of the change process itself. If such behavioural forms become established in a new set of system arrangements, then they eventually may form part of its routinized institutional features. However, some behavioural forms will simply represent interactional fads and fashion (what could be termed "behavioural idioms") as in Goffman's example of Hippie dress codes and forms of "address" that were destined to remain part of cultural life without giving rise to fundamental systemic changes in the established hierarchies of power and control.

However, the focus of analysis here is on the productive and reproductive effects of *routine* everyday encounters rather than the circumstances in which non-routine social changes flow from, or are precipitated by, such conduct. In this sense a crucial defining feature of routine behaviour is its non-change outcome – the sense in which it serves to reaffirm an established set of arrangements (not simply or necessarily legitimate – or part of official practices). This may be contrasted with the realization of the transformative potential of routine behaviour in a wider (structural or systemic) sense that forms part of the analysis of social change and as such is beyond the scope of this present study. However, a great many encounters represent what Goffman (1983: 10) describes as the "one-time intersection of variously impinging interests . . . and nothing beyond that". In terms of the theory of social domains this indicates something of the evanescent quality of situated activity – its tendency to fade away as the participants disperse in time and space – that is also reflected in Goffman's notion of encounters as "created by arrivals and killed by departures". Even though the participants may have met before and may meet up again, the creative products of these encounters – in terms of presentation of self, negotiated meanings, definitions and shared understandings – will be inextricably linked to particular situations of their use or to episodes of behaviour involving the same people.

As I argued in Chapter 3 in speaking of the duality of social relations, the degree of latitude for creative departures from the reproduced aspects of social relations depends to a significant extent on the kinds of settings in which encounters are located. This also means that the extent to which general reproduction is either emphasized or undercut depends not only upon the emergent outcomes of situated and psychobiographical production and reproduction but also on the degree to which these processes are subject to the influence of constraints imposed by different kinds of social organization, power and control (system elements) – and the extent of their sedimentation in time and space.

Psychobiographical production and reproduction

Situated activity is also a medium for the production and reproduction of self-identities, personalities and behavioural predispositions and these are characteristically overlooked in sociological accounts (often in a mis-guided attempt to steer clear of psychological reductionism). As I stressed in Chapter 2 the emotional underbelly of social life and social encounters must be registered in social theory in a way that it has not been hitherto. The continuous and diffuse dispersal of emotion in social behaviour and activities has to be understood in relation to other issues such as ontologi-cal security and the dialectic of separateness and relatedness in order to obtain a full understanding of the link between emotion and processes of production and reproduction.

Pivotal in this respect is the manner in which individuals (considered as unique pyschic units) participate in their everyday encounters and the kinds of psychic issues that are thus implicated. Goffman has skirted around these issues in discussions of deference and demeanour and the social organization of embarrassment but more attention needs to be given to the psychodynamic implications of participation in social events such as face-to-face encounters. As I have already hinted, some of Laing's concern with ontological security is central to these questions, as is the issue of self-esteem (J. Turner 1988). The extent to which a person feels secure or anxious in particular encounters is important in determining the success of the encounter, as well as the willingness of the person to remain, leave or repeat the encounter as Turner has observed. Collins (1983) similarly refers to the connection between the flow of emotions in encounters and the relation between status and power. Interactions between equals results in a "ritual bondedness" while those between superiors and subordinates involve asymmetries in the flow of emotional energy – the person who dominates picking up more emotional energy while the reserves of the one who is dominated are steadily depleted. This also links with Scheff's (1990) notion of an emotion-deference system (see Ch. 2).

The point about these aspects of the individual's psychic predisposition is that they all have implications for the processes of production and reproduction. Both situated and psychobiographical aspects of reproduction and production take place within the envelope of general or system reproduction and are therefore factors that may either undercut or add to the overall reproductive contribution. As with situated activity, the productive and reproductive concerns of psychobiographical elements may take precedence over the other two kinds (without of course extinguishing them entirely). For example, this occurs when dominant or forceful personalities "take over" situations and monopolise the topics of conversation or manage to turn all the interactional exchanges into an egocentric display. A similarly disruptive effect may occur when a participant's nervousness, shyness, or anxiety "infects" the whole encounter (see comments on the contagion of embarrassment in Chapter 2). Although the consequences for the encounter may be different, both examples point to the manner in which elements of psychobiography such as self-identity, self-esteem, behavioural disposition and so on, take centre stage in the proceedings, displacing and reconfiguring the needs of the interaction order as well as placing in abeyance the wider demands of reproduced social relations and practices. In a sense another "membrane" surrounds the psychobiographical domain that filters in and out the influences of institutional and interaction orders.

Of course such psychological elements interweave closely with the situated and emergent aspects of situations creating the conditions under which certain aspects of the interaction order are sustained by the deployment of psychological skills such as the role-distancing technique observed and described by Goffman. Although the deployment of such techniques is related to the needs of the interaction order (such as preservation of self-identity, or maintenance of continuity and meaning) Goffman failed to emphasize that their use is also closely dependent upon the psychological and social skills of the person who deploys them. In this sense role distancing skills may be used appropriately or inexpertly, with finesse or clumsily and so on, according to the judgements, perceptiveness, sensitivity and experience of the person employing them. In this manner the combined demands of situated activity and psychobiography may take precedence over those of general or system reproduction. It is these combined effects that highlight and make possible the individual's ability to "stand apart" from the constraints (including expectations, rights and duties) of wider social settings and system elements. In this sense neither individuals nor their situated activities are "determined" by system or structural forces. In the case of individuals there always remains a decidedly unsocial or anti-social impulse (represented in the tension between relatedness and separateness) and which may cut-through the insistent demands of both system elements and face-to-face encounters. Such an ability is a necessary precondition for the emergence and sustenance of autonomous and unique self-identities.

Creativity and social agency

This brings us to the issue of the relation between agency and structure (or system) and the extent to which individuals are creative and transformative in social encounters. In the light of the above distinctions it is apparent that assertions of the kind that "we create society at the same time as we are created by it", or that "every act of reproduction is also a novel enterprise", are rather vague and lacking in substance. On the one hand, a great deal of system reproduction is about just that – the reaffirmation and replication of already established system features – requiring only the minimum of creative skills and virtually nothing in the way of transformative implications at the system level. On the other hand, much routine situated activity requires a great deal of creativity and ingenuity with respect to the notions of self, meaning, situational propriety and so on – that is, the needs and requirements of the interaction order. In this localized sense a fair amount of transformative activity is implicated in the shaping and reshaping of the interactional fabric at the face-to-face level.

235

Those schemas that do not take into account the relatively independent constraints and requirements of the interaction order therefore underestimate the degree of creativity involved in generating face-to-face encounters. At the same time they overestimate the extent and type of creativity involved in institutional (or system) reproduction by assuming that there is a direct link between agency, structures and systems (primarily institutional phenomena). This is most apparent in Giddens's notion of the duality of structure, but it is also implicit in many of the other schemas that neglect the influence of the interaction order (Bourdieu, Foucault, Habermas, Paci, Bhaskar, Berger & Luckmann). These authors similarly underestimate the extent of creativity channelled through psychic and emotional energies as they are "discharged" by individuals in their routine everyday encounters. In this sense individuals display true resourcefulness, creativity and skilfulness in making social encounters happen.

Habitus, agency and social reproduction

This brings us to the question of the tie between individuals (agency) and the wider social environment (systems, structures) to which they belong. This involves identifying the basic cognitive mechanisms that connect the activities thoughts and intentions of individuals with the wider society. Bourdieu has used the concept of "habitus" to refer to such a mechanism. By habitus he means the durable motivations, perceptions and forms of knowledge that people carry around in their heads as a result of living in particular social environments and that predispose them to act in certain ways. Social class background, for instance, influences one's habits and dispositions – as does participation in any social grouping such as, for example, an occupational group. In a study of routine police work in Northern Ireland, Brewer (1990) found that the police were sensitively aware of the signs of danger (such as particular sounds or unusual silences) as they patrolled the streets. Their training and experience ensured that they were continually alive to the possibility of trouble but it also equipped them with the technical and psychological means of handling it. An important element of psychological support was to be found in the typical forms of talk (vocabularies) that allowed the police to express their feelings about being potential targets of paramilitary attack and (to some extent) to "normalize" the threat of political violence. As a consequence this occupational vocabulary of feeling and motive rendered the constant threat of violence a more manageable feature of the routine aspects of their jobs.

Thus the habitus (in this case of an occupational group) provides a conduit that allows the collective influences of the group to enter into the actual practices of individuals (and conversely, to provide a connection between an individual's practices and the group). For Bourdieu, habitus is the key link in understanding why it is that routine activity is to some degree predictable and patterned while at the same time the individuals concerned are creatively involved, producing novel solutions to the problems thrown up during face-to-face encounters. In this respect habitus reflects the way in which individuals' social backgrounds are represented in their mental make-up and general orientation to the world, but which allow them to deal with situations as they arise in terms of their own personal styles and biographies. Through the habitus, individuals do not simply act according to the dictates of social structures and systems, but neither do they simply act in terms of their subjective intentions. The habitus allows improvisation within the limits set by the social environment.

This is very similar to Giddens's notion of the duality of structure wherein the individual is directly linked to the wider social environment and the two are mutually constitutive. But as with Giddens's model, Bourdieu's notion of habitus leaves out of account the crucial mediating role of situated activity (and the interaction order in general) and thus leads to the overestimation of the creative or productive implications involved in general reproduction that I have already discussed. However, further than this, although Bourdieu's notion of habitus endeavours to register a "subjective" element in the link between activity and social forms (as does "the duality of structure"), it does not go anything like far enough. In this respect habitus has a definite bias towards the social side of things in that it refers to the dispositions and motives that result from the experience of particular social backgrounds and groups. It does not incorporate the fullness of an individual's psychobiography. A person's unique psyche and biographical experiences produce dispositions, motives and attitudes that may be at variance with those that have been imprinted by social contexts, pressures and influences. Although there should be no presupposition that these psychological dispositions will necessarily override those enshrined in the social habitus, neither should there be any general assumption that social influences will be more important. (The same argument can be made for the conditioning and modifying influence of situated activity on habitus since it is closely entwined with psychobiography.)

Bourdieu, Giddens and others propose that reproduction and production are two sides of the same coin and therefore imply that the integrative effects of everyday behaviour are largely routine and taken-for-granted. However, empirically the reproductive potential of routine encounters varies according to the kinds of settings, fields and resource-contexts in which they take place. It also depends upon the mood states of the people involved, their overall personality traits and their behavioural predispositions. Furthermore, the emotional undercurrents that run through particular situations as a result of the dynamics of the situations themselves or the gelling or otherwise of the personalities involved will also play a significant part in influencing the extent to which face-to-face conduct is reproductive or integrative. Instead of a smooth and unproblematic process by which the habitus draws into play the reproductive aspects of social behaviour, social encounters should be seen against the backdrop of a potentially uneven, ruptured and conflictual relationship between psychological and social worlds. The more we take account of the psychological inputs and emotion-work in encounters, the more we are led to the conclusion that the processes of social reproduction are rarely perfect and complete; they are always "in process", tenuous and uncertain.

As I hinted earlier, in cases where emotional energy is the primary fuel of the encounter and self-interest is at a premium, social reproduction takes a back seat to psychic reproduction in so far as the display and contestation of egos feed into a reaffirmation of personalities and behavioural styles. Thus psychic interiors are reproduced and given new life while general social reproduction is reduced to a background accompaniment. Bourdieu's notion of habitus and Giddens's views on the duality of structure do not adequately deal with some of the more subtle and anti-social strands implicated in processes of production and reproduction. In particular they do not properly come to terms with the fact that processes of social reproduction are multi-form and layered. Nor do they acknowledge that such processes are forever tenuous, incomplete and only potentially integrative in their effects. If the affectual underbelly of everyday encounters is taken into account then it is clear that social reproduction and integration can never be viewed as an automatic or taken-for-granted outcome of routine encounters – they are contingent features of social interaction. Moreover, reproduction and integration (of individual and society) are always potentially under threat from invasive influences brought to bear by psychic, anti-social and deviant behavioural styles, and thus are most sensitive to the variability of empirical circumstances.

238

Conclusion: creativity and constraint in social life

I have approached the more general question of the nature of creativity and constraint in social life on three broad fronts. First, I examined the nature of constraints themselves and argued that they must be understood as multidimensional in character. This is necessary to overcome the limitations of viewing them purely as "internal" phenomena reflecting people's reasons and motivations or as the outcome of intersubjective negotiations. Both of these latter views radically underestimate the objective and compelling character of constraints understood as primarily *social* (rather than psychological) phenomena. The theory of social domains insists that registering the external aspects of social constraints (and their complementarity with internalized constraints) in no way minimizes the creativity, skilfulness or knowledgeability of human social actors. In fact it underscores these capacities by pointing to the dynamic relationship between subjective and objective aspects of social life and the manner in which reasons and motivations are shaped by wider cultural resources. By contrast those approaches that endorse only an internalist or intersubjective point of view (for example structuration theory and social constructionism) are unable to define properly the contours and limitations of human skilfulness and knowledgeability since they exclude the external and objective nature of constraints.

An adequate understanding of the nature of human creativity can be achieved only in the context of an appreciation of the nature of social constraints and the manner in which they form an integral part of the routine processes of social repoduction. This led me to a depiction of the relation between discourse and social reproduction and the issues of communicative understanding in social interaction that it entails. My main argument here was that there is a certain sense in which human beings can be understood as nodal points at the intersection of the array of culturally available discourses. This is the kernel of truth in the poststructuralist preoccupation with the function of social discourses and the formation of subjectivity. I further argued that there is a push towards idiomatic stylization that is a consequence of routinely arising problems of communicative understanding in social interaction. However, idiomatic stylization is always only a preliminary holding point for communicative understanding that allows temporary shelter for the temporal unfolding of emergent agreements and understandings. However, innovative elements (and the discursive departures they entail) always arise since meaning not only is discursively assigned but is always a partly achieved and emergent outcome of situated activity and the psychobiographical inputs of the participants, including feelings, emotions and personal powers. Thus people are never *simply* nodal points of overlapping discourses; they are social agents capable of subverting, reformulating and reinventing the discursive resources that are available to them. People cannot be viewed as conduits of discourses, as if their subjectivity was constructed only in discourse. Subjectivity must be understood as an outcome of psychobiography and the anti-social and unsocial (egoistic) pressures and impulses that subserve it. People are active selectors and shapers of the limited array of discourses that is available for them to draw upon in their daily lives.

Finally, I approached the question of creativity and constraint from the point of view of the different modes of production and reproduction in social life and pointed out that it is necessary to distinguish between general, situational and psychobiographical production and reproduction. By conflating these modes and speaking of production and reproduction as if they were unimodal and uniform, existing approaches either overstress or understress the role of either or both of these processes and also mask two major sources of variation in them. First, during routine interaction the degree of transformative creativity that makes itself felt at organizational or institutional levels is severely circumscribed during routine "everyday" interaction and in that sense is overwhelmingly reproductive. Secondly, under the same circumstances (of organizational continuity), most of the creative work that people do remains fixed in situated activity and is buttressed by psychobiographical reproduction. Further, the importance of psychological and situated elements of social life has been frequently overlooked in so far as understanding how social reproduction is conceived. Social reproduction cannot be understood as a perfected (or even perfectible) process because it is constantly "in question" and liable to be undercut by emotional and psychological undercurrents (among other things related to the maintenance of self-esteem, ego enhancement and collective deviance) working themselves out in actual situations. Thus even the "successful" accomplishment of instances of reproduction must be thought to be intrinsically serrated affairs. Thus although replication is always present in social interaction at some minimal level, in particular circumstances, it may be more appropriate to conceive of it as "hanging by a thread".

6

Conclusion

Encounters, subjectivity and integration

In order to underline the distinctiveness and the boundaries of the position I have outlined in this book, let me briefly say what I have had to exclude from my account. First, it follows from the centrality of my focus on situated activity, and its embeddedness in the other key domains of social life, that I have had to limit my concern with collective phenomena in a special sense. This has been a matter of emphasis rather than logical or theoretical exclusion. There are two very obvious senses in which collective phenomena are incorporated within the remit of the analytic framework that I have employed. First, collective phenomena are entailed in the notion of contextual resources both as society-wide distributive effects (as in inequalities of wealth or cultural capital) as well as cultural phenomena like ideology and forms of signification that feed into social activity in various ways.

Secondly, collective aspects of social life are present in the notion of settings as the reproduced forms of social life that provide the immediate environments and arenas of social activity. However, my concentration on face-to-face interaction has meant that a focus on collective agency (such as that involving gender, class and racialized groupings) has had to take a back seat. Therefore questions relating to incompatibilities between various groupings with regard to the distribution of resources and "unequal access to economic, political, legal and cultural technologies" (Mouzelis 1995: 99) as well as the conflicts that are often involved in issues of collective agency (Scott 1995) have also been secondary to my immediate concerns. Questions about collective agency clearly bear upon issues of both social and system integration as Lockwood (1964) defines them. Although I would claim that what I have argued has to do with social and system integration, I have not concentrated on the relation of collective action to these elements of social life.

In this respect my attention has dwelt on the question of the relation of face-to-face activity (or "encounters") to social and system integration. However, one justification for this preoccupation has to do with the fact that all too often in sociological analysis there has been an implicit assumption that social and system integration are "fundamentally" about collective phenomena (and this is reflected in Lockwood's original con-strual of the problem). Now in a certain sense sociology and social analysis are (and must be) predicated on a collectivist assumption and I would not want to deny this in the least (see Alexander 1985). In my view social analysis must start from a collectivist premis in order adequately to account for the non-random and ordered nature of much social organiza-tion and social life (which is not to deny that there are elements of social life that seem to be random and disordered). However, to acknowledge this epistemological starting point it does not follow that the collective aspects of social life are entirely formed from other collective elements. In other words it does not follow that system integration is predicated on col-lective agency in the sense that system elements like the economy, polity and so on are exclusively dependent for their continuance on the outcome of collective forms of agency.

Although Giddens does not begin from an endorsement of an objectiv-ist point of view (which I would argue is entailed in the collectivist premise), he has recognized the intimate tie between individual forms of agency, face-to-face behaviour (everyday life) and the more institutional-ized features of social systems – even though I disagree fundamentally with many aspects of his view of this problem, as well as his attempted resolu-tion of it. (This connects closely with what I take to be Giddens's misinter-pretation of Goffman's notion of the interaction order and his consequent rejection of situated activity as a partially independent aspect of social life.) The theory of social domains suggests that the institutionalized features of social life rest on both collectivist and objectivist assumptions (the latter being entailed in the former) but that individual agency and interactive encounters are also strongly implicated in the larger forces of social life and organization. A major difference between the theory of social domains and structuration theory is my insistence that psychobiography and situated activity have to be treated as separable aspects (domains) of social behaviour and that they in turn are ontologically distinguishable from systemic aspects such as settings and contextual resources.

Nevertheless the theory of social domains has links with a tradition of sociology that is not generally associated with questions concerning social and system integration although I would argue that, in fact, it does and must. I am referring principally to Goffman's work here although in a different way that of some symbolic interactionists and ethnomethodologists could also be said to bear on these questions. In this respect social integration has to be understood not only as the outcome of various socially emergent phenomena such as the division of labour (Durkheim) consensus on values (Parsons and Durkheim) or the orderly or conflictual relations between actors or groups (Lockwood), but also as the outcome of psychological production and reproduction within the arena of situated activity. As with much of the analysis I employ throughout this book (in particular in relation to power and the processes of production and reproduction) I believe that social integration must be conceived of as a multi-form, multidimensional phenomenon with several different but connected aspects. Thus the areas of psychobiography and situated activity can be conceived of as localized aspects of social integration that are part and parcel of the more generalized processes of social production and reproduction – particularly general or system reproduction (which, of course, includes institutional features).

Much of Goffman's work has been in this area although he himself was never concerned with explicating the links between face-to-face behaviour and these more general aspects of social integration – or indeed social reproduction. Goffman's main preoccupation was with describing the form of various kinds of encounters (their internal structure so to speak) and his project necessitated that he developed a series of concepts related to these issues. However, he never developed a general and encompassing framework of concepts (à la Parsons or Marx) that would enable him to link his microstudies of encounters and public order with the wider operation of societies and social systems. As I have indicated, Giddens has tried to co-opt Goffman in this respect and while I thoroughly endorse Giddens's attempt to link Goffman's work with general social theory, in the process I think he has misconstrued some of the central axioms and implications of his work.

In outlining the main elements of the theory of social domains I have endeavoured to carry forward the idea that Goffman's work is essential to any project that involves the development of a body of systematic and general social theory. In this respect the thematic of continuity hinges on an overlap in substantive focus with Goffman's work in that domain theory treats the areas of everyday life, face-to-face behaviour, encounters or focused gatherings (as they have been variously termed) as problematic and essential to the project of general social theory. Although I have not always explicity used the term, one of my main arguments (particularly in Chapter 5) has been that social integration has to be understood as something that is continually worked at through the processes of production and reproduction that exist in different modes and operate at different levels of generality. Central to these processes is the notion of an interaction order in which meaning, morality, trust and so on are implicated in actual episodes of situated activity. Such everyday encounters are essential to any account of social integration since they represent both contributions to, and expressions of, wider collective and systemic elements of integration (or mal-integration) such as collectively held beliefs, particular manifestations of the division of labour, or the orderly or conflictual relations between various groupings in society.

So often the area of the production and reproduction of everyday life as it is accomplished through situated activity has been either ignored completely, or assigned a marginal role in the more general processes of the constitution of social systems by sociologists who have concerned themselves primarily with macro-structural or social systemic issues. In this vacuum interactionist and phenomenological sociologies have been left to arrogate this subject matter to themselves, and by viewing it as solely linked to the phenomenon of intersubjectivity they have hermetically sealed it from wider macro or systemic issues. I have argued that this cannot and should not be the case since situated activity and psychobiography are directly implicated in these wider systemic processes and practices even though as domains they are ontologically distinct and relatively autonomous from each other. These domains and the processes of production and reproduction that they embody do not simply "reinforce" one another (as implied in phenomenology and structuration theory) in the sense that they can be said "automatically" to give rise to mutually supportive consequences for social life. As I have been at pains to point out, processes of psychic reproduction as well as those germane to the situated activities that form their immediate environment often undercut, fissure or qualify the integrity of processes contributing to general or system reproduction. In this sense social integration is something that is expressed on a micro-scale (irrespective of the power of the interactants) in face-to-face enounters and may complement or subvert wider elements of integration depending on the actual circumstances and personalities involved.

Thus at the micro-level there is always a profusion of "molecular" activity that hangs on the coat-tails of larger, more precipitous and sweeping forces contributing to overall levels and modes of social integration. This molecular activity is a hotbed of creativity that not only includes positive and supportive inputs to the social fabric but also contains and reflects anti-social and unsocial impulses that are equally essential components of all social orders. However, I have stressed that much of this creativity is "contained" within the ambit of the local circumstances in which it is produced even though it frays the edges of general or system reproduction. That is to say, that much or most routine or everyday behaviour must be considered to be locally productive rather than transformative at the system level. It is a mistake to think of social activity as inherently transformative (as Giddens and some symbolic interactionists imply). It is more accurate to say that given the right circumstances, all social activity is *potentially* transformative. But these "right circumstances" are never simply routine even though they may be initially embedded in deeply sedimented traditions and relations of power. What makes them ripe for transformative potential is the extraordinary (or non-routine) quality of the circumstances that surround them and that are themselves inextricably entangled in the evolutionary hold of specific historical forces.

In this book I have concentrated on the pockets of routinized continuity that exist in the spaces between periodic structural or systemic changes and that ride on the back of the recurrent everyday activities of people in relatively entrenched and established institutional circumstances. Therefore I have generally bracketed questions of social change since they are clearly beyond the remit of this present book. Structural or systemic changes may entail quite gradual forms of evolution or "structural elaboration" as Archer (1995) terms them. Indeed Archer has provided a framework for the analysis of these kinds of social change with which I would broadly agree (see also Layder 1993: Ch. 9, for a discussion of social change and historical analysis). I have, then, concentrated on the problem of persistence or continuity in social life, which, I insist, has to be characterized as a kind of "fluid equilibrium" because it is a continuity achieved "in spite of" the volatility and creativity of the human activities that produce it. However, I would reiterate that its importance for the question of social integration should not be underestimated.

Although I have largely bypassed questions associated with collective agency, and the problem of system integration that goes hand in hand with them, there are qualified senses in which I have countenanced the problem of system integration. One of the areas that I have obviously navigated around is the question of the historical emergence of system elements. The very scale of this question (as reflected in Habermas's treatment of it for example) and the limited space available has meant that I have not been able to do more than hint at some of the implications that flow from it. Some of these are entailed in sorting through the question of the relation between lifeworld and system elements and the exact nature of the "interpenetrations" involved but I have not dealt with the question of the evolution of system features like political or economic institutions even though such issues are implicated in them at a deeper levels.

Contours of the theory of social domains

I shall try to bring the general strands of my arguments together by looking at the theory of social domains in relation to other approaches that have provided its main impetus both as competing frameworks and as sources of inspiration. It has to be said that the fact that the theory of social domains endorses a moderate objectivism and sees some virtues in dualism in social analysis ensures that it parts company from those contemporary theories that have become disillusioned with both these strands of thought. My view is that this is based on very narrow and erroneous assumptions about the nature of objectivism and dualism and thus the disillusionment is premature and misguided. I shall not attempt to repeat the detail of my arguments here but the upshot is that moderate objectivism is not linked to reification, claims to universal truths (as in positivism), structural determinism, or even functionalism. Instead, it simply registers the relative autonomy of external objective (and collective) features of social life. Likewise "analytic dualism" (Archer 1995) must be recognized as the only viable way of registering and representing the distinct properties of lifeworld and system phenomena (agency and structure). In this respect dualism is a valuable starting point for understanding the more inclusive backdrop to the four principal social domains.

These commitments of domain theory take it quite away from phenomenology, interactionism and structuration theory that are founded upon a rejection of objectivism and dualism and a corresponding celebration of an intersubjective ontology. While Giddens's suggestion that agency and structure are implicated in each other is a laudable programmatic statement, his complete rejection of objectivism means that he can do nothing other than adopt an ontology of "doing and being" with its exclusive preoccupation with actors' reasons, motivations and memory traces and its consequent rejection of a relatively independent social world. Thus instead of incorporating both agency and structure, Giddens's conception of the duality of structure dissolves them into each other while the analytic focus is trained on social practices. But this is the worst of all worlds since the independent properties of both action and structure are lost to analysis and as a result, the exact linkages betwen the two cannot be traced over time (see Layder 1981, Archer 1995).

As with phenomenological and "synthetic" approaches, structuration theory incurs far too many costs in the way of limiting the breadth, depth and explanatory power that social analysis may achieve. Dissolving agency (or activities) into structure through the duality of structure principle misses out the crucial mediating role of situated activity in the process. Conversely, impelled by the rejection of objectivism, these approaches absorb structures into action (practices) and as a result, the whole realm of institutional or macro-structural phenomena are rendered ontologically "flat" since they are said to exist only in activities or practices. Not only does the theory of social domains endorse the notion of analytic dualism of which Archer speaks but goes further and unpacks the dualism of "lifeworld" and "system" elements (this time using Habermas's terminology) into their component units. Thus the concept of "agency" has to be decomposed into the constituent elements of psychobiographical inputs and the emergent dynamics of situated activity while structural or system elements are broken down into settings and contextual resources.

Instead of artificially reducing the complexity and finely differentiated nature of social reality to an intersubjective uniformity and unimodality, the theory of social domains underscores its textured, multidimensional and stratified nature. Recognizing the "open" and "expansive" (rather than compressed) character of social reality in this manner has the effect of allowing more explanatory possibilities (in the form of sensitizing concepts, analytic strategies and procedures, models of, and relations between theoretical elements) that reflect this complex reality. The constrictions, compressions and compactions imposed on the nature of social life and its analysis by those approaches that indulge in "central conflation" (as Archer phrases it) have the effect of reducing the range of analytic devices available since they represent an ontology that stretches no further than a concern with "doing and being". Relatively autonomous properties of the social world that cannot be understood in terms of the intersubjective boundaries of human activity and perception are thereby simply lost to social analysis.

Other things too are missing from these accounts. In particular the complexity of the dimensions of time are obscured in an exaggerated emphasis on the continually productive nature of social activity. Such approaches mask the conjuncture of different temporal dimensions because the idea that social life inheres only in the doing and being of active subjects confuses and compacts "evolutionary" (institutional) time with that of the unfolding temporality of situated activity. Since the aspects and rhythms of social life (reflected by the two timeframes) are qualitatively different, their intersection cannot be simply characterized by a simultaneous "instantiation". Rather it has to be understood as a conjuncture of different elements that meld into one another without any dissolution of their distinct but connected characteristics.

The theory of social domains recognizes that social life is constituted by unfolding situated activity and preexisting historical forms that simultaneously condition this activity. It therefore registers the very limited sense in which people "construct" social organization as an ongoing accomplishment of their activities. As historical emergents, as well as ongoing social processes, these conditions impose varying degrees of constraint on the behaviour of people who live out their lives within the orbit of their influence. Although such systemic factors and resources also function as "enablers" or facilitators of activity, people do not construct the social world anew each time they act. Phenomenological, interactionist and structurationist approaches overemphasize this feature of social life by appearing to overlook the way in which enablements are often circumscribed by pre-existing (and thus external) cultural, organizational and systemic resources (including power relations and forms of domination).

Written-out also is an appreciation of the compelling character of the (relatively independent) constraints that stem from the continually revivified standing conditions (present as ongoing social circumstances) that are independent of *specific* activities, individuals and collectivities – but not, of course, of activity or collective phenomena *per se*. Although it is true to say that social organization is utterly dependent for its *general continuity* on the productive activities of knowledgeable human beings, it is wrong to claim that it has no existence independent of specific forms of knowledgeability,

248

and the reasons, motives and intentions of particular people in specific social circumstances. As a result of their limitation to questions bounded by an ontology of doing and being, reasons and motives, phenomenological and interactionist approaches (including structuration theory) have great difficulty coming to terms with phenomena that lie outside this range. By contrast the theory of social domains attempts to accommodate an expanded conception of social ontology by proposing a moderate form of objectivism. There are several ways in which this objectivism impinges on the central axioms of domain theory but perhaps two of the most important concern the concept of discourse and the idea of world 3 phenomena.

Foucault's work on power, discourse and social practices has been an important influence both positively and negatively on the theory of social domains. In a positive vein Foucault's notion of discursive practices is pitched at a level above human agency and subjectivity in an individual sense, and I have wanted to endorse such a conception in order to posit a view of cultural resources, including ideology, that has an existence beyond, and independently of, the consciousness, awareness and control of individual people. On this view discourses are social constructions that possess an objective existence external to people and are thus not reducible to the realm of human agency. It is this sense of Foucault's formulation that I have adopted and which is at odds with the fixities of the ontological position of Giddens's and phenomenological and interactionist approaches more generally. However, it is also true to say that I have not adopted Foucault's position *in toto* here because his notion of a subjectless social terrain of discourses and practices excludes the active subject from social analysis. In this respect I have adapted Popper's notion of a "third world" of cultural products (including discursive phenomena) or "knowledge without a knowing subject". This more adequately buttresses the view that while discursive phenomena do most definitely have independent characteristics, active subjects also play a resistant and transformative role in social life in general (even though in many respects these capacities are more qualified and limited than in Giddens's formulations).

The problem of the nature of power and its role in social life is of massive significance for the theory of social domains. While here again Foucault's work has been an important influence, I have also been critical of his general views on power. Without doubt Foucault's identification of disciplinary and bio-power and his insistence on the close links between discourse, knowledge, power and practice are important insights for social analysis. However this adds to our existing knowledge and conceptions of power, it does not (as Foucauldians often seem to assume) require the abandonment of previous views of power and power analysis. In this respect the theory of social domains maintains that such one-dimensional views must give way to more flexible and embracing conceptions that capture something of the multifaceted character of power as it is reflected in the social domains. This is at the root of my claim that while Foucault's notion of power as ever-present and ubiquitous is an essential ingredient of an adequate view of power, we must understand these characteristics in rather different terms from Foucault. In domain theory, power is ever-present and ubiquitous because it is multidimensional (an effect of the interlocking nature of the social domains) and capable of transmutation (or "shape-shifting" as I have characterized it in Ch. 4). By contrast Foucault's notion of the "diffuseness" of power rests on the assumption that it circulates in a unitary flow of discourses and practices – and this, of necessity, excludes a multidimensional view.

In order to undergird my own views on power I have drawn upon some of the insights offered by Giddens and Habermas although I have also been critical of them on several grounds. The notion of the "dialectic of control" is useful but generally Giddens overemphasizes the link between power and agency, and as a consequence, he ignores the conditioning influence of both psychological characteristics and system elements (settings and contextual resources) as independent sites of and formative influences on power. Ironically the duality of structure principle also means that the independent contribution of the interaction order – and situated activity in particular – is bypassed. Although very different from Foucault's conception, Giddens also offers a one-dimensional view of power and this prevents him from appreciating its variegated nature. Habermas's approach to power as a system steering mechanism is an important corrective to the idea that power is an exclusive property of agency. However, Habermas's position does not incorporate the fact that power is not simply an aspect of domination but is also an enabler or facilitator of communicative interaction and understanding because of its implication in situated activity and individual personality. The idea of power as personal capacity having to do with emotional, anti-social or egoistic tendencies is an essential component of the position I have outlined.

Power though is of further significance for the theory of social domains in that it is intimately tied in with the question of the nature of social relations and the discourses and practices that they embody. As I have emphasized, social relations (and the powers and practices inscribed in them) establish and fashion the points of contact, convergence and overlap between the social domains. Social relations therefore bind together a multiplicity of social processes and temporal dimensions. As it runs through these social relations, power feeds into the social circumstances that are represented in particular configurations of psychobiography, situated activity, settings and contextual resources. A major feature of this patterning of social life is what I have termed the duality of social relations since this represents the manner in which power conditions both the emergent and reproduced nature of social relations with regard to particular domains and conjunctions or "overlayerings" of their influence. The duality of social relations therefore is able to underwrite a conception of social life as constituted by the independent but interconnected influence of the domains (and hence does not reduce the complexity of social reality to some unitary principle as in Giddens's duality of structure).

Foucault's work is limited by its rejection of human agency and in this respect I completely endorse Giddens's idea that individual human agency is important and an essential ingredient of social analysis. Thus the radical implication of Foucault's work that the individual subject has to be "decentred" or, in other words, effectively eradicated from social analysis because such talk is irretrievably mired in psychological reductionism, must be rejected. The associated notion, that the individual is nothing more than a cipher or conduit of social discourses and the powers they facilitate, has to be similarly consigned to the waste-bin of social theory. The nature and implications of individual agency in social analysis need to be explained not ignored. The only way to accomplish this is to insist that although people must in one sense be understood as nodal points at the intersections of discourses (including ideology), they can never be viewed entirely in these terms. By utilizing in a critical manner some of Habermas's ideas on communicative understanding, I have tried to outline a view of this aspect of social encounters that stresses a push towards idiomatic stylization as a means of facilitating the simultaneous unfolding of shared understandings that emerge from situated activity.

Foucault is also remiss in overlooking the formative influences of situated activity as a separate domain in its own right. (This provides a paradoxical but startling parallel with those phenomenological theories that underestimate the partly independent impact of this intersubjective world by viewing it as the *sole* domain of social life.) In this respect I have drawn on the work of Goffman in underpinning some of the central tenets of the theory of social domains, especially in my formulation of the nature of situated activity and its relation with other social orders. A concern with Goffman's work alongside a discussion of Foucault's ideas on discourses, practices and powers, and Habermas's on the relation between lifeworld and system elements, is perhaps a surprising juxtaposition of influences since Goffman is usually associated with phenomenological and inter-actionist schools of thought – or at least those that centralize agency and the human subject. However, I believe there is nothing in Goffman's work that necessarily commits it to these latter schools of thought in any dog-matic way; indeed there is much to suggest that he entertained various aspects of dualism in his account of the interaction order and sociological analysis more generally. Yet, although Goffman was intimately concerned with the nature and dynamics of face-to-face interaction, he was strangely unresponsive to the need for an account of subjectivity as reflected in indi-vidual psychology and thus his work provides a parallel version of social constructivism that bears comparison with that of Foucault.

As I have already intimated, Habermas's theory of communicative action has also been a source of positive support in the development of domain theory. While I have been careful to distance myself from some of the claims that Habermas makes, especially with regard to the nature of, and relationship between, lifeworld and system elements, I have drawn upon this as fundamental distinction in social reality and social organiza-tion that enables us to assess something of the mutual impact of these "meta-domains". As this latter comment reveals, domain theory insists upon the deconstruction of these elements into the four domains I have identified in order that more refined and adequate statements can be made about the the subtle interconnections between aspects of social real-ity. Also, in a critical manner I have drawn upon some of Habermas's formulations to bolster my arguments about idiomatic stylization and the influence of discourse in the achievement of communicative understand-ing in social interaction. Of course a major problem with Habermas as it is with many others, is the absence of an appreciation of the workings of situated activity (the interaction order in Goffman's terms) as a domain in its own right.

However, unlike Goffman (and phenomenology and interactionism), Habermas at least opens up the possibility of the notion of individual psy-chology as an important arena of of social life with his notion of psycho-logical reality as differentiated from social and physical reality. Although Habermas does not pursue this in any detail as far as a social psychology of the individual is concerned, his ontological distinction is absolutely crucial for such a project. This indeed is what I have endeavoured to do in Chapter 2 of this book where I give an account of some of the main issues involved in psychobiography and self-identity as they mesh with situated activity, settings and contextual resources. A central feature of such an account has to be that there exist relatively independent anti-social and unsocial aspects of the individual psyche that must be taken into account in any general rendering of the relations between social activity and more encompassing system elements. In their zeal to underwrite the importance of social factors in the construction of social reality and subjectivity (identity), and at the same time to avoid psychological reductionism, many if not most schools of social theory simply do not entertain this possibility and thus they contribute to an inappropriate sociological imperialism of the subject.

Perhaps the most advanced, but none the less crude form of this neglect of psychobiography has stemmed from poststructuralist and postmodernist attempts to abandon and decentre the subject. However, many interactionist and phenomenologically inspired approaches to social analysis (as well as many unaffiliated individual theorists) have offered us equally impoverished notions of individuals and their contribution to social processes. I think that this neglect of a central problem in social inquiry has been entirely mistaken and it is difficult to understand why such a glaring omission continues to be defended in the various guises of social constructionist dogma. There are several important voices that have recently swum against this current (Scheff 1990, Craib 1992, Crespi 1992, Archer 1995) and I can only hope that the theory of social domains lends much needed support to this important aspect of modern social theory.

In particular I have outlined an image of the individual as an emotional being who is simultaneously social and asocial and who, as a consequence, constantly grapples with the dilemmas posed by the dialectic of separateness and relatedness. From this basic nexus of pulls and tensions there flow a number of other dualities and contradictory pressures that have their effect on individual behaviour and consciousness. There is here also a conjunction between a view of individuals as emotional beings and issues of power and control in social life that feeds into a number of subsidiary social psychological problems centring on the intersection of the social and psychological worlds. The issue of self-identity, of course, is one of these, as are less familiar problems such as those associated with the maintenance of self-esteem, composure and a sense of contact with the changeable flow of social encounters. In all I have attempted to develop a conception of individuals who experience contradictory impulses, are sometimes only partly aware and in control of their behaviour and reactions and who are both rational and irrational at various times. It is important to stress that such a view does not posit individuals as the sole originators of meaning, and moreover, concedes that meaning and subjectivity are to a limited extent constructed through impersonal social discourses. None the less, individuals inhabit an interpersonal world that is also defined in non-discursive terms and thus they are actively involved in constructing the situated meanings that emerge from face-to-face encounters, and are equally capable of subverting, reformulating and resisting discursive influences in the service of other social and psychological factors, needs and interests.

Bibliography

Abercrombie, N., S. Hill, B. Turner 1980. *The dominant ideology thesis*. London: Allen & Unwin.

Ackroyd, S. & P. Crowdy 1990. Can culture be managed? *Personnel Management* **19**, 3–13.

Adam, B. 1990. *Time and social theory*. Oxford: Polity.

Alexander, J. 1985. The individualist dilemma in phenomenology and interactionism. In *Macro-sociological theory: perspectives on sociological theory*, vol. I, S. Eisenstadt & H. Helle (eds). London: Sage.

— 1995. *Fin de siécle social theory*. London: Verso.

Alexander, J. & P. Colomy 1985. Toward neo-functionalism. *Sociological Theory* **3**, 11–23.

— 1990. Neo-functionalism: reconstructing a theoretical tradition. In *Frontiers of social theory*, G. Ritzer (ed.). New York: Columbia University Press.

Archer, M. 1995. *Realist social theory: the morphogenetic approach*. Cambridge: Cambridge University Press.

Austin, J. 1971. *How to do things with words*. Oxford: Oxford University Press.

Barrett, M. 1991. *The politics of truth*. Oxford: Polity.

Becker, H. 1953. Becoming a marihuana user. *American Journal of Sociology* **59**, 235–42.

Berger, P. & T. Luckmann 1967. *The social construction of reality*. London: Allan Lane.

Bernstein, B. 1973. *Class, codes and control*, vol. I, London: Paladin.

Bhaskar, R. 1979. *The possibility of naturalism*. Brighton: Harvester.

Bittner, E. 1967. The police on skid-row: a study of peace-keeping. *American Sociological Review* **32**, 669–715.

Blumer, H. 1969. *Symbolic interactionism: perspectives and methods*. Englewood Cliffs, N.J.: Prentice-Hall.

Bourdieu, P. 1977. *Outline of a theory of practice*. Cambridge: Cambridge University Press.

1984. *Distinction: a social critique of the judgement of taste*. Cambridge, Mass.: Harvard University Press.

Brewer, J. 1990. Talking about danger: the RUC and the paramilitary threat. *Sociology* **24**, 657–74.

Burawoy, M. 1979. *Manufacturing consent*. Chicago: Chicago University Press.

Burn, G. 1984. *Somebody's husband, somebody's son*. London: Heinemann.

Clegg, S. 1989. *Frameworks of power*. London: Sage.

Collins, R. 1983. Micro-methods as a basis for macrosociology. *Urban Life* **12**, 184–202.

Craib, I. 1992. *Anthony Giddens*. London: Routledge.

Crespi, F. 1992. *Social action and power*. Oxford: Basil Blackwell.

Davis, F. 1963. *Passage through crisis*. Indianapolis: Bobbs-Merrill.

Denzin, N. 1990. Researching alcoholics and alcoholism in American society. *Studies in Symbolic Interaction* **11**, 81–101.

Durkheim, E. 1964. *The division of labour in society*. New York: Free Press.

— 1965. *The elementary forms of the religious life*. New York: Free Press.

— 1982. *The rules of sociological method*. London: Macmillan.

Edwards, R. 1979. *Contested terrain*. London: Heinemann.

Eisenstadt, S. 1985. Macro-societal analysis: background development and indications. In *Macro-sociological theory: perspectives on sociological theory*, vol. I, S. Eisenstadt & H. Helle (eds). London: Sage.

Elias, N. 1978. *What is sociology?* London: Hutchinson.

Foucault, M. 1977. *Discipline and punish: the birth of the prison*. Harmondsworth: Penguin.

— 1979. *The history of sexuality*, vol. I, *An introduction*. London: Allen Lane.

— 1986. *The history of sexuality*, vol. II, *The use of pleasure*. London: Viking.

— 1988. *The history of sexuality*, vol. III, *The care of the self*. London: Allen Lane.

— 1980, *Power/knowledge*. Brighton: Harvester.

Fraser, N. 1989. *Unruly practices*. Oxford: Polity.

Garfinkel, H. 1967. *Studies in ethnomethodology*. Englewood Cliffs, N.J.: Prentice-Hall.

Giddens, A. 1976. *New rules of sociological method*. London: Hutchinson.

— 1977. *Studies in social and political theory*. London: Hutchinson.

— 1979. *Central problems in social theory*. London: Macmillan.

— 1984. *The constitution of society*. Oxford: Polity.

— 1985. *The nation-state and violence*. Oxford: Polity.

— 1987. *Social theory and modern sociology*. Stanford, Calif.: Stanford University Press.

— 1990. *The consequences of modernity*. Oxford: Polity.

— 1991. *Modernity and self-identity*. Oxford: Polity.

Goffman, E. 1959. *The presentation of self in everyday life*. Harmondsworth: Penguin.

— 1961a. *Encounters*. New York: Bobbs-Merrill.

— 1961b. *Asylums*. Harmondsworth: Penguin.

— 1967. *Interaction ritual*. New York: Anchor.

— 1974. *Frame analysis: an essay on the organization of experience*. New York: Harper & Row.

— 1983. The interaction order. *American Sociological Review* **48**, 1–17.

Gouldner, A. 1971. *The coming crisis in western sociology*. London: Heinemann.

Gramsci, A. 1971. *Selections from the prison notebooks*. London: Lawrence & Wishart.

Habermas, J. 1971. *Towards a rational society*. London: Heinemann.

— 1984. *The theory of communicative action*, vol. I. Oxford: Polity.

— 1987. *The theory of communicative action*, vol. II. Oxford: Polity.

Harding, S. (ed.) 1987. *Feminism and methodology*. Bloomington: Indiana University Press.

Hesse, M. 1974. *The structure of scientific inference*. London: Macmillan.

Hilbert, R. 1990. Ethnomethodology and the micro-macro order. *American Sociological Review* **55**, 794–808.

Hirst, P. 1983. Ideology, culture and personality. *Canadian Journal of Political and Social Theory* **7**, nos. 1 and 2.

Honneth, A. 1993. *The critique of power*. Cambridge, Mass.: MIT Press.

Hughes, E. 1937. Institutional office and the person. *American Journal of Sociology* **43**, 404–13.

Jampolsky, L. 1994. *The art of trust*. Berkeley, Calif.: Celestial Arts.

Laclau, E. & Mouffe, C. 1985. *Hegemony and socialist strategy*. London: Verso.

Laing, R. 1969. *The divided self*. Harmondsworth: Penguin.

Layder, D. 1981. *Structure, interaction and social theory*. London: Routledge.

— 1984. Sources and levels of commitment in actors' careers. *Work and Occupations* **11**, 147–62.

— 1985. Beyond empiricism: the promise of realism. *Philosophy of the Social Sciences* **15**, 255–74.

— 1990. *The realist image in social science*. London: Macmillan.

— 1993. *New strategies in social research: an introduction and guide*. Oxford: Polity.

— 1994. *Understanding social theory*. London: Sage.

Lengermann, P. & J. Niebrugge-Brantley 1992. Contemporary feminist theory. In *Sociological theory*, G. Ritzer (ed.). New York: McGraw-Hill.

Leonard, P. 1984. *Personality and ideology*. London: Macmillan.

Lewis, H. 1971. *Shame and guilt in neurosis*. New York: International Universities Press.

Lockwood, D. 1964. Social integration and system integration. In *Explorations in social change*, G. Zollschan & W. Hirsch (eds). London: Routledge.

Luckenbill, D. 1979. Power: a conceptual framework. *Symbolic Interaction* **2**, 97–114.

Lukes, S. 1977. *Essays in social theory*. London: Macmillan.

Magee, B. 1973. *Popper*. Glasgow: Fontana.

Manning, P. 1992. *Erving Goffman and modern sociology*. Oxford: Polity.

Marx, K. & F. Engels 1968. *Selected works*. London: Lawrence & Wishart.

.ad, G. 1967. *Mind, self and society*. Chicago: Chicago University Press.

.eltzer, B., J. Petras, L. Reynolds. 1975. *Symbolic interactionism*. London: Routledge.

Mouzelis, N. 1991. *Back to sociological theory*. London: Macmillan.

— 1992. Social and system integration: Habermas' view. *British Journal of Sociology* **43**, 267–88.

— 1995. *Sociological theory: what went wrong?* London: Routledge.

Paci, E. 1972. *The function of the sciences and the meaning of man*. Evanston, Ill.: Northwestern University Press.

Parsons, T. 1951. *The social system*. London: Routledge.

Popper, K. 1972. *Objective knowledge: an evolutionary approach*. Oxford: Oxford University Press.

Poster, M. 1984. *Foucault, Marxism and history*. Oxford: Polity.

Rawls, A. 1987. The interaction order sui generis: Goffman's contribution to social theory. *Sociological Theory* **5**, 136–49.

Rosenau, P. 1992. *Post-modernism and the social sciences*. Princeton, N.J.: Princeton University Press.

Rosenhan, D. 1973. On being sane in insane places. *Science* **179**, 250–58.

Roy, D. 1973. Banana time: job satisfaction and informal interaction. In *People and organisations*, G. Salaman & K. Thompson (eds). London: Longman.

Sartre, J. P. 1966. *Being and nothingness*. London: Methuen.

Scheff, T. 1990. *Microsociology: discourse, emotion and social structure*. Chicago: University of Chicago Press.

Schelling, T. 1960. *The strategy of conflict*. Cambridge, Mass.: Harvard University Press.

Scott, J. 1995. *Sociological theory*. Cheltenham: Edward Elgar.

Seve, L. 1978. *Man in Marxist theory and the psychology of personality*. Brighton: Harvester.

Smail, D. 1993. *The origins of unhappiness*. London: HarperCollins.

Smith, D. 1988. *The everyday world as problematic*. Milton Keynes: Open University Press.

Stanley, L. & S. Wise 1983. *Breaking out*. London: Routledge.

Stebbins, R. 1970. Career: the subjective approach. *Sociological Quarterly* **11**, 32–49.

Stryker, S. 1981. *Symbolic interactivism: a social structural version*. Englewood Cliffs, N. J.: Prentice-Hall.

Tannen, D. 1987. *That's not what I meant*. London: Dent.

— 1992. *You just don't understand*. London: Virago.

Turner, J. 1988. *A theory of social interaction*. Oxford: Polity.

Turner, R. 1962. Role-taking: process versus conformity. In *Human behaviour and social processes*, A. Rose (ed.). Boston, Mass.: Houghton Mifflin.

— 1985. Some unanswered questions in the convergence between structuralist and interactionist role theories. In *Micro-sociological theory: perspectives on sociological*

258

theory, vol. II, S. Eisenstadt & H. Helle (eds). London: Sage.

Vaitkus, S. 1991. *How is society possible?* Dordrecht: Kluwer Academic.

Weber, M. 1964. *The theory of social and economic organization*. New York: Free Press.

Weedon, C. 1987. *Feminist practice and poststructuralist theory*. Oxford: Basil Blackwell.

Wieder, L. 1974. Telling the code. In *Ethnomethodology*, R. Turner (ed.). Harmondsworth: Penguin.

Wittgenstein, L. 1972. *Philosophical investigations*. Oxford: Basil Blackwell.

Wolf, N. 1993. *Fire with fire*. New York: Fawcett Columbine.

Wootton, A. 1975. *Dilemmas of discourse*. London: Allen & Unwin.

Wrong, D. 1967. The oversocialized concept of man in modern sociology. In *Sociological theory: a book of readings*, L. Cozer & B. Rosenberg (eds). London: Collier Macmillan.

Index

DATE DUE

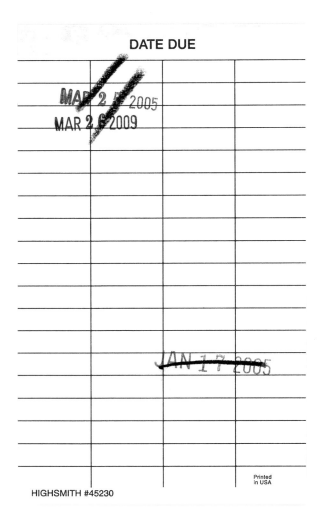

MAR 2 5 2005

MAR 2 6 2009

JAN 1 7 2005

Printed
in USA